Murphy, Apostle of the Smokies

MURPHY, APOSTLE OF THE SMOKIES

▼

The Story of a Detroit Businessman Who Became a Priest at Age 80

Sister Jane Schmenk
In Collaboration With
Jean Battlo
and
Carolyn Nowakowski

Writers Club Press
San Jose New York Lincoln Shanghai

Murphy, Apostle of the Smokies
The Story of a Detroit Businessman Who Became a Priest at Age 80

Writers Club Press
an imprint of iUniverse.com, Inc.

For information address:
iUniverse.com, Inc.
5220 S 16th, Ste. 200
Lincoln, NE 68512
www.iuniverse.com

Cover and book design, graphics, editing, and typesetting:
Carolyn Nowakowski
TOP-DRAWER SERVICES, INC.
Waynesville, North Carolina 28786

ISBN: 0-595-18890-7

Printed in the United States of America

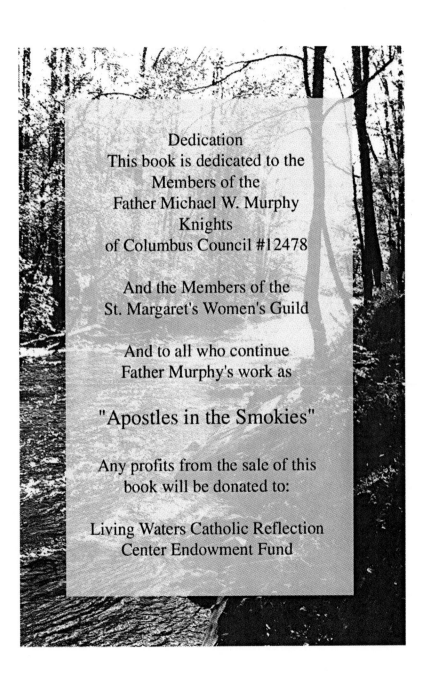

Dedication
This book is dedicated to the
Members of the
Father Michael W. Murphy
Knights
of Columbus Council #12478

And the Members of the
St. Margaret's Women's Guild

And to all who continue
Father Murphy's work as

"Apostles in the Smokies"

Any profits from the sale of this
book will be donated to:

Living Waters Catholic Reflection
Center Endowment Fund

INTRODUCTION

My purpose in writing this book is twofold: I want to preserve the story of Father Michael William Murphy and Living Waters Catholic Reflection Center, and I want to place that story within the framework of Catholicity in the South.

My first task was to gather the stories. I am grateful to all those who have contributed their memories. My second task was to research the history of Catholicity in the South and relate that history to the efforts of Father Murphy to make a change in the way Catholics are accepted in the southern states.

This book would not have happened if it hadn't been for the help of those who prayed me through the process. Neither would it have happened without the efforts of the many people who assisted me in gathering the data, in proofreading the text, and in financing the project. I am most grateful to the following:

My family: Alvina and Jim Ellerbrock, Robert and Pat Kreinbrink, Orville and Audrey Verhoff, Ralph and Kay Herman, Teresa Warnecke, Edna Musch, and Joe Schmenk.

My religious community: Sisters of St. Francis of Tiffin, Ohio, Sisters Jean Linder, Francine Sartor, Virginia Gase, Roberta McKinnon, Germaine Wannemacher, Rosann Morman, Patti Langenderfer, Carolette Grote, Maryann Orians, Diane Mueller, Linda Scheckelhoff, Andrea Inkrott, and Arlid Barrera.

My friends: Maggie Weigel, Ann Trigg, Delores and Ron Arch, Sharon Webb, Patsy Conard, Freeman Owle, Mary Everson, and Catherine Bodenmiller.

A very special thanks goes to Jean Battlo, writer and poet, who collaborated with me to get this book off the ground, and to Carolyn Nowakowski who, after the manuscript was off the ground, patiently edited and prepared the text for the printer. She scanned many photographs and prepared them for black and white publishing. Without their help I'd still be wandering around in the Smokies.

I also thank Sister Timothy Warren, RSM, Vicar for Religious, who presented the manuscript to the Most Reverend William Curlin, Bishop of the Diocese of Charlotte, for his approval.

As you read the story of Father Murphy and Catholicity in the South it is my hope that this Old Gaelic Blessing will descend upon you—

> May the roads rise with you,
> And the wind be always at your back
> And may the Lord hold you
> In the hollow of his hand.

Father Michael William Murphy

CONTENTS

Mountain High

I am taking a late summer evening walk
    along the street of Maggie Valley,
        past the motels with names that lure
            "Rocky Waters"–"Jonathan Creek."

It's August and I am on a brief trip
    away from caring for my much-loved 88-year old mother,
        whose coming earthly conclusion is becoming evident
and the wind whirs its rustle through the full-bodied leaves of elm tree
and oak
    and then burrows into the deepened verdure of the pines.

I've come to a space where a long row of pines circle a road,
    where a tumbling stream sings a constant song,
        and the path winds around what seems to be a motel
            nestled behind the trees,
                tucked snugly into the bottom cusp of a
            mountain.

When I reach the long white building
    and approach the office I find a surprising sign that states
    clearly, curiously–

This is not a motel

What then?
    I will learn. This is a space
        built for a special type of seeker,
            a sojourner who knows of this world,

"This is not a lasting city and wherever thou art,
thou art a pilgrim and a stranger."

And still, perhaps, the comfort and community
　　of lodging in such a space of grace,
　　　　designed as it were,
　　　　　　for my specific style of journey, would be for me
　　　　　　　　the very heaven-haven I was seeking.

I step back from the motel-not-a-motel
　　　　and, as all must, in the massive green arms
　　　　　　of the mountains surrounding the Valley,

I look up
There, high, as with so many symbolic pilgrims, I know I will have
to climb,
　　　　to an apex, a peak where gleaming white in the last soft sun-
　　　　hued tint of gold,
　　　　　　stands the church of

St. Margaret
No matter what peak or valley
　　my personal subjective spiritual journey may be in,
　　　　that sudden sight of the unsuspected shrine in the sky
　　　　　　will cause pause.

Like a mountain magnet,
　　　　it draws me up the steep paved incline toward the plateau
　　　　where the church stands sentinel
　　　　　　over the dimming little town below.

"To Thy Name, O God, give glory."

A sojourner would have to be completely spiritually illiterate
not to hear the refrain, all but audible:

"I lift up mine eyes unto these hills."

An odd startling cacophony of gunshots
     ring out from the other side of the hill where tourists on
another trip
        are being playfully haunted by the frontier past in

Ghost Town–

Incredible twin adventures in

Maggie Valley, North Carolina.

I smile at the congruity in incongruity.

Ghost Town and St. Margaret's

sharing the same hill.

The bells begin to toll the hour's turn, muffling the distant gunshots.

As a partly mis-guided poet, with just enough fancy left to fire the imagination, I step inside the church to find a leprechaun of an aging priest, with whispy strands of white hair, and in stocking feet, pouring water into the font from a Clorox bottle.

As if my entrance were a remote control, and he, a pre-programmed tape for tourists happening into the church at twilight, I hear,

"We can't keep enough holy water in here any more. I don't know how many times a week I have to come in and put more water in the fountain. We have more people coming in here just to see the church than I can keep count of, and on Sunday the church is full for Mass, too. A lot of them are our parishioners, of course, but we get a lot of Catholic tourists and some aren't even Catholic but want to come to services here at St.

Margaret's. You wouldn't know what it was like when I first came here after my good mother died. I lived with her and I was lonesome when she died. So I was driving to Florida when I came here. There were only eight Catholics in the whole region and no church at all in Maggie Valley which had just one Catholic. I stopped here, as I had always wanted to, but my good mother had not wanted to stop. When I saw the beauty of the mountains I bought a house and moved here.

"My mother was a lovely, blessed, holy woman, and when she died it was a sad day for me. We lived in Detroit then, but I moved here, and of course, the name of Maggie, which was what everyone called my mother, made me stop here. And I loved it from the first, but there was no church anywhere in this part of North Carolina so I built one over in Sylva, and then I moved here and made a chapel in my house and later I got the Bishop to let me build a church here in Maggie, though he kept saying there were not enough Catholics here for a church. But he finally agreed so after I built the church I started telling the Bishop that we needed a priest and he said there wasn't one, and I kept asking until finally he said, 'Will, if you want a priest at St. Margaret's, you're going to have to become one.' So I went to the seminary and was ordained when I was eighty. I prayed that the good Lord would allow me to say just one Mass in this church and that was thirteen years ago and I'm still here."

The human tape pauses, looks at me. I look at him, and though I've never heard of him, and though I will go down to the motel that's not a motel and meet Betty and Bob Prier and ask them how much of what I heard was true, and as I am approaching fifty and as I have been one of those people who, for better and for worse, have kept a too-close bond with my mother, and as I've been realizing that the time is near when that bond on this earth is about to break, and as I wondered, approaching fifty, what can I hope to do or accomplish after she is gone, I know that there is some

Source of Guidance, a Divine Spirit
that at this particular time in my life introduced me, **Jean Battlo,** to

Father Michael William Murphy
and now introduces him to

YOU.

CHAPTER ONE

▼

REMEMBERING

Father Murphy, it's brewing up a storm outside and my thoughts are with you as I sit here with your handwritten ledger on my desk. The storm reminds me of some of the turbulent times and disappointments you faced as you ministered in Western North Carolina.

It is now over ten years since you walked among us. One would think that after so many years I wouldn't remember the details of the fourteen years we spent in ministry together in Maggie Valley, but I do remember, and I want to write everything down before it all fades away into the vast expanse of history. I want all your friends and those who read this book to know what a remarkable person you were, especially while you lived with us here in the Valley.

We found your ledger among our treasured blue prints and journals at Living Waters. As I look at the pages you kept more or less faithfully from 1961 to 1980, my memory is refreshed and I learn more about your thoughts concerning your family and those things that mattered most to you.

You remembered and wrote "My Good Father" on January 8 of several different years,

"January 8, 1961. My good Father was born 108 years ago today. Great changes since then.

> *1962,*   *My good father, James Murphy, was born January 8, 1853.*
>
> *1963,*   *Jan. 8, My good Father was born 110 years ago today in Detroit.*
>
> *1965,*   *My good Father, James Murphy, was born in Detroit 112 years ago today. He was baptized at Holy Trinity Catholic Church and lived most of his life on Old Church Road (now Hubbell Road.)*
>
> *1966,*   *My good Father, James Murphy, was born Jan 8, 1853. His mother was Mary Lawlor Whalen of Tralee."*

Even though most of the ledger is a record of "business as usual," there are familial notations throughout that form a homily to what was important in your life—family. Births, deaths, and other such recollections are noted on each year's anniversary dates. The reverence in which you held every member of your family is commemorated in these daily and annual references in your ledger.

Father Murphy, this is your family history as you related much of it to us.

My Good Father

Michael William Murphy, who went by the name of Will until he entered the seminary, traced his "good Father's" roots back to Ireland. There, in Tralee, his paternal grandmother, Mary Lawlor, was born and raised. Mary married John Whalen who was also born on the "old sod," hailing from County Cork. The couple had one young son, Patrick, age two, when they left Ireland for America in 1832.

The departure of the Whalens from their homeland preceded "An Gorta Mor," the great hunger caused by the potato famine, by at least a decade. Grave hardships were, nonetheless, a part of Irish life as the 19th Century began. There were a number of socio-economic factors creating the problems that led to emigration. The population almost doubled in the first half of the century. The approximately four and one half million people on record in Ireland in 1800, rose to over eight million when the census of 1841 was taken. In reference to density, Benjamin Disraeli called Ireland "the most populous country in Europe." Such leaps in numbers are generally paralleled by poverty.

That same census also noted that 45% of the land holdings for a family was under five acres. This scarcity of land ownership sometimes caused farmers to share land tenancy. This system of sharing was called "rundale." Naturally a family's gleanings were sparse. Farming land for a Catholic was also accompanied by a cornucopia of other limitations. Exorbitant land prices generally resulted in an Irishman being a tenant of a wealthy, absentee English landlord.

England's authoritative influence was complete and restricted all facets of Irish life. Catholics could not vote, hold political office, nor pursue an education. They could not serve in the military, nor engage in open commerce. Complete lists of Irish grievances in this era are book length.

Though over a million people died during the great potato famine of "Black 47," there were other reasons besides the famine for the Irish to emigrate. The Irish "homeland" was not really "home" anymore. Often, in history and biography, when not all of the data is available, there is an assumed history from prevailing conditions. It seems reasonable to assume that the existing conditions, combined with the voyager's typical dreams and sense of adventure, led the Whalens away from Irish shores. Mary, John, and little Patrick Whalen became part of that great Irish wave of humanity that landed on the Canadian and American shores.

Though the Whalens would leave Ireland, Ireland would seemingly never leave the Whalens. They and Will Murphy's other progenitors, the Garlands, the McGourkes, and the Murphys, planted the seed of legendary Irish identity so firmly in his bones that even as he aged toward his century mark the lilt of Irish laughter sparkled in old Will's Irish eyes.

What adventures and misadventures were the Whalens on the sea voyage to America must be left to the imagination, but those travels brought these initial sojourners to Detroit in 1832. Soon after they arrived in Detroit, Mary and John bought 80 acres of land. Their land deed was signed by Andrew

Jackson, then President of the United States. What an unimaginable bounty that must have seemed to these Irish Catholics who had left behind them such a dearth of land holdings among their compatriots!

The land which John and Mary purchased from the government was located eleven miles north of the center of the developing city of Detroit. Because they were outside the core of the city there were no roads to the Whalen farm. But that would not deter this industrious couple. They began their rugged frontier lives the same way the other pioneers did. John cleared the land and built a log cabin, beginning a life comparable to that of Abe Lincoln, the teenager who lived miles to the south of the Whalens. That log cabin where John and Mary made their first home was on Indian Trail, north of Puritan Avenue and west of Church Road, now Hubbell Avenue in Detroit.

Typical of the pioneer life, the Whalens started farming, growing corn and potatoes. Did John stand in grateful awe as he looked down at the corn, some of it growing around the tree stumps and some of it in long neat rows? Did Mary, freshly dug potato in hand and filled with unutterable thoughts, whisper a prayer for her starving, dying kind and kin in the homeland?

In addition to these staples, the Whalens gathered wild berries from the region. Necessarily industrious and ambitious as these early settlers had to be, the Whalens added cattle to their economy. According to Will Murphy, when the killing frosts came and claimed the corn, tree bark was sometimes used for the cattle. The Whalens added further to their income by churning and selling butter. They had many trees on their property so they also sold firewood to help keep "the wolf from the door."

Not only for the Whalens, but for all on the great American frontier the 1830s and 1840s were periods of burgeoning growth. It was inevitable, that just as their eastern city sisters, New York, Boston, and Philadelphia outgrew their boundaries so would the more westerly cities like Chicago and Detroit. As Detroit began to seep out into the country-side, the Township of Greenfield constructed a road. The progressive

Whalens then built another cabin on that road and looked toward their future. It was here in Greenfield Township that the Whalens had their second child, a little girl they called "Mary" after her mother.

Of course, homesteading along the American frontier was fraught with its own set of troubles. Though not so grave as the troubles back in Ireland, they were formidable nonetheless. Living at a distance from the great growing capitals of commerce, the head of the house had to find work where work was to be had. When crops were insufficient, or were lost altogether because of weather conditions and roving animals, provisions from another source became a necessity. Twentieth Century Americans have become vividly familiar with scenes in movies and in such TV series as "The Little House on the Prairie" where, sadly, the father has to leave his home and farm to work elsewhere.

Because the Whalens were having a hard time making ends meet, John left home to work on the Erie Canal near Maumee, Ohio. Mary remained behind in Detroit to care for their son, Patrick, and their daughter, Mary. Tragic news arrived for the family one day when Mary, faithful wife and mother, was summoned to go to Toledo because John, her husband, was gravely ill. Before she reached her destination, John was dead and buried. Typhoid fever caused many deaths among the canal workers. Mary was now alone in the New World, a world that must have started to seem like a mirror of the Old World.

And again, typical of immigrants, Mary did not give up. After a few years she found solace and comfort in another Irishman, Charles Murphy. Charles Murphy's parents had also come from County Cork in Ireland. Charles Murphy and Mary Lawlor Whalen were married and, on January 8, 1853, their only son, James, was born. James, who was to become Will's "good Father," began life in hardship also. His father, Charles Murphy, died of a heart attack while trying to help a neighbor dig a well. James was only two years old. Again, sharing the troubles of a legion of her pioneer sisters, Mary Lawlor Whalen Murphy found herself without a husband to help support her and the children. However, given the stature and faith of the family she led into American history, Mary's hard work and integrity helped her as she and her three children, Patrick Whalen, Mary Whalen, and James Murphy, continued the Murphy odyssey in the New World.

In time, James assumed responsibility for the family farm. As with most pioneers the "many devices" of the human spirit surmounted the mountains and continued in the plains and valleys. The legacy of the home, the farm, and the economy of John Whalen and Charles Murphy was such that by the age of twenty-five James was selling cattle.

With this increase in their fortunes the Murphys were able to build their first two-story brick and stone house. This would be the house that Will's father and mother would live in for the rest of their lives and it was where they would die. This would be the house that Will would call "home" for sixty years, the house where he would spend many happy hours playing with his brothers and sisters. It would be the house, the home that he would leave behind him when he moved to North Carolina. Having abandoned the log cabins, the Murphys were now firmly launched on American soil.

My Good Mother

1966, My good mother was born on April 2nd, 1855 in Detroit. Mass for her today.

1967, My good mother was born on April 2, 1855 at 56 Locust Street, now Henry St. in Detroit.

The entries in the ledger continue. Anniversaries of "my good mother" are never to be forgotten. Each year an entry is made to commemorate the date of birth and death of "my good mother," Margaret Garland Murphy.

The Garland fortunes appear to have been a little more fortuitous than those of the Whalens. This branch of the family had its roots in the noted village of Clondalkin, just southwest of Dublin. Clondalkin was founded around 600 A. D. by Chronan. Chronan established a monastery there and the village grew up around the monastery. St. Chronan became the first abbot of the monastery. As with many monasteries the raising of sheep was an important labor of love. At some point near the middle of the Eighth Century, Saint Fugillius became the first Bishop of Clondalkin. Roman Catholicism was becoming deeply rooted in Clondalkin.

This was the era of Ireland's famed artistic manuscripts of the Gospels on "sheep skin," better known as "vellum." The Clondalkin Mass Book, now at the Karlsruhe Library in Germany, was one of these manuscripts.

In the twelfth century, Clondalkin Diocese was united with Dublin. Clondalkin became an even more significant ecclesiastical village of both prayer and learning. However, in 1641, the village and church of Clondalkin fell prey to the ever-present Irish curse–the British. England sent a detachment of troops into the village and they torched the entire region, destroying castles such as the one at Deansrath, and even massacring women and children. Nonetheless, Clondalkin prospered, aided by its proximity to Dublin. A gun powder mill was built there in 1783. A paper mill, established at Sally Park in 1837, produced paper in Clondalkin for the next one hundred and fifty years.

It was in this village of rich history that Michael Kelly Garland, Will Murphy's maternal grandfather, was born. He was educated at Monmouth College and Seminary, and at the age of twenty married sixteen year old Julia McGourke of the same village. The couple was married on August 15th, the Feast of the Assumption, in 1840. Immediate sojourners, the Garlands left Ireland on the very day of their marriage and set sail for America. Their destination at the beginning of their sea voyage was Chicago, but that would change by the time they disembarked.

In those early days of the nineteenth century, the trek across the Atlantic Ocean often took six weeks. This was ample time for the travelers to have a variety of experiences, to meet new people, to conceive new ideas, and to undergo many changes. The most notable encounter for the Chicago-bound Garlands was their meeting with a family named Ford. The Garlands and the Fords struck up a lasting friendship on their trip across the ocean. As a result of that friendship the Garlands changed their plans. They would disembark at Detroit instead of Chicago because the Fords were disembarking at Detroit. How different Will Murphy's life might have been if the Garlands had gone on to Chicago instead of stopping in Detroit.

Detroit–Home to the Murphys

Will Murphy was very much interested in the history of his native city. In various interviews with Sister Jean Linder, Jim Cinque, and Fred Woodall, he spoke of his love for the farm and for the city of Detroit. When he mused, in his later years, on "the big old city," his ardor was somewhat diminished because of what Detroit had now become. However, the old priest would still speak with pride as he related the history of his native city, a history he knew so well and loved to share with others.

The city of Detroit was founded in 1701 by Antoine de la Mothe Cadillac (1658-1730) and a group of French Catholics who settled on the west and south side of what eventually became Detroit. It is germane in a biography of the Whalens, Garlands, and Murphys, to note here that Cadillac had with him two priests and that within the year of founding the city, the foundation of St. Anne's Church was laid. St. Anne's was the first Catholic Church in what became the state of Michigan.

"The sun never sets on the British empire," so goes the cliché. That movement toward worldwide power by the British reached North American shores when the English encroached on the region that was to become Detroit. Consequently, Cadillac, along with approximately one hundred followers and an equal number of Native Americans, built a fort on the straits between Lake Erie and Lake St. Clair, calling it Fort Ponchartrain.

In 1760, the British took Fort Ponchartrain and renamed it Fort Detroit. However, the success of the American colonies in ridding themselves of the mother country eventually reached the frontier regions such as Detroit. In 1796, the British were forced from that territory and, in triumph, the American flag was first raised there. However, as the Whalens were arriving in Detroit, the threat of England, though less in America than in Ireland, was nonetheless a continuing reality. As late as 1813, the residue from the belligerency of the War of 1812 forced American soldiers once more to recapture the fort from the British.

Other woes of developing cities touched Detroit. In 1805, a gust of wind blew a small ember from the tobacco of a pipe and sparked a fire that eventually burned the whole city of Detroit. And then, in 1832, just as the Whalens were settling in the frontier region, a ship of soldiers going west docked and brought cholera with them to Detroit. Eleven soldiers and twenty-eight residents died in the epidemic.

On the positive side, as the Whalens, Garlands, and Murphys were launching their lives in the 19th Century, Detroit was initiating that stream of economic, political, and social activities that would make it one of the booming cities of the America that was moving west.

In 1802, Detroit was incorporated as a town with its own marshal and, first things first, its own tax collector. By 1805, the city had grown to the point that Congress named it the seat of the new Territory of Michigan. A year later, Detroit became the first Michigan city to open a post office. In 1825, Detroit elected its first mayor.

In 1827, Rufus Wells installed the first water works in Detroit. The pumping station was located at the foot of Randolph Street. The first "water mains" were made entirely of tamarack logs bored with a three-inch hole lined with pitch. The logs were connected together with iron bands. Will Murphy's grandfather and Henry Ford's father used to help cut the logs and bring them to the city for the water lines. Charles Murphy was well known around the country for his ability to take an unhewn log and hew it perfectly.

In 1837, Michigan's legislature met for the first time in Detroit.

In 1838, the first city-owned pumping station was erected at the foot of Orleans Street. The wood mains were discarded in favor of cast-iron pipes. Many people secured pieces of the old water main to keep for souvenirs. Catherine Bodenmiller, Father Murphy's niece, gave him a one-foot piece of hollowed log that he kept in a prominent place in his library. After all, it could have been one of the logs hewn out by his grandfather.

In 1847, the first telegraphed message reached Ypsilanti from Detroit. Cities were "growing up" side by side.

Undoubtedly one of the most significant events in American history occurred just outside the city environs. *On July 30, 1863, Henry Ford was born.* The human fabric of this birth would weave its way through American history, going beyond it to thread through most human lives on the planet after first being stitched into the tapestry of the Garland family.

The Fords and the Garlands would remain friends long after the sea voyage from Ireland that brought together the two families, one staunch Protestant, the other fervent Catholics. Henry Ford was destined to transform millions of people into worldwide travelers. However, it wasn't until Michael William Murphy was five years old, in 1896, that Charles B. King of Detroit became the first person to drive a horse-less buggy through the streets of his city.

Julia and Michael Garland always felt their journey to Detroit was guided. And blessed. The couple had fourteen children. Among the fourteen children was a girl born on April 2, 1855, whose name was "Margaret."

The boon of longevity in the Murphy tree can be traced to this branch. Julia McGourke Garland lived to the age of 95, and so did her daughter, Margaret, thus beginning a Garland-Murphy tradition. That flow of long-living stalwart blood would stream down and muster her grandson, Will, well into his ninth decade.

The Marriage Blessing

"My good father and mother were married, June 1st, 1880, at Holy Trinity Church, 6th and Porter Street, Detroit, Michigan."

This ledger entry chronicled the most important event in the life of Michael William Murphy. He would be born of this union eleven years later on August 8, 1891.

James Murphy was hard at work when he met Margaret Garland. He was 28 years old and she was 25. In 1880 the Murphys were still years away from their eventual considerable familial prosperity. In addition to his farm work, James took on the task of making charcoal. Using the age-old method, James placed chopped logs in a pyramid position, leaving an ample center for the fire to be made. Over the pyramidal structure he would put dry leaves and straw that would ignite from the central flames. Once the pyramid was burning, the fire had to be fed every two to three hours, day and night, for two weeks.

James had successfully completed one such pyre-payload just before his wedding day. Reflecting on his father's humility, propriety and deep faith, the legendary Irish twinkle would come into old Father Murphy's eyes a century later as he told his favorite story of his father's "Marriage Economic Development Plan."

In an interview with Jim Cinque and Fred Woodall, Father Murphy told how by the time the wedding day approached his father had finished his pyrotechnic labors and had the product that would provide him with a small nest egg upon which to begin his marriage. The charcoal was ready and his father planned to take it to Detroit to sell on the market. Charcoal was a booming business during this era. In addition to its various home uses in the 1800's, charcoal was increasingly significant in the commercial world. Tailors, for instance, used charcoal to fire their irons. "The law of supply and demand enabled my father to return home with a $20 gold piece, a considerable fortune at that time," Murphy would say.

Continuing his story about his father's wedding day, he told how considerate his father was of his horses. "He drove home after delivering the charcoal. The team was tired, so my father got cleaned up and walked from his home back to Detroit, about 12 miles. He went down to visit a cousin named Lawlor, and then the next morning he walked to Holy Trinity Church to his wedding."

One can imagine with what anticipation the young bridegroom traveled with the shining gold piece shimmering in his hand. What daydreams must he have entertained! Should he use the gold piece for a special memento to commemorate the holy sacrament that would unite him to Margaret Garland, something she would treasure all their lives together? A necklace? A brooch? A ring with a special stone in it? Maybe it should be spent on some unexpected little delicacies for the wedding guests? Or perhaps it would be best to use it with Murphy practicality and buy some necessities for their new home?

Whatever the tune may have been that James' imagination danced to as he traveled that day, one thing was for sure. This good young Catholic man, preparing to be the head of a household, would give the priest who performed the ceremony a full $5 of his charcoal lode. That would leave him $15 with which he could begin married life. Thus, after the ceremony, in the throes of joy and prosperity, and in anticipation of beginning a new life with cash in his pocket, James handed the priest the $20 gold piece and waited for his change.

And waited. And waited. But he did not speak up.

The priest, not knowing what was in the bridegroom's mind and not aware that James Murphy was too good and too timid to ask for change, pocketed the $20 gold piece, rejoicing in having received a stipend that had to be unparalleled in the farmlands of America in 1880. The priest must have experienced a pleasant surprise at the generosity of James Murphy. What a husband, what a father this bridegroom would make!

The priest could not know that James and Margaret Murphy would be starting their new life together with only the thirty-seven cents that James had in his pocket. "But," Margaret Murphy said in closure, "it brought a blessing on the family."

Margaret Garland Murphy and James Murphy, Will Murphy's Parents

Soon the family was increasing, and the thirty-seven cents had to be stretched and stretched and stretched. Five Murphy children, Mary Frances, Julia Gertrude, James Garland, Patrick Whalen, and Louis Aloysius preceded Michael William.

> Michael William Murphy was born to James and Margaret Murphy on August 8, 1891, at the home of his parents in Greenfield Township. He was baptized September 13, 1891 in St. Mary's of Redford Catholic Church in Detroit. His godfather was James Clinton; his godmother was Monica Garland.

Two siblings, Margaret Ellen and Joseph Elliottt, were born after Will. Unusual for the era, only little Patrick Whalen died before the age of two. An entry in the ledger shows that Will Murphy never forgot the little brother who died six years before he, Will, was born. In his ledger for January 10, 1962, he wrote, "Patrick Whalen Murphy was born Jan. 10th about 77 years ago. Died April 19 same year." Some entries seem to indicate that little Patrick died a year later, when he was a year and three months old. That would have been in 1885 or 1886. Will would not be born until 1891. And yet each year he remembered the birthday of the little brother he never knew.

Berries, Berries, and More Berries

With those thirty-seven cents in their pocket, the Murphys set up their homestead on their 80-acre farm located on Six Mile Road and Hubbell. They struggled to farm the soil. It was poor and sandy and the yields were not great. By the time the Murphys and Garlands reached Detroit the French had bought up most of the good land so the new arrivals had to settle on the sandy land 12 miles northwest of Detroit.

"The first two generations of Murphys in the new country barely got by on the poor soil," said Father Murphy, "but then a funny thing happened. It was discovered that the poor soil was ideal for raising berries, and the next generation of Murphys built what was the biggest berry farm in Michigan."

The enterprising Murphys had made a discovery. In time, berries became the family's major economic enterprise. The Murphys would grow and sell strawberries, red raspberries, black raspberries, and blackberries. Will was only three years old when he helped to pick berries.

Even though the other siblings also helped, the Murphys needed additional workers for their fields. They got this extra help from the children of Polish immigrants who would come out from the city to help pick the berries. The children would sing-song their favorite slogan, "One for Murphy, one for me." The Murphys didn't mind. They knew what it was to be poor and to relish every little delicacy that came their way.

According to Will the children rode about ten miles on the streetcar and then walked the rest of the way from the street car stop to the Murphy farm. They carried workingmen's tickets. These tickets, provided by the Murphys, were eight for twenty-five cents, and could be used only for two hours in the morning and two hours at night. A regular ticket would have cost five cents. Enough money was made from the sale of the berries that the Murphys were able to purchase several other pieces of property.

Father Murphy's niece, Catherine Bodenmiller, vouches for the fact that the Murphys not only were good to their workers but they also enjoyed the pleasure others got from the produce they hauled to the fresh market every day. "Indeed," Father Murphy would say, "raising berries was a very good business." But it had its day and the berry fields gave way to housing projects.

With the additional property the Murphys were able to buy and with the city of Detroit touching on their original property, the Murphys got involved in constructing homes. Building took a prominent place in the Murphy family, and Father Murphy, even until his dying day, could tell you where they built their first cabin, then a second cabin, and then a brick and stone house. He could also point out the many homes the Murphys built on the outskirts of Detroit.

"Lead Kindly Light"

The chief guiding light for Will Murphy was, of course, his mother. Margaret's total, unquestioning, simple faith is revealed, first of all, in what Will called "My mother's favorite prayer," a prayer which he often recited publicly after offering the Holy Sacrifice of the Mass and when telling visitors about his mother. Will grew up hearing his mother pray,

Jesus, Jesus, dearest Lord,
Forgive me if I say,
For very love of Thee,
Thy sacred name,
A thousand times a day.
I love Thee so I know not how
My transports to control,
My love is like a burning fire
Within my very soul,
Then teach me, dearest Jesus,
In Thine own sweet loving way,
All the lessons of perfection
I must learn this blessed day.
Give me a heart to know Thee
That loving Thee and serving Thee
Faithfully in this world,
I might adore Thee and love Thee
Forever in Thy heavenly kingdom
Sweet Jesus, hear my prayer.

As with most farm children at the turn of the century, the children of James and Margaret Murphy had to create play where they could. No television, computer, or the rest of the contemporary smorgasbord of technological time-eaters contended for their attention, so Michael William and his siblings often played in the backyard of their farmhouse. One day as they were playing their mother came out on the porch. Margaret stood there a while watching as her children played their games. The children found nothing unusual in this arrival of their constant sentinel. Suddenly Margaret began to shout *"LOOK! LOOK!"*

The children stopped their game and looked where their mother was pointing. They saw nothing. Looking back to the porch they saw with what awe and stunning certainty their mother pointed beyond them. So they looked again in the direction of her pointing. They stared. They saw nothing.

"There! There! Just above you! Don't you see? It's the Blessed Virgin Mary!"

The children did not see anything but knowing, as they did, the depth and ardor of their mother's strong faith, they could not doubt that she saw something.

"Look, now can you see them? It is Our Lady. There are three monks with her."

The children still did not see. However, the apparition was so awesome that Margaret went back inside her house thinking she was going to die. The children were stunned at first. And then they ran into the house to be with their mother. They found her lying on her bed. They thought she was dead. They knew that when people died other people brought flowers so they began to cry and ran out of the house to gather some flowers. They put the flowers on her as she lay on her bed. They sobbed out loud. Their sobbing woke her up. She was amazed to see how she had frightened the children, and so she joined them in their crying. When she saw the flowers she realized how disturbed her children really were. She also realized how disturbed her flowerbeds must be.

The Murphys had a picture of the "Mother of Sorrows," which was a gift from France. Maggie Murphy held it in great reverence; she could identify with the Mother of Sorrows because she, too, had lost a son, an infant son. At some time or other she mentioned that she would like to have that picture placed in her coffin when she died. Little Elliottt never forgot.

The Sunday following the vision, Maggie Murphy was still aglow with her unusual experience. When she came home from church she went straight to her bed, saying that she did not feel well. It was unusual for her to be sick. The children were very upset. They feared that this time she really would die. Will's young brother Elliottt, wanting to be helpful, said, "Mother, shall I get your picture so they can put it in your coffin?" Again, the children were afraid of losing their mother. Again, Will's eyes filled with tears as he recalled her. "My mother was a wonderful woman, but then are not all mothers wonderful?"

Growing in Age and Grace—Wisdom??

The children did what they could to help make the farm a success. Among the manifest plagues of the farmer were the ever-present and miraculously healthy bugs. *Paris Green* was a popular pesticide at the turn of the century, and one day little Will and Margaret Ellen were sent to the store to get some *Paris Green* to kill the potato bugs.

The nearest store was a good two miles away and the children had to walk there. They walked and they walked. They walked at the usual pace of children and by the time they reached their destination they were starving. So they used their heads and listened to their stomachs. They looked at the tempting goodies in the store and succumbed. They bought some cheese and crackers to fuel themselves for the long two-mile trek back home.

With childhood's lusty appetite, Margaret and Will ate well as they marched back to the homestead. As they were nearing home, fairly satiated and down to just a few crumbs, they remembered that they had not been sent on this journey to gorge themselves on crackers and cheese. No. What they had gone to the store to get was still in the store. They had forgotten all about the *Paris Green* until they were almost home. How salty the last taste of cheese and crackers must have been as the little ones realized they had forgotten to get the pesticide! How longingly they must have wished for the salt of wisdom that could keep them from such folly! "I don't remember what my parents said when we got home," said Father Murphy as, in his later years, he would laughingly recount the story, "but I know we didn't get a spanking."

All of Will Murphy's memories about his childhood centered around family, poverty, and "fun" things." "We were so poor!" he would say so often. And, as usual he would add, "I'm so glad I grew up poor and on the farm."

Like his brothers and sisters Will went to the country grade school. The first day he went to school he stayed only until recess. By that time he had had it with school. He was homesick and so he went home! There were many more interesting and challenging things to do at home. Will Murphy always laughed heartily when he told of this early childhood experience. He always added, "And then I didn't go back to school for two years!" After two years he was willing to give school learning another try.

And so he went back to school. After graduating from the sixth grade Will attended the Ypsilanti Normal School, and though such schools generally trained teachers, Will did not become a teacher. He stayed home to help with the chores and to engage in his own hobbies. He loved the great outdoors. When he was thirteen years old, after putting a two-cent stamp on an envelope, he wrote to his brother Louis who, apparently, was spending the winter with his uncle and aunt.

Dec. 15th, 04
My Dear Brother,
I thought I would write a few lines to you. I have not seen you in so long a time. I wish you and Uncle Lewis and Aunt Ella would come out hunting some Sunday.
I have been out hunting several times but I haven't got anything yet.
At school there is only one boy bigger than myself, and we have some great times. The bigest boy is always trying to wash our faces, but some times we get the best of him and wash his face. And some times we have a fight.
I suppose you have a great time playing snow ball in town.
I am in the sixth grade in everything but arithmetic and that I am in the seventh. Have you been out hunting very mutch and have you got many rabbits. I make my own powder and shot but the shot is not very good, I cannot make it round enough. I think that is about all that I can think of this time.
I remain yours truely
Ans. Soon. William Murphy

The letter is in his handwriting. The handwriting is legible but not A+. And the spelling is his original.

Will was a great lover of sports. Hunting, fishing, camping, and swimming all kept him out of trouble. Swimming was one of his favorites. In the wintertime, he took his mother to Florida where he could swim in the ocean. When he wasn't making use of the swimming pool he built at the Falling Waters Motel he explained, "Once you swim in the ocean you'll never swim in a pool again. Too small."

Climbing telephone poles also provided Will with a way to get rid of some of his youthful energy and it fit right into his daring spirit. It also fit right into his way of exciting his mother. He said, "When I was young I used to climb up the telephone pole to amuse my nieces and nephews. I would stand there on the very tip of the pole and wave my arms. My mother never really liked that."

That wasn't the end of his daring. His niece, Catherine Bodenmiller, recalls how some beautiful Sunday afternoons Mrs. Murphy wanted the boys to take her and the girls out for a ride. The boys much preferred tinkering with the car. Because this always happened on a Sunday afternoon she wasn't at all pleased with her sons. Sundays are not to be "tinker with the car" days! Sundays are for the Lord—and the Ladies!

So what did the boys do to make things right with "my good mother?" Will bragged when he told how they did take his mother and the girls out for a ride, not so much to please them as to show off the car and what it could do. After giving the ladies a nice smooth ride they would find an icy field and speed around in that, deliberately putting on the brakes so the car would go into a spin. They loved to hear the ladies yell out at them. It seemed there was nothing the boys enjoyed more in their daredevil youth than giving their mother and sisters some heart-stopping scares. For them it was not a scare but a thrill, and something that Will remembered years afterwards and retold with glee.

When he was still Mr. Murphy, one of his favorite Sunday afternoon activities, when he wasn't taking his mother and sister for a ride, was to take young girls to the convent, to the Immaculate Heart of Mary Convent in Monroe, Michigan, and the Dominican Convent in Adrian. He had one of the few Cadillacs in the neighborhood and enjoyed sharing it with others in this way. He felt it was a real privilege to be of service to anyone who wanted to pursue a religious vocation.

One of the Adrian Dominicans recently related how some of the younger Sisters would hide when he stopped to take the Sisters for a Sunday afternoon ride. They didn't want the Superior to know where they were for fear they would be the ones assigned to go with Will Murphy for a ride. The young Sisters weren't anxious to go with him primarily because he was so taken up by everything he saw along the way that he drove at a snail's pace.

He also chauffeured young men who were entering the Jesuit Seminary in Milford, Ohio. When asked why, as long as he was at the seminary, he didn't apply to enter, he thought for a moment, smiled sheepishly, and then began to sing, "Don't fence me in!" He enjoyed freedom in the wide open spaces. He wasn't ready yet to be fenced in by seminary rules and walls. Besides, his mother was still living and he wanted to take care of her. However, he never totally abandoned the idea that maybe, just maybe, some day he would pursue the priestly vocation. He once said that even though he was a prominent businessman he never felt totally at home in the secular world.

Long before cars became an important part of Will's life he was fascinated with horses. He had a particular love for horses because the Murphys had horses on their farm. He inherited his love for horses from his father who walked to church on his wedding day in order that the horses could have a rest. Will practically went into ecstasy in his later years when friends took him to a circus and he saw the beautiful horses perform. "Oh my, oh my, oh my!" he would say while giving his famous "dominus vobiscum" hand gestures. He sensed though, that the performances were not a part of the horse's normal routine and feared that the trainers whipped the horses to get them to perform.

One day one of his friends gave him a miniature model of a Clydsdale horse. When he saw it he remarked, "Oh my goodness! This is just like the horses we had on the farm that I used to take care of. My mother used to be so afraid because I would ride them around standing on their backs."

While the great outdoors provided Will with much to do in the line of play and work he needed other outlets. He needed to exercise his inventive mind and explore his creative genius. He loved to "tinker" as is evident in the penny postcard he sent his sister, Mary Francis,

Dear Sister,
When you come home please bring some sandpaper for the violin. We are well. Hope you are the same.
From Your Brother Wm. Murphy

And then on the front of the card, as if it were a PS, he wrote, *"If you didn't send some glue by mail, I wish you would bring some too. You can get it at the Hardware Store."*

This post card was sent on December 30, 1908. Murphy would have been seventeen at the time and he was building his own violin. In an interview, many years later, Father Murphy said, "My Uncle Louis Chevillot was asked to play for the different county functions. He was well known for his violin playing. When I was a young man I played at the county dances on Saturday nights with my uncle's violin. They said I had a natural talent for music and I took some lessons. I loved to play the violin!"

When he retired years later he would show visitors the one violin that he made and the back of another one that he started but did not finish. He carried that partial violin with him wherever he went, evidently hoping that some day he could finish it. When displaying that unfinished violin he would stroke it and comment on the fine wood that was in it. When questioned about his violins he said, "I built a violin once and the back of another one, but I never finished it. It was beautiful." That "aborted" violin seemed to be just as much his friend as was the one he finished.

Occasionally Will would pick up his violin and play an Irish tune. He would even give out a few dance calls. In his later years, however, he declined the invitation to play saying his fingers were too stiff. The spirit was willing but the flesh would not cooperate.

Will Murphy would move from violins to radios. When an interviewer said to him, "Father, I hear not only do you build big things, but you also have built small things, like radios."

He answered, "Oh, yes, we used to build crystal radios and sell them." He added, "I did so much soldering that my brother said that when I die they'll put a soldering iron in my coffin. An electrician once told me that I could pass the exam." Marconi, an Italian electrical engineer and inventor, was seventeen years older than Will. It seems safe to say that this man who installed the first radio in the Vatican was an inspiration to young Will.

Labor is the Sweetest Joy

As the "Gay Nineties" swept into American History the Whalens, the McGourkes, the Garlands, and the Murphys were safe and at home. Though hard work and hard times were a part of their lives, Detroit and its environs were the safe haven, and the developing frontier American character was stamping its image on the budding Murphy household.

Having been born in 1891, when the infant country was just over a century old, William Michael Murphy was about to enter an era filled with challenges. In just the opening decades of his life, events in the United States occurred that were to impact negatively and positively on his world as it moved into the next century. In the twenty-six years after the end of the Civil War, the United States had experienced social, technological, political, and economic heights all but incomparable for any nation in a similar period of time.

Alexander Graham Bell had improved human communication. The dull ring of phones would gradually, household by household, connect the whole sea of humanity.

John D. Rockefeller endowed the University of Chicago. The developing sense of philanthropy that families like the Carnegies and Rockefellers were pioneering would become a part of the tradition Will Murphy would continue.

Thomas Edison's light bulbs were flashing out from Menlo Park to materialize in astonishing new inventions that made the 20th century bubble with expectation. Edison, with his kinescopic camera, was taking the first steps that would end, for better or for worse, in Hollywood. Will Murphy would be among the first to buy his own movie camera, an early edition of the 8-millimeter variety, and would delight in making his own home-made movies, movies of his travels in Europe, of weddings and other important events in the family.

In 1892, when Will was just a year old, the Populist Party held its first convention in St. Louis. This party was established essentially for the southern and western agricultural interests but the advances made by this strong third party were also of significance to the booming berry farmers in Michigan, the Murphys.

Also in 1892, at the increased urgings from the Pacific coast territories, the Chinese Exclusion Act was passed. This act again evidenced the concern that second and third generation Americans felt about being invaded by "new" foreigners. There were no nationalities or races exempt from prejudices. The same Irish who experienced prejudice from the Boston Brahmin might themselves move on to New York and practice discrimination against the African Americans who came up from Alabama. In the southwestern states, it was the Mexican and Latin Americans who suffered from discrimination. In the west, it was the Orientals; and throughout America it was the "new" European immigrants from Italy or Hungary, from Germany or Poland, of Slavic or Jewish descent. In New Orleans eleven Italian immigrants were lynched as a result of the acquittal of three Italians in the killing of a sheriff.

The World's Fair was held in Chicago in 1893, and was full of new wonders, heralding a provocative new century ahead. Since Chicago was the original destination of the Garlands and since there was a growing interest in automated vehicles it can be presumed that some of Will Murphy's relatives visited the fair.

At the World Exposition in 1893, Frederick Jackson Turner delivered his classic thesis on frontier life as the mode of existence that would define the best of America's unique character. Turner, noting the importance of the movement that drove intrepid settlers farther and farther west, suggested that the cross-country journey was the "most fundamental, dominating factor in United States history." He claimed that the frontier shaped, "not only the character of Americans, but also the nature of their institutions."

In 1894, the marching of Coxes' Army on Washington, D. C. was a declaration of war on management by American labor forces. That declaration would be succeeded by years of strikes and battles and the eventual creation of unions. The Murphy berry farm that employed children of Polish immigrants might have been affected by some of the new legislation resulting from labor's demands.

By 1896, Sears Roebuck had begun a mail order business that offered free delivery. Though the Murphy's proximity to Detroit enabled them to have better access to commodities than many other people had, they must have rejoiced with most other Americans as the 19th Century glided into the era of the greatest consumerism recorded in human history up to that time.

In 1898, the sinking of the American ship, *The Maine*, saw America become involved in a foreign war. This involvement was interpreted by many, at home and abroad, as the nation's first baby steps toward becoming a great power. America was courting imperialism. The fear of imperialism was of such concern that in 1899 the American Anti-Imperialist League was formed. The sympathizers with the new League must have felt justified because the same year there was an uprising in the Philippines over American control.

As a boy, Will Murphy saw first hand the daily hardships of frontier life. As an aging priest living in the warmer climate of his beloved Maggie Valley, he commented on the long, cold winters in Michigan. When asked in an interview if he was poor as a boy, Father Murphy answered lengthily and somewhat disjointedly, "I don't know how much we had. We were poor, poor farmers. We didn't have much. I never went to bed hungry in my life. But the trouble was my father…of course I don't blame him a bit but, you see, our people way back bought the land from the government."

Father Murphy went on to explain that his father went into debt to make land purchases, which, as land was so available at the time, seemed foolhardy. Later, however, as Detroit began to "bust out" of its city seams, the purchases would become a considerable investment. However, for a time, the land purchases were simply a debt hanging over their heads and rough, unpredictable farm life would be the route of Will Murphy's early boyhood.

It must have been during those early years of struggle that Will learned the lesson of the value of work. Though he could not recall who had taught him the verse, he recited the following for Sister Jean Linder, in an interview in February 1987, when he was 95,

Labor is the sweetest joy
The poor man works that he may live;
The rich man lives that he may work,
Each has his duty to perform;
Folded hands are ever weary;
Selfish hearts are never gay,
Active be, then, while you may.

Folded Hands Are Ever Weary

Yes, folded hands are very weary unless they are folded in prayer. Truly "my good mother," Margaret Mary Garland, would walk only a few steps behind the Blessed Virgin Mary, mother of God, on the spiritual voyage of William Michael Murphy. And so Will got involved in projects that would honor them both.

The vision of the Virgin Mary that Margaret Murphy had when the Murphy children were playing influenced the lives of all the Murphys but none as much as young Will. His mother's vision in his early childhood would forever be a port of faith from which he would set sail.

For their Golden Wedding Anniversary, Margaret and James, with their sons Will and Louis, took a trip to Italy. After seeing the most magnificent works of art and architecture, most of them tributes to Our Lady, they erected a small chapel on the sacred ground where Margaret experienced Mary.

When telling the story of their travels in Europe, Father Murphy could not identify the shrine after which they modeled their "St. Mary, Queen of Heaven Chapel," but did note that there was a shrine they had seen in Genoa, Italy, that impressed them so much they wanted to make a chapel like it. And so they did. Murphy had been constructing homes. This was his first attempt at a chapel. Later when he went to building churches he was well acquainted with the requirements.

Catherine Bodenmiller sent this article, written by Mary Nelson, and evidently intended for publication in some newspaper. It describes the chapel very well.

A tangible and melodious reminder of the fast disappearing days of the slow moving, gracious living of dignified old Detroit at the turn of the Century is an exquisite little chapel out on Hubbell Road near Six Mile in the northwest section of that now bustling and dynamic city.

The little chapel is situated on the property of the Murphy family. Mr. William Murphy and his mother occupy the seventy-five year old brick house on the same grounds as the chapel. This house with modern innovations is the same as it was when built by Mr. Murphy's grandfather four-score years ago.

Fifteen years ago, on a spot once covered by the early Missionary priests as they traveled up and down the rutted lanes on their visits to the scattered members of their parish, William Murphy gave tangible expression to that pioneer spirit with his erection on the family estate of a beautiful little shrine to the Blessed Virgin.

The perfect little Chapel, a replica of an ancient Romanesque cathedral, surrounded by the spacious and well kept grounds of the Murphy estate is one of the most beautiful spots in Detroit. This little chapel is an illustration of art, poetry, architecture and music all combined. It is indeed a lasting memorial to the esteem and honor for the Blessed Virgin. The name AVE MARIA over the door proclaims to the world the purpose of the shrine.

A life-size statue of the Blessed Mother made of marble was brought from Italy to crown the top of the building. At night a concealed spotlight illuminates the statue and causes it to cast a welcoming glow for many miles around the section. The "coldness of stone" is belied in the beautifully arched entrance of the Chapel. The perfect proportion and delicate tracery of windows and arches lend a glowing warmth to the welcome which invites any and all to this spiritual haven.

Within its walls, the exquisite altar, distinguished by its simple dignity and beauty of line, is banked daily with beautiful flowers, grown in the adjoining conservatory by Mr. Murphy. The sanctuary brackets are cast bronze figures. The entire work differs from ordinary lighting effects, being strictly ecclesiastical and suggesting medieval church lighting. The stained glass windows are made of the finest glass through which the light falls with a soft radiance on the beautiful interior. The Stations of the Cross, designed in Germany especially for the Shrine, and in perfect proportion, are bordered with the same mosaic as the altar.

A blue wrought-iron door invited entrance into the chapel. A beautiful altar, featuring mosaic tile of blue and white highlighted the interior of the chapel. The cloth adorning the altar was brought from Ireland by Mary Lawlor Murphy, Will's grandmother. Completing the aesthetic melting pot were statues of the Infant Jesus and St. Joseph from Germany, and stained glass windows from Czechoslovakia.

The most unique and outstanding feature of the Shrine is housed in the adjoining alcove to the left of the altar. Inside this alcove is an Estey Organ. Connected to the organ are two complete sets of chimes which may be played at the organ keyboard, either separately or together. The distinguishing feature of these chimes however, which sets them apart from any of their kind is a control box, hand made by Mr. Murphy himself, and which automatically controls the chimes. *Every hour after the chiming of the hour, there peals from the sounding tower outside, the AVE MARIA. At noon the chiming bells call the faithful to prayer with the ringing of the Angelus. At the conclusion of the century old melody the bells ring out sweetly and harmoniously the hauntingly beautiful refrain of "Holy God, We Praise Thy Name"*

The feature of this control which makes it unique is the fact that every detail of its construction was planned and made by hand by Mr. Murphy. Although he modestly shunts away praise and acclaim for his achievements, it is quite apparent even to an unscientific observer that hours of intense study and concentration have gone into the making of the control box. In as much as any human thing can be perfect this apparatus may be said to be perfect. Completed after months of painstaking labor and attention to the minutest details it proclaims in dulcet tones honor and glory to the Mother of God.

Five years ago in response to numerous requests, Mr. Murphy inaugurated a chime recital for an hour every Sunday night. At this time the control box is turned off and hymns honoring the Blessed Virgin and also hymns appropriate to the Ecclesiastical time of year are played over the Public Address system outside for the enjoyment of the surrounding section. The popularity of these recitals may be judged by the number of cars parked for blocks around the vicinity of the chapel every Sunday night as the time for the recital approaches. It is considered an honor for a musician to receive an invitation to play on this Sunday evening hour.

Many non-Catholics have found their steps turned toward the Church after a visit to the Chapel on a Sunday after the last dulcet tones of the bells have gone winging up to the star-sprinkled sky.

Inside, for those who are curious, there are numerous pamphlets explaining the origin and customs of the Catholic Church. Within, from every point, from windows and walls, to the statue above the entrance and the ringing of praises to her name, the visitor sees glowing around him the tokens and memorials to MARY.

Truly, *folded hands are ever weary,* and so Will Murphy, not wanting to be idle on his many "vacations" with his mother in Florida arranged for similar chimes to be placed in St. Ann's Church in Palm Beach, Florida. On December 8, 1946, the *Palm Beach Post-Times* printed the following,

"One of the finest sets of power chimes in the state of Florida will peal out today at services in St. Ann's Catholic Church. Installation of the amplified power chimes was announced Saturday following a week during which the instrument was installed by the Kimball Organ Co. The chimes are suspended beneath the Rose Window in the choir loft."

When Will Murphy built St. Margaret's church in Maggie Valley, he made sure this new church also was well equipped with chimes. Visitors who came to Falling Waters Motel at the foot of the church, and retreatants who came to Living Waters to pray, were enthralled when several times a day the chimes would send forth their melodious rendition of favorite hymns.

CHAPTER TWO

▼

CATHOLICISM-ALMOST NON-EXISTENT IN THE SOUTH

Although Will Murphy read the Bible and spiritual treatises most of his life, it was articles and pamphlets about the needs of the Church in the South that got his attention in his later years. When he read during the 1940s and 1950s of the church's scarcity in some southern states, Will developed a missionary zeal for spreading Catholicism there. There were reasons why Roman Catholics were scarce in the South.

South Carolina

According to historians of the period there were only two Irish Catholics living incognito in Charleston in 1775. When it was discovered that they were Irish and Catholic, they were tarred, feathered, and banished from the city. The accusation made against them was that they had conspired with Negroes in ways that "threatened the liberty of the country." Perhaps, if there was any legitimacy to the accusation, it resulted from Catholics being opposed to slavery.

As eternally, so now, law and spirit contended. The need for tolerance as mandated by the ideals of the Declaration of Independence (spirit) and the commands of the Federal Constitution (law) were at odds in town, county, and state. 1776 was a year when the concept of "all are created equal" was the "in-thing."

South Carolina eased up on the restrictions against Catholics when drafting its Constitution. Taking strides in stepping forward, South Carolina echoed, in its new Constitution, the spirit of the nation. It became one of the first states in the south to decree that Roman Catholics **could live** in the state "as individuals and as an organized group."

North Carolina

Organized religion had made very little headway in North Carolina during the proprietary period before it was made a state. As early as 1717, Governor Eden had referred to the deplorable state of religion in this " poor province." What could be done about it? What should be done about it? England was concerned about the lack of organized religion, not only in North Carolina, but in the entire South.

One solution would be to get the Governors moving. An edict went out. Every royal governor received official instructions from England to get laws passed which would give support to the Established Church of England and which would permit liberty of conscience to all persons **except Papists**.

That edict succeeded. In 1775, William Tryon, then governor of the North Carolina colony, reported to the Crown that "Every sect of religion abounds here **except Roman Catholicism**." Tryon was a Loyalist. As a Loyalist he was opposed to separation from Great Britain. As a Loyalist in charge of the North Carolina colony, he needed to report to the Crown what the Crown wanted to hear, and what the Crown wanted to hear was that the Church of England was growing in the colonies, and that Catholics were practically non-existent. Tryon was so devoted to the Crown that during the Revolutionary War he led Loyalist raids in New England.

When North Carolina finally had its own Constitution it made sure the restrictions on Catholics would be the standing order. Article 32 of the state Constitution forbade public office to anyone who denied the "being of God or the truth of the Protestant religion." This article was in direct violation of Article 19 of the Bill of Rights. It was, therefore, ignored to some extent. A few Catholics, Jews, and deists had been elected to public office in spite of Article 32.

In 1833, William Gaston, the most noted Roman Catholic in North Carolina, was elected to the Supreme Court of the state. He found Article 32 of the state Constitution particularly irritating because it forbade public office to those who did not belong to the religion that the Crown favored. At the Convention of 1835 Gaston worked hard to have Article 32 changed. For two days he addressed the Assembly, arguing in favor of dropping religious tests for public office, but no change was made except to substitute the word "Christian" for "Protestant." Catholics could now legally hold public office, but Jews and atheists still could not. However, the Carolinas would remain chiefly Anglo-Saxon and Protestant. Gaston felt that he had failed in his attempt to abolish religious prejudice.

Carroll–Prefect Apostolic

It goes without saying that, because of the level of anti-Catholic hostility, Catholics in these colonies would necessarily have kept any sign, suggestion, or sacramental of their faith hidden during those colonial days. However, following the Revolution, the awesome wave from the "Spirit of '76" sent rippling waves of democracy like a cleansing mist throughout the new states, creating a new exuberance seldom seen before in human history.

It was only after the Revolutionary War that the Holy See in Rome saw the need to take a look at what was going on in the States. In 1784, the Holy See named the Reverend John Carroll of Maryland's famed Catholic founding family, "Prefect Apostolic" and "Head of the Missions in the Province of the New Republic of the United States of

America." Now there would be a religious figure, an authority figure, to take an interest in eradicating some of the hostility that was so evident in the southern states. This authority figure would remain, however, subject to the authorities in Baltimore.

Assessing the situation, the new Prefect Apostolic concluded that the most immediate need was to arrange for clergy for the south. He sent Reverend Matthew Ryan to Charleston in South Carolina. Father Ryan was astonished that in a region so apparently bereft of Catholics there were approximately 200 Catholics gathered for his first Mass in Charleston.

Georgia and the Carolinas–A New Diocese

Despite the positive notes the struggle had only just begun. Problems arose that needed immediate attention. Baltimore was too far north to understand these problems and too far away to do anything about them. It was understandable, then, that a new See needed to be created.

On Sept. 1, 1820, Archbishop Carroll received a letter from Bishop-Elect John England that said,

My Lord,
I beg to inform Your Grace that I have received from Rome, a few days since, a Bull creating a new See in the United States of America, comprising North and South Carolina and Georgia, and appointing me to be the Bishop of Charleston, which is the capital of that See–and that the Bishop of Charleston is Suffragan of the Archbishop of Baltimore.

A new diocese was created. South Carolina, North Carolina, and Georgia now made up one diocese. This new diocese made it much easier for the Church to function in the South. This diocese would be known as the "Diocese of Charleston."

North Carolina, South Carolina and Georgia remained one See until 1850. Progress was being made and soon this one big diocese would have to be broken down. Further division was necessary. Bishop Ignatius Reynolds, the second Bishop of Charleston, had recommended that Georgia become a separate diocese. There was enough growth and activity in the Charleston Diocese to warrant the creation of a new diocese. Thus in 1850 the Diocese of Savannah came into existence. Consequently now only North Carolina and South Carolina comprised the Diocese of Charleston.

Catholics were beginning to come into their own. They were being accepted in the South and their numbers were increasing, necessitating more changes.

North Carolina–A Vicariate

At the Second Council of Baltimore, held in 1866, a proposal was made to the Holy See for the creation of a Vicariate in North Carolina. When a vicariate is created a vicar apostolic is chosen to rule the mission territory that has not yet been established as a diocese. A vicar apostolic, generally a bishop, has authority in the name of the Pope. He is the local ordinary of the territory to which he is assigned and he has most of the rights and obligations of a bishop who governs a diocese. A vicar apostolic, however, differs from a resident bishop of a diocese in that he does not exercise power in his own name. (Source, Grolier's Catholic Encyclopedia)

Bishop James Gibbons became the Vicar Apostolic of all of North Carolina. Only South Carolina would belong to the Charleston Diocese. Now there were two dioceses and one vicariate in the South where less than 50 years earlier there had been none.

Bishop Gibbons, accompanied by Archbishop Spalding, arrived at Wilmington on October 30, 1868. There he was met by Reverend M.S. Gross, his sole clerical companion, who had a congregation of about 400 persons in Wilmington.

It was one hundred years after Bishop Gibbons visited Wilmington that St. Margaret's church in Maggie Valley was dedicated. The South was yielding.

In his visitations around his juridical territory Bishop Gibbons noted that Catholic families were scattered throughout the state. While he saw their isolation as a danger to their faith, he also realized that these families were a means for enlightening many others. Books of religious instruction were in great demand. Catholics needed to know their faith. They needed to understand and appreciate their religion better. It was at the urgent request of Father Gross from Wilmington that Bishop Gibbons wrote *The Faith of Our Fathers.* By 1891, his book had sold nearly 200,000 copies. It was used all over the United States.

In 1862, the city of Wilmington was stricken with a yellow fever epidemic. Three Sisters of Charity of Our Lady of Mercy, a congregation that had been established by Bishop England in Charleston, responded to the call for help until the epidemic had subsided. This eventually led the Sisters of Mercy, allied with the Sisters of Mercy in Dublin, Ireland, to make a permanent foundation in Belmont.

Awaiting an opportunity, Bishop Gibbons planned the foundation of a Benedictine college. He found his opportunity in 1873, when he was able to petition the Venerable Reverend Archabbot Wimmer of St. Vincent's Abbey, Latrobe, Pennsylvania, for a foundation for the vicariate. The Archabbot had received a similar petition from a more favored diocese but Bishop Gibbons said it was the true spirit of God in the Archabbot that moved him to make the new foundation in Belmont, North Carolina. The vicariate would now have its own Catholic College.

The new vicariate of North Carolina was in the midsection of the Bible belt. The area would remain predominately Protestant. However, the increase in church membership and in priests serving the North Carolina vicariate continued and finally in 1924, the Diocese of Raleigh was established. North Carolina was no longer a Vicariate. It had attained the status of a Diocese. Raleigh would be the See city.

On December 5, 1925, Bishop William Hafey was consecrated the first Bishop of the Diocese of Raleigh. He was consecrated in the historic Cathedral of Baltimore by Archbishop Curley. At 37, Bishop Hafey was the youngest Bishop in the United States. Bishop Eugene McGuinness became the second Bishop of Raleigh in 1937. He had been an associate editor of the *Extension Magazine*, a magazine that Will Murphy read regularly. As the new Bishop, he continued to campaign for the South.

Most Reverend Vincent S. Waters, a native Virginian, was installed as the third Bishop of Raleigh on June 6, 1945. He wrote articles for the *Extension Society* on the needs of the Catholic Church in his diocese, articles that Will Murphy and his mother read. He visited parishes up North to seek financial assistance in order that he could carry on the work he felt needed to be done in his diocese. He had a tremendous influence on Will Murphy.

Bishop Waters of Raleigh, a Committed Leader

Bishop Waters provided forceful leadership for the North Carolina Diocese when he was appointed Bishop of Raleigh in 1945. He committed himself to establishing a parish in every county and to ending racial discrimination in every parish. He also committed himself to promoting Christian education in his Diocese. In the late fifties, the church was in the exciting days that led up to the Second Vatican Council. Liturgical and educational renewal was in the air.

On February 25, 1959, Bishop Waters wrote to Sister Madeleva, President of Saint Mary's College in South Bend saying, "I'm sending you under separate cover *Catholic Education in North Carolina* and wonder if you might be available for a session June 24-27 at Asheville to talk about what should go into a new type of college with people from CU & ND and everywhere? This is the beginning." Bishop Waters wanted a new-type of college in his diocese and he wanted it in the Asheville area. Belmont, which is near Charlotte, already had two Catholic Colleges, one operated by the Benedictines, and another by the Sisters of Mercy. "This is the beginning" refers to the new type of college he hoped to establish.

Sister Madeleva responded, "I would look forward very much to returning to Asheville this June except for the fact that I am under obedience to spend the summer in Europe. Perhaps another year I can bring much more back to you. Please continue to pray for all of the causes that are so dear to both of us."

Sister Madeleva had the same interest in higher Catholic education as Bishop Waters did. On May 15, 1959, he again wrote to Sister Madeleva,

"During the past ten years in the Diocese of Raleigh, curriculum preparation and improvement have been a major project. Although this will remain for some time a constant endeavor, we have come to the point where a new college curriculum for use in the preparation of our teachers, priests, and seminarians, as well as lay teachers would be helpful.

"Towards this end, we are forming a college planning group of some of the better known educators of the country to join with us two days during June in remote preparation of such a college curriculum. During these two days, the need and what should go into such a curriculum to prepare our sisters, priests, and lay people adequately for life and for the teaching profession will be principally discussed.

"I would be signally honored if you would be willing to join this group and enter into this discussion with us in Asheville on June 25th and 26th.

"This remote preparation shall proceed for several years before any actual steps will be taken to found such a college. However, I am sure you will appreciate how much we can get out of these sessions in these pioneering efforts."

This time he received a note back from the Secretary to the President of St. Mary's College that, "Your letter to Sister Madeleva arrived just as she was preparing for her departure to the east. She therefore asked that I send a word of acknowledgment to you. I need not assure you that Sister

Madeleva would be only too happy to help you if she were here. Your Excellency will understand her deep regret in the matter and her wish for success in your undertaking."

On March 14, 1960, Bishop Waters again wrote to Sister Madeleva saying, "Last year we formed a college planning group of some of the better-known educators of the country to join with us for two days during June in discussing the ideal college and its curriculum. I would be greatly honored if you would be willing to join our group this year and enter into these discussions with us in Asheville, July 5th-July 8th. May I hope to receive an affirmative answer from you and expect you in the beautiful mountains of Western North Carolina on July 5th?"

Sister Madeleva responded, "How very good you are to remember me in the farsighted and excellent plans that you have for your priests, seminarians, sisters, and lay teachers. Both you and your projects are irresistible. Some of our richest experiences in missionary activities have come to us through our days in your diocese. Unless something which I cannot at all anticipate should prevent me from coming, I shall be with you from July 5 to July 8."

Later that same year, after the July meetings were over, Bishop Waters wrote to Sister Madeleva, "Towards the end of this year's discussion, you will recall that you suggested that we take this discussion out of the ideal order and bring it down to the practical; then after we had picked out a great number of these Ideal Catholic Teachers and listed them that we ultimately call them "Master Professors." You suggested that we open a workshop next summer in Asheville under the auspices of a Steering Committee of the group that had made this study during the two years, and invite one or two or three of these "Master Professors" to conduct this common workshop for college teachers. We would keep the student body to about 40; that these "Master Professors" be brought up to date on our ideas and ideals and agree to help us to the extent of three weeks. Only two members of any community would be permitted to attend this workshop, to keep it small, and that they promise to follow through on their reading assignments, as well as attendance at future summer workshops to the extent of at least two or three.

"It was decided that the workshop would be called CONFERENCE ON CHRISTIAN HUMANISM and that the principle subjects to be covered in at least a three-year period would be the orientation of a college teacher for an Ideal College from the point of view of theology, philosophy, sociology, the humanities, and science, by two or three of these "Master Professors," each year for the three-year period.

"We hope to have a dormitory building completed by next year and to purchase additional property behind the high school which would contain a faculty residence. We already have two nice convents for the Sisters."

Sister Mary Madden, CSJ has also been helpful in providing the following information for us. She attended the lectures for two summers. She says, "After the release of the encyclical, *The Christian Education of Youth*, by Pope Pius XI the Catholic University of America was commissioned to develop curricula for Catholic elementary and secondary schools based on the integrated Christian values expressed in the encyclical. By the mid-fifties, Bishop Waters envisioned the development of the ideal Catholic College whose foundation would be those Christian values brought up to a higher level of learning.

"He consulted his good friend, Sister Madeleva of St. Mary's, Indiana. She helped him see the impossibility of his task, since Raleigh, N.C. was the poorest diocese in the U.S.A. However, she suggested that he could start a "Christian Humanism Conference" that could be spread over four or five summers. Each summer would be devoted to certain college subjects until all the important departments of learning were covered. The Bishop would invite Master Professors in each particular field and the Diocese of Raleigh would invite all college teachers to attend who would be interested in approaching their fields with new vitality and insights. In this way, many Catholic Colleges would be improved and move towards the ideal Christian vision of education.

"All the sessions were held in Asheville where Bishop Waters had built a new seminary. Professors with outstanding personalities and expertise came from as far as the Angelicum in Rome, Notre Dame, Columbia, etc. Some presenters came for only two or three days to contribute their expertise, like the writer Anne Fremantle. Others came for the full session such as Dr. Barry Ulanov from Columbia University. Father Nogar, OP, author of *Wisdom Of Evolution* and *Lord Of The Absurd* was quite outstanding and Sister Josetta, RSM, president of Xavier College, gave insightful lectures on Contemporary Trends in Higher Education."

Along with many others who dropped by for a day or two to speak was Reverend Ricardo Lombardi, SJ, founder of the "Better World Movement." He was accompanied by Reverend Stanley Kusman, SM, who was often called "The John Baptist of the Better World Movement in the USA." Bishop Waters invited the Better World Movement to make its USA headquarters in Asheville at Mount St. Mary's.

Bishop Waters was highly interested in any trend or movement that would further the cause of Catholic education on all levels. After all the sessions were over Bishop Waters requested Dr. Ulanov to put together a book containing the important lectures from each session.

Besides providing classes for those attending seminars, Bishop Waters took those attending the session on interesting side trips to the Cherokee reservation, the play, *Unto These Hills*, the Biltmore Estate, Mt. Mitchell, the Smokies, the Blue Ridge Parkway, concerts, plays, etc. He was very much interested in everything cultural and aesthetic.

Though Will Murphy appreciated the good work that Bishop Waters was doing for the Diocese, he was not invited to attend the Christian Humanism Conferences because he was not involved directly in education. He was instead very busy in what he considered HIS mission, the establishing of places of worship in the western-most part of the state so that the Gospel could be spread throughout the area. Bishop Waters encouraged him in his endeavors.

Sister Madeleva died in 1964. All plans to establish a college must have been abandoned at that time. There is no Catholic college in Asheville today.

St. John Vianney Hall

At the same time that Bishop Waters was working towards the establishment of a Catholic College he was also looking at other needs of the church. He saw the need for more priests, especially in the South, and sought to do what he could to encourage vocations to the priesthood. These were pre-Vatican days and the church was not yet giving much attention to the ordination of older men to the priesthood, nor to the ordaining of lay men as permanent Deacons.

Will Murphy knew what Bishop Waters was doing but he was more interested in building churches than in providing clergy for those churches. He had his heart set on fulfilling his mother's dying wish. She had requested that he build a church in the south. Bishop Waters could concentrate on education and vocation work; Murphy would concentrate on providing churches for those who would be ordained.

Bishop Waters had told Sister Madeleva that he hoped to have a residence hall ready in time for the use of those attending the Conferences on Humanism. The residence hall was ready and was named after the patron saint of parish priests because it was intended to be a resident center for young boys who were thinking of the priesthood.

In early May 1960, Bishop Waters sent a special-delivery letter to the parishes of his Diocese announcing the examinations that would be conducted to determine who would be accepted into the pre-seminary program. He wrote to the pastors, "I would like you to make the following announcement this coming Sunday, May 7th, at all the Masses.

"Scholastic examinations for those wishing to enter Saint John Vianney Hall at Asheville to study for the priesthood in September will be given in the following places this coming Saturday, May 13th. (Seven places listed). The examinations will take approximately four or five hours.

"We are hopeful that many will apply to take these examinations, as vocations to the Priesthood are very much in demand in North Carolina."

Evidently enough students applied to make the program for the next few years worthwhile. The Hall was located on the campus of the Asheville Catholic High School, the former St. Francis High School. Students living in the Hall were encouraged to participate in all school activities such as sports, student council, glee club, and the production of a school newspaper called the *Pathfinder*. The high school was co-educational.

Msgr. William G. Wellein, the Rector of St. John Vianney Hall, was pleased with the progress being made in the Diocese toward the education of young boys for the priesthood. Four years after the opening of the pre-seminary he wrote the following for the *North Carolina Catholic*, the Raleigh Diocesan publication. It was dated March 7, 1965, and entitled *Our Venture in Asheville–Four Years After.*

"Looking back, now, we can see that God HAS stood with us in this venture. With HIS help, we have graduated eight young men, during the past three years, into Seminary-College. Previously we were fortunate indeed, if we had even ONE high school graduate from North Carolina to enter Seminary-College in any given year.

"If all goes well, we shall have six more graduates in June ready for this step, four of whom are "charter" members having been at St. John's Hall since it began four years ago. The other two have been here three years.

"No one who has an understanding of the "vocation crisis" facing the Church in this modern age of ideas and changing values pretends anymore to have a "pat" answer as to how we can best meet the Vocation shortage.

"So far as the Diocese of Raleigh is concerned, we believe St. John Vianney Hall is a large part of the answer. It may not be the final answer; but it is better than merely sitting on our hands, theorizing or waiting for God to dump priestly vocations on our door step. We must think NOW about the future."

The future was dim. In spite of the efforts of Msgr. Wellein and all those connected with St. John Vianney Hall, enrollment in the pre-seminary did not increase significantly. The Hall was closed as a residence for young boys interested in the priesthood after the enrollment dropped considerably. An article in the Asheville daily paper, dated July 3, 1969, stated, "A decision to discontinue operation of St. John Vianney Hall and a program here for boys who desire to study for the priesthood was announced today by the Most Rev. Vincent S. Waters, Bishop of the Roman Catholic Diocese of Raleigh."

The closing of the Asheville Catholic High School, so closely connected with the pre-seminary, would follow in a few years. An article in the Asheville paper for May 1, 1972, announced *"Asheville Catholic High to Close."* Bishop Begley, the Bishop of the newly formed Charlotte Diocese, had made the decision to close the school. The paper quoted Father Ed Sheridan, at that time the principal of the school, as saying that "a lack of religious personnel for the faculty, low enrollment, and rising costs in education" were the reasons for the Bishop's decision to close the school.

Bishop Waters had made persistent and heroic efforts to promote Catholic education in western North Carolina, particularly in the Asheville area, but he never achieved the success he was looking for.

In 1974, the Asheville Catholic High School was sold to the Asheville-Buncombe Technical Institute, commonly known as AB Tech.

After its closing as a pre-seminary, St. John Vianney Hall continued to be used by the Diocese for various functions such as Cursillos. When the House of Prayer in Maggie Valley burned some of the events scheduled there were relocated and accommodated at St. John Vianney Hall.

In May 1979, St. John Vianney Hall was also sold to the Asheville-Buncomb Technical Institute.

Before the Hall was sold, Living Waters in Maggie Valley was given the opportunity to transfer some of the furniture and altar accessories to the new retreat facilities there. A gold-plated tabernacle, now in use at St. Margaret's Parish in Maggie Valley, was among the treasures retrieved from the seminary. The stained glass windows in the seminary chapel designed by the students under Msgr. Wellein's direction depicted some of the history of the Diocese as well as the symbols for the sacraments.

These windows were brought to Maggie Valley and installed in the chapel and hallway of the new Living Waters addition. Books from the school library were also given to Living Waters.

While Bishop Waters was arranging for the seminars in Asheville and was concerned with the seminary in Asheville he came on down to Maggie Valley to see how Mr. Murphy was coming along with the building of St. Margaret's. It was during these visits that he encouraged Will Murphy to consider the priesthood.

Evangelization Moves Farther Westward

The work of evangelization in Western North Carolina had begun long before Will Murphy arrived in the area. The Catholic presence moved even more westward when in 1925, Father Peter G. Marion of St. Lawrence in Asheville, purchased a home in Waynesville. It was remodeled and opened as a mission church in May 1926 with 27 members.

Father Jack McNearney, Glenmary, shares from the history he wrote regarding the growth of Catholicism in western North Carolina,

"Back in the 1930's the few Catholics (less than 50) that lived in the six most western counties (Cherokee, Graham, Clay, Macon, Jackson, Swain) of North Carolina were served from Waynesville. In 1936, Father Lane was pastor of St. John's Church in Waynesville and of all Western North Carolina. He gave a series of lectures on the Cherokee County Courthouse steps in Murphy in 1937.

"In 1938, Father Ambrose Rohrbacker became pastor of St. John and the western part of North Carolina. He occasionally celebrated Mass in Murphy or Franklin or Sylva or Bryson City. There were no Catholic Church buildings in those days so Mass was celebrated in the house of one of the parishioners. Or sometimes it was offered in a hotel like the Regal Hotel in Murphy or the Carolina Hotel in Sylva or in a funeral parlor or in a theater."

Father Ambrose Rohrbacker built a new church in Waynesville across the street from the old chapel on the site of a former Baptist Church and cemetery. The new St. John's was dedicated in 1941. On the same day a small church of the same design as St. John's, was dedicated in **Bryson City**. It was placed under the patronage of St. Joseph and seated about 80 people.

Father Rohrbacker also purchased the property adjoining St. John's Church. It was a "historical building" having been the home of Will Thomas. Will was born in 1805 about two miles from Waynesville. Thomas was the person who helped the Cherokee Indians regain some of their land after the infamous "Trail of Tears" forced them from their native land into Oklahoma. He was the only white man ever to become chief of the Cherokee nation.

Young Will Thomas went to work for an Indian trader, Felix Walker, who became a Congressman. He tended Walker's trading post on Soco Creek where all his clients were Indians. He learned their language, their customs, their lore, and their religious rites. He attracted the attention of Chief Yonguska, also known as Drowning Bear. When the chief learned that Thomas had neither father nor brothers he adopted him as his son and told his people that when he was gone Thomas was to be their chief. By the late 1820's, Will Thomas owned a dozen trading posts and was elected to the state legislature. He was instrumental in making some of the Smoky Mountain Indian Trails into passable roads.

Father Rohrbacker converted the Thomas home into a school in 1939. The Sisters of St. Francis from Milwaukee taught in the school. They lived on the second floor of the Thomas house. Boarding students had rooms on the third floor. Classes were held on the ground floor. In 1944 a high school was added.

After Father Lawrence Newman became pastor of St. John's, in 1950, he saw the need for a new school building in Waynesville. He built the school, a modern state-of-the-arts building. It was dedicated in 1956.

Father Vincent Erb, the next pastor of St. John's, moved the rectory into the Thomas house which now was no longer needed as a school. He tore down the old rectory to make a playground for the school. In 1963, the school closed for a year. It was reopened by the Sisters of St. Francis of Tiffin, Ohio, with Sister Miriam Miller as Principal. Sister Dionne Sartor and Sister Patricia Miller joined her on the staff. Sister Miriam's book, *History of the Charlotte Diocese,* furnished some of the historical data included in this treatise.

Later, Sister Veronica Nowakowski and Sister Stella Magers, teachers in the school, held many "flea markets" and used every means possible to raise funds to keep the school going. They even put on little theatrical performances in the county courthouse where the *Ten Commandments* are displayed in a neat, artistic arrangement on the wall behind the judges bench. Separation of church and state was not an issue at the time. Years later a local citizen, a declared atheist, would try to get the *Ten Commandments* removed from those walls. By that time the Sisters no longer needed to use the courtroom for fund raising purposes.

When the Franciscans withdrew from St. John's in 1979, the Daughters of Charity came to teach in the school. The school had had financial problems all along. It was difficult to keep this tremendous Catholic presence in Waynesville alive.

The school closed permanently in 1980. In his ledger, Father Murphy makes mention of small donations given to St. John's School. While he disliked playing bingo (the prizes were too small and the numbers were called too fast) he often went to the bingo games in order to show his support for the Catholic school in Waynesville.

When St. John's school closed, *The Mountaineer* ran an editorial that said in part, "When St. John's closes, Haywood will lose a strong community force in education, in personal discipline, and individual development. But it will not fall completely into the shadow. The good it has done, the knowledge it has conveyed, have shaped many of us, and through us it has helped shape the community. Its benefits will still be felt long after all of us are gone."

▼

CHAPTER THREE

MURPHY'S APOSTOLIC WORK IN NORTH CAROLINA BEGINS

"Build A Church"

> August 4, 1950
> Father Murphy's beloved mother died in her home in Detroit.
>
> An entry in Murphy's ledger for August 4, 1965 reads
> "My good mother died 15 years ago today at this home
> 16201 Hubbell, Detroit."

It seemed important to Will Murphy to note that when, on August 4, 1950, Margaret Murphy died, she died quietly at the Murphy home on 16201 Hubbell Street in Detroit. "Home" was everything to him. But it never would be the same again. Will Murphy was heart-broken. For the rest of his life whenever he thought of her, he would refer to her as "my dear, dear, sweet Mother." The loss of a nurturing, beloved parent is one of life's greatest sorrows and it is in no way minimized by the fact that such a loss is felt by every human being at some time or other.

Just one month after her death, with his mother's last words, "Build a church" ever on his mind, Will Murphy left his beloved home in Detroit and headed for Florida. The echo of his mother's oft-repeated commandment while he was growing up, "Stand erect, shoulders back, head up," helped him to face the days of loneliness that were ahead of him. Her last commandment to build a church also echoed in his ears as he headed south.

Heading for Florida, Landing in Murphy, North Carolina

Missionaries were becoming more and more active in the western part of the Diocese of Charlotte. Father Lane made many sacrifices to bring the Gospel to the people in the Murphy area. Already in 1942, the people of Murphy saw the need for a church. Under the direction of Father Brendan Burns, SA, they began a fund-raising campaign. That campaign was interrupted by the war. For some reason, probably the lack of priests, the Bishop of the diocese decided to discontinue sending a priest to Murphy for Sunday Mass.

That announcement spurred the people to begin the fund raising again. Maybe if they had their own church they would be more likely to get a priest in their area. An appeal for funds was made to all the families in the United States whose name was "Murphy." The people collected $5,000.00. That sum was then matched by the Catholic Extension Society. The Society of the Propagation of the Faith also gave a generous contribution toward the building of the church, which was called St. William.

Finally, the church was finished. It was dedicated by Bishop Vincent Waters on August 12, 1952. When Jim Cinque and Fred Woodall interviewed Father Murphy about the fund raising he said, "They missed our family, but they collected a sum of money, enough to build a church in Murphy—St. William." Interesting enough, "William" was Father Murphy's middle name, the name he used until he went to the seminary. And "Murphy" was, of course, his last name.

Will Murphy did not even realize there was a town in North Carolina by the name of "Murphy" until, a month after his mother's death, when he decided to drive to Florida. He and his mother had made this trip to their home in West Palm Beach every winter for thirty years.

This time the trip to Florida was supposed to be a healing one. Will Murphy needed time to think, to pull himself together, to mourn, to spend time in the Florida home that he had shared with his mother. He could be close to her there. He could review the good times, the loving times they spent there together. He could mourn in private.

As he drove along "something" lured him to drive through the mountains. He had often seen them at a distance but because his mother didn't like mountains he avoided them on the trips to Florida. He said, "My mother died on August 4th and one month later, September 4th, I visited this lovely state of North Carolina." This visit was supposed to be just a short one. Murphy really was on his way to Florida but as he drove along, the beauty of the mountains beckoned to him, and this time he stopped.

After an interview with Father Murphy, Kim Shaver wrote an article for the July 1984, issue of the *Catholic Digest* in which she relates a sequence of events,

"On September 4, 1950, a Cadillac rolled into a gas station west of Maggie Valley. Inside was a stranger, a Yankee. The Yankee told the gas attendant his name was "Murphy" and asked where he was. The attendant told him that he was in a place without a name, but about 10 miles west there was a town named Murphy. Lured by the name, Will drove into Murphy, North Carolina, where he eventually found one man who informed him that he was from the north originally but was now the only Catholic in Murphy.

"Then Will heard a unique story from the lone Catholic, who told him that years earlier a traveling priest had come through the town and was struck with a church-building idea. The priest, along with a number of supporters, began contacting as many Murphys in the United States as possible, and requested money to build a Catholic church in a town named Murphy."

Murphy was a small town, and to find even one Catholic there in 1950 was a surprise. In 1937, Father Lane, pastor in Waynesville, gave a series of lectures on the Cherokee County Courthouse steps in Murphy. Because of the efforts of earlier missionaries, there probably were more Catholics in the area, but there was just this one who identified himself as such when Will Murphy made his inquiries. In fact, the ratio of Catholics in all of North Carolina in 1950 was less than three-fourths of one percent, the lowest ratio of any state in the union.

Murphy, North Carolina, was initially the site of Fort Butler. General Winfield Scott established the fort during his notorious roundup of the Cherokee people. Located near Hiawassee Dam and Lake, it was not the town that would hold Will long, because it was already in the process of getting a church. Will Murphy drove on to Sylva.

Sylva, the Promised Land

Sylva was the county seat for Jackson County. At the time of Will Murphy's visit, Sylva, with a general population of around 2,000 but a Catholic population of one, was swallowed up in Father Lawrence Newman's large pastorate that included all the counties west of Asheville. The only churches in those counties were St. John's in Waynesville where Father Newman resided, and St. Joseph's in Bryson City.

When Mr. Murphy arrived in Murphy, North Carolina, he heard that the people in Murphy were building a church. He also heard that there was no church in Jackson County. His next move was to approach Monsignor Newman with the offer to build a church on any site that suited Monsignor Newman. The faith-filled meeting between these two spiritual stalwarts would lead to increased progress of Catholicism in the region. Because there were so few Catholics in the county, Msgr. Newman had been offering Mass only once a month in Sylva in the American Legion Hall, or the old Carolina Hotel, or in private homes such as that of Mr. and Mrs. William Wise.

After careful study and consideration, Monsignor Newman chose the site for the church. It would be in Sylva, the county seat. Seven miles south of Sylva, in Cullowhee, there was a small college that appeared to be growing rapidly. Thus the church would serve both "town and gown." Will purchased the land from the owner, W.B. Dillard, whose company was also awarded the contract to build the church. Murphy purchased 10 lots, 100 x 50 feet. Msgr. Newman would later add another 8 lots.

The church was finished in 1955. It seated approximately 100 but there were less than 12 parishioners at the time of its dedication. Bishop Vincent Waters dedicated St. Mary's on August 30, and on that same occasion administered the Sacrament of Confirmation, the first Confirmation in this new parish. An estimated 125 clergy and lay persons attended the services and enjoyed a festive dinner afterward at the Carolina Hotel. Soon after the formation of the Diocese of Charlotte in 1972, St. Mary's became a parish in its own right. Father John Loftus, Glenmary, was named the first pastor.

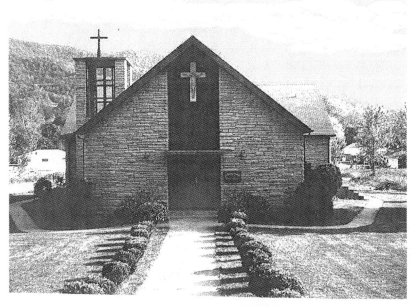

St. Mary's Church, Sylva, NC, first church built by Will Murphy in memory of his parents

Will Murphy had finally fulfilled his dream and that of his mother. He had built a church! There is a plaque in St. Mary's that commemorates the fact that Will Murphy built the church in memory of his parents, James and Margaret Murphy.

Because Will Murphy always had a great respect for the Glenmary missionaries, it was with delight that he learned, in 1954, that Bishop Waters had arranged for the Glenmarys to minister in the counties of Cherokee, Clay, and Graham. The following year, 1955, the Glenmarys were asked to serve in the counties of Macon, Jackson and Swain. Will Murphy's "pride and joy," St. Mary's in Sylva, would now be cared for by dedicated missionaries.

It was while Father Jack McNearney, Glenmary, was the pastor of St. Mary's in Sylva, that the need for more space was obvious. A church built for 100 people in 1954 was already inadequate in 1984. A hall was built and annexed to the church. That was followed by a renovation of the church and rectory. When Father Murphy went to see what was going on at his beloved St. Mary's, his "first born" church, he was dismayed and surprised. It looked to him like the church was being rebuilt. But when Father McNearney explained that the remodeling was necessary because of the growth of the congregation, Father Murphy rejoiced! It was proof to him that it was, after all, very much worthwhile to have built a church in Sylva. Msgr. Newman had shown good judgment in choosing the location for the church. It was serving the Diocese well.

Murphy Donates Newman Center

Will Murphy wasn't finished in the Sylva area yet, although by this time he, himself, had moved to Maggie Valley and was staying in Fred Henry's motel. He needed to do one more thing. He had heard about the need for a Newman Center in Cullowhee. He decided to act. In 1959, he purchased a house and land on Dix's Gap Road for $12,000. With his long history of development and construction behind him, it was a simple matter to renovate the house and create a chapel for the students. Father Jack McNearney, in the personal history he has written, gives this information:

"In 1951, Nell Morrill, the wife of Dr. Maurice Morrill, Dean of the Graduate School of Western Carolina University (in Cullowhee) began to gather the first Catholic Student Group from Western Carolina College. They met in the dorms, over one of the stores in downtown Cullowhee, and at several other places. In 1957, Father Frank Schenk organized the students into a Newman Club. He was replaced the next year by Father John Loftus who offered Mass on campus in one of the dorms or in the local barbershop.

"Michael William Murphy purchased a house at Dix's Gap, adjacent to the campus of Western Carolina College in 1959. This house was converted into a chapel, and a meeting room. Mrs. Neva Grady moved in the next year to act as housemother. There were about 2,000 students at the

College. Father Loftus was living at Sylva and he served the Student Center as well as the people of Jackson County.

"I was first assigned to the Franklin, North Carolina parish on 4/15/1963 to replace Father John Gilhooly as assistant to Father John Barry. I stayed till 9/30/1965 when I was made pastor of Murphy, North Carolina. During these years I was in contact with Michael William Murphy at least once or twice a month."

Will Murphy was happy with his accomplishments in Jackson County. Now it was time to move on. Move on he did, to the little town of Maggie Valley in the County of Haywood, North Carolina. It is here that he was to achieve his crowning victory.

In the Verdant Hills of Maggie Valley

In the September 23, 1984, issue of *Our Sunday Visitor,* Father Vincent J. Giese painted a nicely done verbal portrait of the 93-year-old priest in *"The Story of Father Michael Murphy."* He wrote, "Father Michael Murphy is etched into the Great Smoky Mountains of North Carolina. His features reflect the awesome serenity of the hills around him. His powerful large-boned hands tell the story of his 93 years, most of them engaged in farm and construction work. His eyes reflect the changing beauty of the trees, the haze of the mountains, the grandeur of a valley located halfway up the Smokies. And his voice constantly praises God for the breathless beauty of these surroundings."

Father Michael Murphy of Maggie Valley in North Carolina is no ordinary priest or man. How Michael Murphy, born of Irish ancestors who came to the United States 150 years ago, and raised on a farm near downtown Detroit, eventually settled in North Carolina some 36 years ago and became a priest at age 80 is a personal odyssey unique in American Church history.

Father Murphy had been a priest for thirteen years when Giese wrote the article with a subtitle, "In the Verdant Hills of North Carolina 'There is nothing I shall want'." With photos of Father Murphy, ever in the shadows of St. Margaret's Church in Maggie Valley, Giese notes that he was pastor there those years in "the very church he built as a layman, was ordained in, and where he will die."

Though Will had seen the Maggie Valley exit sign many times on his trips to Florida his mother never wanted to stop there. Will said that on those trips when his mother's disdain for traveling mountain roads prevented his exploration of western North Carolina, he had already made up his mind that some day he would retire and live in the mountains.

It was just a month after his mother's death that Will Murphy arrived in North Carolina to begin his apostolic ministry in the mountain area. Just as the town of Murphy had appealed to him because of his family name, so did the town of "Maggie Valley." His mother, Margaret, was called "Maggie" by her friends. He had a personal interest in the valley.

Maggie Valley is ideally located in the foothills of the Smokies. It is approximately an hour's drive from the Tennessee, South Carolina, and Georgia borders and it is sixteen miles from the Cherokee reservation. It has a moderate climate and is a favorite destination for tourists. The town consists mostly of motels, restaurants, and craft shops. Maggie Valley was founded in 1904, but was not incorporated as a town until 1974, long after Will Murphy settled there.

The name "Maggie" was given to the valley in May 1904, when the region had enough people to open its own post office. John Setzer, a native in the valley, wrote to the US Postmaster requesting permission to use his private home as a post office. He had been traveling by horseback down the mountains to the Plott Post Office miles away in order to provide mail service for himself and his neighbors. The task was becoming more than he could handle. After receiving application papers Setzer presented the case in depth to the Postmaster General, providing the necessary facts and figures that the government required for the establishment of a new post office. The Postmaster told Setzer that the figures he presented justified the establishment and the only other thing he still had to do was to come up with a valid name for the post office.

Setzer's first choice for naming the post office was "Jonathan," an apt choice for the name of a post office located in the Bible belt. Jonathan also was an appropriate choice because it is the name of the creek that runs through the valley. However, there already was a North Carolina post office using the name "Jonathan." Mr. Setzer was told to try again. He next submitted the names of his three daughters. The Post Master General chose the name "Maggie" which was the name of Setzer's twelve-year-old daughter.

Young Maggie was not too happy about the choice. Like most twelve-year olds, she resented the use of her name for business purposes. "Maggie" was a girl's name, it was her name. As she grew older she realized it really was an honor to have the post office named after her. It was the post office that gave the town its name. Maggie married and moved to Texas where she died in 1979 at the age of 88. Today an image of a pioneer mountain woman, vividly arrayed in bright yellows, reds, and green with the traditional bonnet, is the symbol for the beloved valley. The image represents the strength, integrity, and beauty of the mountain culture combined with its spirit of southern hospitality, it's gentle invitation, "Come on down, ya'll."

Will Murphy did exactly that. He "came on down." His first obvious effort in his apostolic work in the valley was to find a place where the Mass could be offered. In 1956, he purchased 33 acres of land along US 19 (later Soco Road) from Wade and Ruby Cordell. The property Murphy bought had on it a large building with a craft shop on the lower level and an apartment where he lived on the upper level.

Beautiful scenery, good neighbors, good climate, and pure drinking water—now Murphy had everything. Everything except a church. When he first bought the property on US 19, he maintained the craft shop just as the owner did before him. However, he was readily willing to abandon that business. He said, "No one stopped there anyway." By any standards, he reasoned, a chapel would make better sense than a craft shop.

Where Two Or More Are Gathered

The dreamer-believer, Will, had to take literally the promise, "Where two or more are gathered in my name I am in their midst," because that was, as far as it could be determined, the number of Catholics who would accompany him on his first steps in Maggie Valley—two or three. The general consensus that there were two or three Catholics living somewhere in the Valley was just what Mr. Murphy needed to spur him on "to move mountains."

It wasn't long before the crafts disappeared from the lower level of his home and in their stead there were pews, an altar, a podium, and an organ. Like St. Paul who traveled through Ephesus, Corinth, Athens, and Antioch to preach the Gospel, Will traveled through Murphy, Sylva, Cullowhee, and into Maggie Valley to share the GOOD NEWS, the good news that was so much a part of his Irish heritage and spirituality.

It was in no way a "Pauline" epistle but Will Murphy did write to the motels and restaurants in the area to let them know that hereafter the Holy Sacrifice of the Mass would be offered in the Valley on Sundays. He had removed his craft shop sign, replacing it with a sign that indicated that here, in this very house, there was a chapel where the Mass would be offered by a visiting priest on Sundays and Holy Days. He apparently had the chapel "up and running" in 1961 because in his ledger he made an entry on August 4, writing "Mass–Chapel–Mother's anniversary."

Shortly after he converted his craft store into a chapel, Will Murphy asked Bishop Waters for permission to build a church in Maggie Valley. He was told that there were not enough parishioners to support a church. Will did not give up easily. There was something in him that kept whispering, "Build it and they will come."

In his eagerness to serve the Lord, and ever gifted with the business man's need for records, Will made numerous entries in his ledger indicating the number of persons who attended each Mass. These were pre-Vatican days and the law of the church stated that communicants could take no food or drink until after communion; therefore, when Mass was offered late in the morning not many received Communion.

Although by the time he was keeping record of Mass attendance in his little chapel, he may already have had permission to build the church, still Will wanted to prove his case. He wanted statistics to show that there were summer-time visitors who would profit if a Catholic Church would be built in the Valley.

His first entries, in 1964, indicated the following,

> Sunday, June 7–27 present
> Sunday, June 14–26 present
> Sunday, June 21–39 present—about twelve received
> Sunday, June 28–44 present

Another Loss, Another Time to Mourn

Will Murphy, in his own unique way of keeping a debit-and-credit ledger, did not hesitate to record spiritual experiences right next to business entries. It is in this ledger that he tells the story of his mother's vision and his own vision of the angels and the Eucharist. While he was extremely brief when he made note of his brother's death it is the very brevity that tells us his grief could not be put into words. We can feel the ache in his heart as we read the entry he made on August 6, 1963,

> *"My good brother died today—Joseph Elliottt Murphy."*

Elliott, as he was called, was the last of the Murphys except for Will. His mother and father were gone; his brothers and sisters were all gone. His uncles and aunts–gone except for Aunt Frances Garland. Will would mourn the passing of the last of his brothers for many days to come. Elliott, the youngest in the family, was the brother who got into "mischief" with Will in their younger years. He was the brother that, when mentioning his name or relating an incident that happened when they were young, Will Murphy always broke out into a smile as if the incident had just happened last week. The baptismal font in St. Margaret's church was donated by Mr. Murphy in memory of his "good brother," Joseph Elliott.

The Garland Name Lives On

As was his custom, Murphy recorded more than money and Mass statistics. His ledger was also a family register. On June 16, 1965 he wrote in his ledger,

> "Aunt Frances Garland died today. She was the last sister of my mother. Buried June 19th in Mt. Elliott Cemetery, Detroit."

Father Murphy often spoke, always with fondness, of his Aunt Frances. Now there were no more close ties with his mother's family, the Garlands. There were no more brothers and sisters left. He was the only surviving member of the Margaret Garland and James Murphy family, and his name was "Murphy." But the Garland name would live on.

The Garland name would remain in the public domain for years to come. Shirley Pinto explained that after she and Al had opened Alfredo's Restaurant, Father Murphy came to eat there often. It was Thanksgiving time and anyone who wished could go to Alfredo's for Thanksgiving dinner. Al had brought home five turkeys from a turkey shoot and the family wished to share them. After the meal Father Murphy was given a tour of the kitchen. When he saw that the Pintos were using a Garland stove he said, "That stove was named after my grandfather."

When Shirley was preparing the *Little Bits of Heaven* cookbook she wanted to mention that the stove was named after the Garlands who were the ancestors of Father Murphy. She wanted to get in contact with the International Stove Company to see if the story was true and to see if she could print it.

One day when she was doing dishes in Father Murphy's kitchen, some visitors stopped in. The gentlemen stayed in the living room to talk to Father Murphy while the lady who was with them went into the kitchen where Shirley was working. The two ladies struck up a conversation. Shirley mentioned that she was working on a cookbook that would tell Father Murphy's story. She said the cookbook was nearly finished but that she still had one thing to do; she needed to track down the president of the International Stove Company to verify the Garland story and to get permission to put it in the cookbook.

When the lady heard what Shirley was saying she gasped and said, "The president of the company is sitting there in the next room talking to Father Murphy." Shirley then talked to the gentleman and he confirmed the fact that when the Garlands were coming over on the boat his grandfather was on that same boat. His grandfather had already manufactured a number of stoves but he was coming out with a new sturdy line for restaurants and institutions. He wanted a name for it. He liked the name "Garland" so he went to Father Murphy's grandfather and asked for permission to use his name for the stove.

The Fords, who came over on the same boat as the Garlands, went into the car business and named their automobiles "Ford." And thus their family name lives on. The Garland name also lives on having become prominent because of the stove, even though the Garlands did not own the business.

Murphy, Always An Evangelist

Will Murphy kept recording the attendance at Mass and Communion each Sunday during the summer months until 1967, the year the corner stone for St. Margaret's was laid. The number of persons attending Mass in his little chapel, and receiving Holy Communion, kept increasing each month during the summer. Catholic tourists were becoming more aware of Murphy's chapel. When they stopped in, whether for Mass or for a visit, Mr. Murphy would give them pamphlets to take home.

Will's "being about his Father's business" during those years included his personal purchases of literature to distribute. In the spring of 1961 he bought Confraternity Home Study pamphlets which included "Facts everyone should know about the Catholic Church." He was very much aware of the many false rumors about the Catholic Church that were circulated in the Valley. He had hoped, through the written word as well as through his own example, to dispel those rumors.

Besides all the notations of family anniversaries, strewn throughout the ledger, there are records of purchases from religious publishing houses such as *Our Sunday Visitor, Abbey Press, Paulist Press, Divine Word, and Liguori*. Will Murphy trusted the written word more than any verbal message he might give. He considered himself a poor preacher. He thought the written word would more adequately express what he thought and felt but could not say. If he had read the life of St. Francis of Assisi he would have learned that St. Francis told his followers to "Preach the Gospel at all times. If necessary, use words." Without a doubt Murphy preached the Gospel at all times in his own way.

Falling Waters Motel

In interviews with people who knew Will Murphy during the early 1960's as he established himself in the heart of the valley, it is generally agreed that he got along well with the local people, not an easy hurdle in any community, and considered quite difficult amid old mountaineer stock. Sometimes the people become like the mountains–strong, sturdy, unrelenting.

It was because of the goodness of these southern folks, mostly Anglo-Saxon protestants, that Will felt accepted. He, a Yankee, a Roman Catholic, an Irishman, felt right at home among the people. His own charisma, his concern for the people, his praise and appreciation of everything they loved, and his developmental projects for the region won him friends. Over and over again he said, "I want to give work to these good mountain people. They are such good people. They would never hurt anyone." Indeed, he was on his way to becoming the "centerpiece" of Maggie Valley.

It can be understood, then, why it was that when Will went looking for property it was a local business man who recommended that he buy the 19 acres upon which he built the Motel, and eventually the church, convent, and house of prayer.

In an interview with Jim Cinque, Father Murphy explained how he happened to buy that particular piece of property. He said,

"Going into the valley one day, I saw a 'For Sale' sign on a mountain piece of property and thought to myself who would ever want to buy that piece of property.

"While at the Maggie Valley Restaurant, I mentioned the property to the owner of the restaurant, Mr. Carver, and he said, 'You go and buy that land.' Well, I thought, he is from this area so he must know what he is talking about. So I bought it.

"The best move I ever made was to take his advice and buy that piece of mountain property. The owner of the property was Reverend Walter Rathbone, a retired Methodist Minister.

"On the property was a one-story building that was a gift shop and later became a restaurant for many years known as 'the Pancake House.' Then I built a 25-unit motel called Falling Waters.

"My greatest desire was to build a church, but Bishop Waters said there was not enough collection to support a church. But in 1961, they built Ghost Town and Bishop Waters saw a possible need now, and he gave me the go ahead to build the church."

In addition to building a church in Sylva, remodeling a house into a Newman Center in Cullowhee, and changing a craft shop into a chapel in Maggie Valley, Will Murphy had to have an occupation that was ongoing. He needed something that he had to care for on a daily basis, something to attract his attention while dreaming dreams about the church he would build in Maggie Valley.

Will Murphy had never owned a motel, but that was as good a reason as any for going into the motel business. A motel would be a different kind of challenge. A motel would keep him in contact with the people and a motel would give work to residents in the area. He needed the people. They needed him. With the businessman's acumen in construction and in economics, the details of building a motel would not present a problem.

In May 1961, Will Murphy broke ground for the motel. He made a ledger entry on January 2, indicating that he paid Wm. Rathbone & wife $4000 + $800 interest for the property that Mr. Carver had encouraged him to buy. Later he would make more payments.

A final entry in his ledger for December 31, 1961 indicates that up to this time Will Murphy paid $8,324.18 for furniture for the motel, and $77,289.18 for construction, a total of $86,906.07. There are a few more entries for construction costs in 1962. The motel was opened for business in May 1962.

According to Mattie Killian, an employee at the motel from the very beginning, the general contractor for the motel was James Picket who lived up the road just across from where Mr. Murphy lived. Bill Franklin, John Killian, Joe Kirkpatrick, Clyde Ramsey, Ben Moody, Bill Finger, Houston Sutton, and Mattie's son Robert Killian, all helped to build the motel.

Will Murphy would come to know these workers well. It was with great sadness many years later when one evening in the depth of winter, when the thermometer registered four degrees above zero, he responded to a call to give the last blessing to Ben Moody. Murphy had already been ordained when Ben, who was returning from a visit to his family, had a heart attack. The pick-up truck he was driving left the road and landed in the creek right next to Murphy-Garland Hall, then called "the White House."

Father Murphy had offered Mass that evening at 7:30. Sister Lucy Comer and Sister Judith Pask, who were living in the apartment that Father Murphy formerly lived in, noticed the truck in the creek when they were returning to their apartment after the Mass was over. They knew the truck had not been there when they went up to Mass so they returned to the rectory and told Father Murphy. They also called the Maggie Valley police. Father Murphy went to the scene immediately. When he was asked if he knew the man in the truck he responded, "I knew him well. He was a wonderful, wonderful man."

Will Murphy took to inn keeping as he had taken to berries and building and everything else he tried, bringing the Murphy gusto to the job. Mattie Killian, who worked for Falling Waters explains further:

"Before Mr. Murphy opened the motel in May, 1962, Tela Peeples, Lelia Rathbone, and I began working for him. We cleaned the motel and made the beds and hung the drapes, getting ready to open. The furniture from Scotch Bargain furniture and Butler Furniture was already here. It took us a while to get the motel ready. There have been lots of improvements since the opening day. Later the pool was built and the driveways were paved.

Falling Waters Motel in 1962 before church was built

"Tela Peebles managed the motel for about seven years. Then her health failed her and one day she just gave up. So I kept the office and Mr. Murphy took the evening shift for a while. Then Lelia's daughters stayed at night. Bishop Waters came and wanted Mr. Murphy to go to the St. Meinrad's seminary in Indiana and study to be a priest. So I got Blye Caldwell to stay at night. When Mr. Murphy came back from Indiana, and after his ordination, he went to Williamston, North Carolina, and then later on he came up to St. Margaret's church. The workers from the motel helped to keep the rectory and the church clean until the Sisters came.

"When we all began to work for Mr. Murphy he had an accountant in Waynesville make out the pay roll, but Mr. Murphy wrote the checks while he was here. When he was away I kept the time sheets for the employees and his accountant wrote the checks and brought them to us once a week. The ledger was kept at the Motel and I made entries in it so Mr. Murphy would know. I wrote down how many rooms were rented each day and how much money was taken in. I also wrote down all the little expenses for things that we needed to keep up the place, like cleaning supplies. Everything was written down—even doughnuts for breakfast for some of the guests.

"Mr. Murphy got along well with the local people and they were all glad to work for him. He designed the stairway for the motel lobby. He measured off every inch and made the stairway come out just right. It was circular. He had been told nobody could build that kind of stairway, but he built it. A few years later Mr. Hoppi used Murphy's idea for the stairway when he made one just like it in the rectory up by the church.

"Jonathan Creek, which runs in front of the motel, flooded but that did not stop Mr. Murphy from building the motel where he did. The creek was worked on after the flood and routed further in. Bill Henry and his wife Pat lived very near the creek. Their bridge washed away. They had no access to the main road so Mr. Murphy told them they could use the bridge he was building.

"The motel guests enjoyed Mr. Murphy because he always greeted them when they arrived. He was so friendly. He would get up early in the morning and get down to the motel to greet the people. He would walk up and down the porches talking to them, telling them where the beautiful spots of scenery were. I think Water Rock Knob was one of his favorite places. Everyone who knew Mr. Murphy loved him. He always said Maggie Valley was a great place to live in but a poor place to make a living.

"He constructed his own waterfalls with colored lights. The water no longer flows and the colored lights are all gone but the concrete forms are still there. Maybe some day some one will restore those waterfalls. I hope so.

"Father Murphy will always be in my memory. He was always nice to everyone. I am glad I had the privilege of knowing him and working for him, because he was a good person to work for. In the fifteen years I worked for him, he never gave me a short word. He was a blessing to me."

Murphy also had a huge sign out by the road. It said "largest heated pool." Mattie said, "It was Murphy's idea to put up the sign but after he had it up for a while he had it taken down because he didn't think it would go over too good. He wouldn't hurt anybody."

Falling Waters sign

Leila Rathbone also enjoyed working for Mr. Murphy. She said, "I helped Mr. Murphy set up the motel when he first opened it in 1962. I continued to work for him for about ten years. He was a good person to work for. He took an interest in everybody and appreciated everything that we did for him. He would walk around on the motel porches to talk to the guests. There was a lot of laughing going on when he was around.

"One day Mr. Murphy went up to Water Rock Knob just to look at the view. It was so pretty that day that he came back to the motel to get Mattie and me so we could enjoy it, too. When we got up there we saw that the clouds had fallen down and we were above the clouds. The little clouds were moving like they were playing. And there we stood watching them. It was so beautiful. I will never forget what I saw that day. It was like we were in heaven with the clouds all around us. I guess we were.

"Mr. Murphy used to pick up my girls, Mary, Donna, Jean, and Jackie, and take them to church with him at St. Mary's in Sylva for Saturday afternoon Mass. We aren't Catholic but Mr. Murphy didn't mind. Then after Mass he would take the girls grocery shopping and they would all gather at his place on Soco Road for a good home-cooked meal that the girls would prepare for him. He said it was just like his good sweet mother's cooking. Later on, when the hotel became a retreat center my son, Bobby, worked there on maintenance."

Many expenditures in the ledger related to establishing Falling Waters as a motel. There was a ledger entry indicating a $400.00 deposit for a city sign listing the motel. In addition to the city signs, Murphy had billboards advertising the motel erected near all the entrances into Maggie Valley.

Serving a Need

Business was good. Falling Waters Motel was serving a need in Maggie Valley. For years to come it would be Mr. Murphy's pleasure to go out in the early evening to check on the other motels in the Valley. He drove up and down the Valley. He wanted to see how many "NO VACANCY" signs he could find.

Years later, after Falling Waters Motel became Living Waters Reflection Center, people came by wanting rooms. It was necessary for Living Waters to put up a sign on the lobby door saying, "This is not a motel. Sorry!" Sometimes the visitors did not believe the sign. They would enter the lobby and argue, saying, "This is where we spent our honeymoon" and "we had our pictures taken on those steps." They seemed to think that, having stayed at the motel in previous years gave them some sort of priority status, even if the building was no longer a motel.

Motels in the Valley tend to be "sold out" on holidays. One July 4, after Falling Waters became Living Waters, a distraught mother came in early in the morning. When told that Living Waters could not, because of its tax exempt status, accommodate tourists but could only give rooms to people who came to pray, this mother said, "Ma'am, I have children. We slept in our car all night last night and we prayed all night that we would find a room in the morning." That did the trick. Needless to say the family was given a room. Prayers do get answered!

Both church and motel projects continued to get the attention of Will Murphy during the early 1960's. More important than all of his projects combined was the impact that he, personally, had on the people that he met. Charles and Harriet Jimison of Canton, North Carolina, met Mr. Murphy, the businessman, in January 1963. They had recently been married. Charles explains,

"Mr. Murphy needed someone to live at Falling Waters during the winter months. We went to him and told him we would like to stay there until the spring when he started renting rooms again. Since Mattie Killian, my mother-in-law, was already working for Mr. Murphy he was glad for Mattie's daughter to be living there.

"When we moved in we were both working at Dayco Corp. I was working the day shift and Harriet was working the three-to-eleven shift. Mr. Murphy would come by the Motel almost every day to see if everything was OK. He was always talking about the beauty of this area. He couldn't get over it. He would bring fruit from Florida and leave it at our door.

"At that time Mr. Murphy had a house about half way up Soco Road where he lived. We knew he had to do his own cooking, so on weekends we would invite him to eat supper with us. He really enjoyed those home-cooked meals.

"He was always asking me to eat supper with him at his place when Harriet was at work. One evening I told him I would go to his house to eat supper with him. He opened a can of green beans and heated them. He didn't put any seasoning in the beans at all. We had a supper of unseasoned green beans and white bread with butter. I ate the green beans even though they squeaked in my teeth when I chewed them. We had water to drink and some cookies for dessert. Mr. Murphy lived a simple life. No fuss. He liked to share.

"We lived at Falling Waters Motel until April, 1963. Then we purchased a mobile home and moved to Canton. Harriet and I were always very grateful that we had the opportunity to know such a fine person."

Will Murphy was a man of this world who loved to eat and play cards and visit with people. He was not a plastic saint, but the "sinner" that is part and parcel of being human. He never tired of telling people, "I am just a poor sinner."

Murphy Touches Lives

But that was not always the way others saw him. It is one of the gems in his crown of legacies that, though so strongly and thoroughly devoted to Roman Catholicism, he made it obvious to all that his was not a faith that was exclusive, but that it was inclusive. He prayed over and over again, "That we all may be one." He treated everyone as an equal in the Lord. Bruce and Lois Carden remember his acceptance of them and how he seemed to enjoy coming to their home for a good home-cooked meal.

"As seventh generation Baptists, Lois and I do not count ourselves as Protestants because we do not protest anything. We wish to count ourselves as poor, simple believers who worship the same Savior that Father Murphy worshipped."

Before the Cardens met Father Murphy they had been reading in the local papers about the work that Will Murphy was doing in memory of "his saintly mother and his Lord Jesus Christ."

Bruce gives a personal definition of Father Murphy, "What was Father Murphy made of? Why, just love, humility, and concern for others. He was one who never sought to impose his faith on another except by demonstrating through his own strong faith the true and right way, the only way!"

Retreat work in the valley began long before the House of Prayer or Living Waters Reflection Center was a reality. Already in 1964 the Motel was used for retreat work. Father Jack McNearney wrote,

"In 1964, I gave a retreat for the women of the Franklin and Murphy parishes at Maggie Valley, NC. At that time William Murphy had a chapel in the downstairs of his two-story house on Highway 19. We used the chapel for our conferences and liturgies and Brother Dick Walsh did the preparing of the meals using Mr. Murphy's kitchen upstairs. The women stayed at the Falling Waters Motel, which was owned by Mr. Murphy. He didn't charge the women for the two nights they stayed."

▼

CHAPTER FOUR

UPON THIS ROCK I WILL BUILD

St. Margaret's Church

"And then it was time for the great project–his life's dream, the final glorious climax of all his work."

Thus begins the article *"Man for this Season"* that Bishop May wrote for the *Extension Magazine* in December 1968. The article was written to acquaint the magazine readers with Michael William Murphy, the church builder.

Indeed, it was time for the great project. Finally, years after he had first requested permission to build a church in Maggie Valley, he had that permission from Bishop Waters. Finally, he knew where he would put the church that he was about to build in memory of his mother, Margaret. At least he thought he knew where he would build until he ran into some obstacles.

Father Jack McNearny, who often visited Murphy, said that Mr. Murphy showed him where he wanted to put the church. It was on the 33 acres that he had purchased from the Cordells. He would build the church behind the house he lived in. In fact he had already cleared a road that went up the hill to the proposed site. First snag–Bishop Waters did not approve of the site. Murphy then went out looking for more land to buy.

One of the difficulties of building a church in the Valley was the resistance of some local people who had not been exposed to Catholicism but had heard bad things about it. To sell land to a Catholic required second thought. Mr. Murphy would try one more time. He thought he found the right spot for the church when he saw four acres of land for sale on a side road near where he lived. The view was beautiful and the land would not have to be cleared of trees before construction could begin. Mr. Murphy approached the owner. Yes, the owner wanted to sell. Mr. Murphy made a down payment on the land and returned to his home satisfied that he now knew where to build his church.

Second snag–when he went back to the owner to make the final payment on the land the owner no longer wanted to sell. It had become known that Mr. Murphy wanted to build a Catholic Church on the property and the owner told him right out, "We don't need any of those Catholic Churches in the Valley." With only a few known Catholics in the Valley in 1962, there was no real need for a church. Mr. Murphy did not want to offend by insisting he had a right to build a church in the Valley. He simply promised that he would not build a church on the property upon which he had made the down payment. He purchased the land and later on he had Claude Phillips, his master builder, erect homes on the lots.

Today we say, "Thank God for Bishops who speak decisively" and "Thank God for property owners who either through foresight or prejudice don't want a church on their property!" Because Murphy could not build on the properties he had singled out, he went back to his residence to think things over. He said, "Finally I had permission to build a church but now I had no place to put it." And then he added, "I thought if God wants a Catholic Church in the Valley there will be a Catholic Church in the Valley."

It was then that Mr. Murphy took another look at the property he already owned, the property that Mr. Carver had suggested he should buy, the property where he had already built a motel. Yes, just maybe he could build farther up on the hill. He had already carved out part of the hill for the motel. Why not carve out more? So he went to work figuring out how he could put a church high up on the hill. For many days he tramped through the wooded area until he found the exact spot for a new church, a spot where the surrounding hills would reveal their splendor and make it easy for people to pray.

Mr. Murphy said it took him three years to clear the land and another three years to build the church. One of the reasons it took so long was that Mr. Murphy would not work on clearing the land or on erecting the building during the tourist season. He did not want to offend the people in the valley who depended upon tourism for their living. He often mentioned how grateful he was that the hill was not solid rock. Murphy said the Lord could build a church on solid rock but he didn't think he could.

St. Margaret's Catholic Church 1968

To Thy Name, O God, Give Glory

Will Murphy had his mother's favorite prayer painted on a board that was placed on some two by fours. The sign stood 6-8 feet high. It read, "To Thy Name, O God, give glory." Father Murphy said, "We had to keep moving the sign because the construction workers moved around, but we kept the sign there all during construction." Mr. Murphy said ordinarily the construction company keeps a sign on the work site but he preferred to keep his mother's prayer on the site. Undoubtedly, he felt her presence around him as he was building the church in her memory. Because the builders brought in more and more equipment, Murphy kept moving the sign around so that it would never be in the way of the workers.

One day Bishop Waters came out to see how much progress was being made on the church. When he saw the sign Mr. Murphy was moving around, he told Will that he should be a priest. "My answer," said Mr. Murphy, "was that I was only a poor sinner and did not have much education." He continued, "Each time the Bishop came to see what progress was being made on the construction of the church he spoke to me about being a priest."

No one knows what happened to the sign after the church was built. Up until a few years after Will Murphy was the pastor of St. Margaret's the concrete space in the arch above the double doors of the church was just that—unfinished concrete. It needed something, but what? Finally, Charlie Blanchard, a parishioner skilled in metallic sculpture and art media, used mosaic tile to fill in that space, printing out the prayer that was on the sign. Father Murphy was very pleased when Charles finished his work. The prayer from the movable wood sign was now immovable. It was imbedded in concrete.

Little Bits of Heaven

And so the work proceeded. In 1987, a committee which included Jo Ann Woodall, Esther Quirk, Trudy Cinque, Rose Waxenfelter, Helen Tabacek, Jeanne Perry, and Mary Triana, under the direction of the coordinator,

Shirley Pinto, created a cookbook for the parish entitled *Little Bits of Heaven*. The ladies were all from St. Margaret's and had easy access to first-hand information because Father Murphy was still living. By that time he was pastor-emeritus of St. Margaret's. He was willing to share his story with Jim Cinque and Fred Woodall, giving them an interview, which they taped. The following is from the cookbook regarding some of the details of the construction of the church:

"The stone work was done by the master mason, Raymond Hoppi. The crab-orchard stone was cut from the quarries in Tennessee. The great beams came, already formed, from Georgia and were delivered by trucks. Mr. Murphy was going to use brick inside the structure but Mr. Hoppi convinced him to use stone. Mr. Hoppi was called to another job before the work on the church was completely finished. Cherokee Indians from the reservation completed the work."

There were many decisions, naturally, that Will Murphy had to make when designing the church. One question Will Murphy had to deal with was, "stained glass or no stained glass?" It didn't take Murphy any time at all to make a decision on that question. He would forgo the usual stained glass windows in favor of all clear glass. He would use what the Creator had already made, all of nature, in place of something made by creatures. The wall behind the altar and one of the side walls are made entirely of plain glass, affording worshippers a magnificent view. Murphy said, "Stained glass or any work of human art cannot compare with the marvelous beauty of nature."

He did allow for one exception. There would be a stained-glass rose window in the rear of the church that would depict the patron saint of the church, St. Margaret of Scotland.

St. Margaret of Scotland

According to Grolier's *Catholic Encyclopedia*, Margaret was brought up at the court of Stephen of Hungary where her father, Prince Edward, was exiled during her early childhood. She was a member of the English ruling house deposed during the Norman Conquest. She escaped from England with her mother and brother after the Battle of Hastings in 1066, and took refuge at the Scottish court.

There, in 1070, she married King Malcolm III at the castle of Dumferline, thereby becoming Queen of Scotland. She became a "pious and benevolent influence" in the kingdom. She and Malcolm had six sons and two daughters. Three of their sons became kings and one of their daughters married a king, Henry I of England.

With her husband she founded several churches, among them the Holy Trinity at Dumferline. She introduced the observance of the Lenten fast in her country and worked toward the proper observance of Sundays. She made a great effort to get rid of superstitious practices. Margaret made it her constant effort to obtain good priests and teachers for all parts of the country. She formed a kind of embroidery guild among the ladies of the court to provide vestments and church furnishings. She was very strict with the embroidery guild, allowing no men in the area and allowing no nonsense in the special room she set aside and equipped for the guild. She made that room into "sacred space" for all who would sew there, and she carefully chose which members of her court would be members of that guild. She purchased the finest of cloth to be used in the making of sacred vestments.

St. Margaret is best known for the love she had for the poor. She often visited the sick and tended them with her own hands. She erected hostels for strangers and ransomed many captives. Invariably, when she appeared outside in public, she was surrounded by beggars, and she never sat down at table without first having fed nine little orphans and twenty-four adults. She died in Edinburg, Scotland on November 16, 1093, just four days after her husband, the king, died in battle. She was canonized in 1250, and named the patron of Scotland in 1673.

Both Butler's *Lives of the Saints* and Grolier's *Catholic Encyclopedia* give her feast day as June 10. On June 10, 1968, Father Murphy wrote in his ledger, "First Holy Mass in new church of Saint Margaret. Most Rev.

Vincent S. Waters officiated. Feast of Saint Margaret. About 40 persons present." Evidently the Bishop got his information from the encyclopedia or from Butler's *Lives of the Saints* when he decided to celebrate the feast day for the first time in St. Margaret's church. There are several saints on the church calendar who are named "Margaret." The Bishop chose Margaret of Scotland because many people living in the Valley have Scottish ancestors.

Butler's *Lives* has a footnote to the story of St. Margaret's life that says that in Scotland the feast of St. Margaret is celebrated on November 16. The Roman Missal gives her feast day as November 16.

One day late in the afternoon Father Murphy was walking in the yard behind the church. When he looked up at the large window that formed the entire back wall of the church, he discovered that the mountains were reflected in that window and that the rose window was centered in the midst of all the trees When visitors came in the afternoon to see him, Father Murphy delighted in showing them this unusual sight. "Come here," he would say, "I want to show you something that you can't see anywhere else." When John Zierten, a photographer working for *Our Sunday Visitor,* stopped in to see Father Murphy, he took a picture of the unusual reflection.

Image of Rose Window as it appears on opposite front window in the afternoon

Construction Questions Needing Answers

There were other construction questions, besides that of stained glass that Mr. Murphy had to answer as the church was entering into the final stages of construction and he had to think of the furnishings. Statues or no statues? By the time Mr. Murphy was building St. Margaret's, the Vatican Council was in session and there were many changes in church structures and furnishings. Mr. Murphy was aware of these changes. Churches all over the nation were being remodeled to reflect the Vatican II thinking. One of the concerns after Vatican II was "statues." Do they stay or do they go? Mr. Murphy approached Bishop Waters about putting statues in the church he was building in Maggie and was told to use his own good judgment. When talking about his decision not to put statues in the church he said, "The good people in Maggie Valley may not understand about the statues. I don't want to offend them." And so he did not put any statues in the church.

Later on when the Carmelite Sisters in Asheville closed their monastery Bishop Begley offered their beautiful outdoor bronze statues to Living Waters. The statues were life-size. When Father Murphy was asked if he wanted any of the statues around the church he said, "You can put them way up on the hill on the reservoir up there." He still wasn't sure it was appropriate to have statues anywhere in sight. "Way up on the reservoir" was definitely out of sight. Eventually the Lourdes statues were placed in a little cove-like area near the Convent and the Crucifixion scene was given to the Catholic Center in Hickory, North Carolina.

However, recently a statue was placed in the church. When Father Eric Housenecht was the pastor of St. Margaret's, he understood the spiritual value of having a small shrine in the church. With the help of some of his parishioners he erected a beautiful shrine to Our Lady of Victory. He provided the people with an opportunity to honor the Mother of Jesus with their prayers and with the lighting of votive candles at her shrine. The shrine was erected in memory of Velma and Bernard Utendorf.

Our Lady of Victory Shrine and a copy of a plaque in Westminister Roman Catholic Cathedral in London explaining why we light candles at a shrine

The question "chimes or no chimes" was easy to answer. There probably never was a doubt regarding chimes for the church. Mr. Murphy already had chimes in the chapel he built near his home in Detroit.

When St. Margaret's was nearly completed Mr. Murphy brought the organ and the chimes from the family's private chapel in Detroit to his new church in Maggie Valley. For years the chimes sounded the Angelus from the church tower and played pre-Vatican Catholic hymns, much to the delight and edification of the retreatants who came to pray. Early in the 80's the "home-made" device was replaced by a commercial one.

Jim Bodenmiller, Father Murphy's grandnephew, left a note in the bell tower that explained, "This tape was recorded in approximately 1968-69. It was recorded at the church in Maggie, using the chimes formerly mounted in the small chapel at 16201 Hubbell in Detroit. The music was recorded one afternoon for the purpose of being played automatically at designated intervals over the original speakers in the bell tower which also were first used in the chapel in Detroit. A control box containing time and audio sensors was used to control the tape player. This tape was played for many years over the valley until it was replaced by a modern commercial system. The music was played and recorded by Father Murphy's grand-nephew and the electronic control system was developed by the nephew as well in 1968 at the age of 20 and installed in the summer of 1968 during summer vacation." Evidently talent for "messing with" electronic equipment runs in the Murphy family.

It was on the occasion of Father Murphy's ninetieth birthday celebration in August 1981, that the new commercial chimes were dedicated. Bishop Begley had a Pontifical Mass that day at which he blessed the chimes, offering the following prayer,

"O God, who decreed through blessed Moses that silver trumpets should be made and be sounded at the time of sacrifice in order to remind the people by their clear tones to prepare for your worship and to assemble for its celebration, grant, we pray that these chimes and bells, destined for your holy Church, may be blessed by the Holy Spirit so that when they are tolled and rung the faithful may be invited to this house of God.

"Let the people's faith and piety be increased whenever they hear the melodious pealing of these bells; may those who are weak be strengthened in faith; may unbelievers be aroused to look toward this mountain and come to know their God.

"When the peal of these bells resounds in this valley, may a legion of angels stand watch over the assembly of your Church. Bestow your ever-abiding protection upon the people both in body and in spirit. We ask this through you, Jesus Christ, who lives and reigns with the Father in the unity of the Holy Spirit, one God, forever and ever. Amen To the honor of St. Margaret. Amen."

Father Murphy with parishioner, Eleanor Wilson, whose niece, Marie Sherwin, gave a new set of chimes in her memory

From the *Little Bits of Heaven* cookbook we learn more about the other furnishings in St. Margaret's.

"Father Joseph Bumann (pastor at Waynesville) was asked by Bishop Vincent Waters to see to the furnishings of St. Margaret's. He selected the pews, carpeting, and furniture. Father Bumann asked Father Patrick O'Donnell, a Glenmary priest who at that time had an artisan workshop in Vanceburg, Kentucky, if he would commission his local artisans to make a set of Stations of the Cross and the tabernacle. Father O'Donnell took it upon himself to design and form the tabernacle.

"The Stations of the Cross were made in December 1954, by Vicki Graves of Columbus, Ohio, a long-time friend of Father O'Donnell. Father O'Donnell acquired the Stations of the Cross when he visited Mrs. Graves on her sick bed. She requested that he find special places for her religious articles that she had made. When Father Bumann inquired about the Stations of the Cross, Father O'Donnell said, "I have the perfect set for you. Vicki would be delighted to know that they have a home in St. Margaret's Church, if she were alive."

Father Bumann and Mr. Murphy went to the quarry in Marble, North Carolina, near Murphy, to select and commission the cutting of the marble that is now the altar.

Stones Laid, Blessed, And Dedicated

It would be impossible to describe the feelings Mr. Murphy had when in 1967 the corner stone for his memorial church was put in place by Mr. Hoppi, who was in charge of the construction of St. Margaret's. He was assisted in laying the cornerstone by Father Joseph Bumann, pastor at St. John's in Waynesville, and Mr. Murphy. For Mr. Murphy it was a high point in his career to be equaled only by the dedication of the church and his own ordination in it.

Now that the corner stone was laid it was time to make plans for the dedication of the church. At long last the great day for the dedication of St. Margaret's arrived. It was August 15, 1968, the feast of the Assumption.

The *Extension* magazine article, written by Bishop May, president of *Extension* at that time, summarized the event:

"The great day for the dedication arrived. Down from Detroit came Mr. Murphy's nieces and nephews and all their families. From Washington, D.C., came Archbishop Luigi Raimondi, the Apostolic Delegate who had been informed of the project by Bishop Vincent Waters of Raleigh. Archbishop Raimondi offered to dedicate St. Margaret's personally, assisted by Bishop Waters, Bishop Ernest Unterkoefler of South Carolina, and by the President of *Extension*. It was a grand and glorious day for Maggie Valley, but especially for Michael William Murphy.

"St. Margaret's was packed for the dedication Mass—full of Michigan Murphys and Carolina Catholics from all the surrounding counties invited by their Bishop to join the visitors. Probably Mike Murphy will never see St. Margaret's full again. But from time to time Father Joseph Bumann of Waynesville will offer Mass there and before long a priest will be available to live in the quarters provided in connection with the church. "It will come," Mike Murphy insisted, looking out over the haze of the valley. "I don't expect to see it, but it will come."

The article continues:

"The local folks couldn't believe it when they saw the steel work going up. There are only 80 Catholic families in all of Haywood County served by St. John's Parish in Waynesville, and in Maggie Valley there are exactly 3 Catholics including Michael William Murphy. The newly completed St. Margaret's seats 200 so 'you can see I didn't build this church because of the demand' grinned Murphy. 'I built it for the future—strong so it will last for ages. Some day it will be full every Sunday.'"

Bishop May, who attended the dedication ceremony, was also the President of the Catholic Extension Society. When Mr. Murphy's savings account was nearing rock-bottom he appealed to Bishop Waters for help. Bishop Waters referred him to the Extension Society. The Society gave him a donation of $10,000. All churches receiving assistance from the Extension Society must acknowledge that assistance by putting a plaque somewhere in the church. A small plaque in the vestibule of the St. Margaret's gave the Extension Society credit for assisting with the construction of the church. Mr. Murphy never liked that plaque. After he became the pastor of St. Margaret's he paid back the money to the Extension Society and took down the plaque. In its place he put another plaque that read, "Please pray for Murphy-Garland and Whalen Families."

Though there were only 80 Catholic families in all of Haywood County at the time of the dedication of St. Margaret's, the enthusiasm and expectations glow from the ledger entries. Mr. Murphy was obviously and rightfully delighted with the response of the people,

June 10, 1968	First Holy Mass in new church of Saint Margaret. Most Rev. Vincent Waters officiated. Feast of St. Margaret of Scotland. About 40 persons present.
June 23, 1968	First SUNDAY Mass at St. Margaret's. Father Joseph Bumann, pastor of St. John's, Waynesville, officiated. 30 present; 12 received.
June 29, 1968	Mass at St. Margaret's. Bishop Waters. First confession on June 30th.
August 4	About 90 present for Mass at St. Margaret's Church.
August 11	80 present for Mass.
August 15	St. Margaret's dedicated by Apostolic Delegate, Luigi Raimondi. Four Bishops present. About twenty priests, fifty sisters and three or four hundred people. Holy Mass at noon."
August 21	Mass at St. Margaret. About 90 present.

Further entries up to the end of October list the number present at each Mass, numbers ranging from 23-90. Mr. Murphy was obviously pleased with the way the Lord was directing worshippers to the memorial church he had built for his mother. She had told him to build a church in the south. He built not one, but two! While St. Mary's in Sylva was his first church and was dedicated to both his mother and father, it was the church in Maggie Valley that would receive his love and attention for the rest of his years. Mr. Murphy was more and more convinced that St. Margaret's should have its own priest.

Church Rectory

Mr. Murphy desired to provide ample living quarters for those associated with the church. At first his plans were to have a one-story rectory, but when he got the project started he decided on a two-story rectory. He failed to ask the Bishop for permission to make the Rectory larger than originally planned. While Mr. Murphy thought it was a grand idea Bishop Waters did not think so. Why Bishop Waters did not think so is a mystery. Possibly it was that he was taken by surprise and his surprise registered as disapproval in Murphy's eyes.

Whenever Father Murphy talked about this change in plans his eyes would get watery and he would say, "I never would have done it if I had known the Bishop didn't want me to." He had expected praise and gratitude from Bishop Waters but he got the opposite. His feelings were hurt because he held Bishop Waters in such high esteem.

The old saying, "Into every life some rain must fall," was very true for Will Murphy. While many lauded Murphy's efforts at providing worship space for so many, and loved the man for his goodness, few knew the agonies and the hurts he endured in order to fulfill his dreams. No worthwhile achievement comes easy. Visitors who come to admire Murphy's work will never know how often the very stones cried out as Mr. Murphy proceeded on his mission.

Divine Providence had a plan. Mr. Murphy put the second story on the rectory because he wanted priests, brothers, sisters, and laity to come to spend time in prayer in the Valley. He wanted them to drink in the beauty of the mountains that so much enthralled him. He did not want individuals who wished to enhance their spiritual journey to have to go to a motel. One wonders today how different everything might have been if that second story had never been added.

Because there was ample space in the Rectory, the Mercy Sisters from Belmont brought their formation group to Maggie Valley for their summer program. Because the Mercy Sisters came, Mr. Murphy became acquainted with Sister Carolyn Coll. Because Sister Carolyn took an interest in Mr. Murphy, she gave him the encouragement, and the shove, he needed to become a priest.

Because there was ample space in the rectory six Sisters of St. Francis from Tiffin, Ohio, Sisters Laurene Toeppe, Thomas Kill, Eleanor Rahrig, Roberta McKinnon, Maurice Kleman, and I, made a retreat in the Rectory.

Because we made our retreat in the rectory, we got acquainted with Father Ron McLaughlin who, in 1971, was the pastor at St. John's in Waynesville. He invited us to return the following year to help him with the liturgies at the four churches he served. We would live in Cherokee and be a Catholic presence there.

Because Sister Roberta and I returned to the area the following summer to work on the reservation and to be the "Catholic presence" there, we got acquainted with Mr. Murphy and offered to assist him with the House of Prayer.

And, finally, because there was ample space in the rectory there are now five Augustinian Friars living there and administering to the people at St. Margaret's, at Living Waters, and in neighboring parishes. Father Murphy, in those heart-aching days of building the Rectory could never have known that his tears were watering the soil and making it fruitful.

Yes, indeed, Divine Providence had a plan. Every spiritual director knows that sometimes God writes straight with crooked lines. Mr. Murphy was hurt when he realized the Bishop did not approve of his plan to enlarge the Rectory, but many new births and many straight lines came out of his suffering and continue to come.

No Area Of The Rectory Was "Cloistered"

Even though the second story on the rectory caused some suffering it was also a cause of joy to Mr. Murphy after he began to live in the Rectory. At first when he was ordained and left the Raleigh Diocese to administer in Maggie Valley, he went back to his former home on Route 19. His chapel there was still intact. When Bishop Begley found out, he told Father Murphy to live in the rectory and to take care of the people who came to St. Margaret's. And so he did.

Father Murphy moved into the rectory but for some reason or other he never thought of the place as his private living quarters. Everything was open to the public. His hearing was still keen. When he heard people come into the church he went out to meet them. After all, that was what the Bishop told him to do—take care of the people. After pointing out the beauty of nature from the church he would take the visitors to the large bay window in his living room and rave about the beauty of the mountain side, adding, "It's like my mother always said, 'If this is such a beautiful world how much more beautiful heaven must be.'"

Father Murphy never thought of his rectory as being cloistered. He would tell the visitors to walk around the house and "be sure you see the upstairs." The visitors were, up to this time, complete strangers. Amazed at his warm hospitality they walked all through the house. While they oh'd and ah'd as they peered through every window, Father Murphy was free to sink back into his favorite chair, smile at their obvious pleasure, and continue his reading. He didn't have to entertain his guests. He just sent them on a tour of the house. When the visitors left they thanked him graciously, convinced by this time that they were on his "favorite-people" list. He had that way about him of making everyone feel at home, and he always invited the visitors to come back.

And come back they did, bringing others with them. When they came back they would say, "Remember us? We were here last year. We even went upstairs." Father Murphy wouldn't remember, but he didn't let them know that. He never lied, but he had that unique Irish way of pretending in order not to offend anyone. He always gave a nice courteous reply to the question, "Remember us?" while indicating that the visitors were most welcome to go upstairs again! Father Murphy met hundreds of guests every year and always gave them the impression that they were "best friends." He knew how to make people feel good. He wouldn't hurt anyone's feelings by letting them know he didn't remember them.

Indeed all who stopped in to see him were his friends. They felt honored to meet him. He was happy he could share with them. Many a guest was invited to have lunch with him. When they accepted the invitation they had no idea that lunch consisted of a slice of bread with peanut butter on it and a cup of tea, tea without sugar.

But Some Areas Should Have Been Cloistered.

Father Murphy began the custom of inviting anyone and everyone in to see the rectory long before he made his home there. He got into that habit when he was still Mr. Murphy. Father Tom Walsh, the pastor at St. John's in Waynesville at that time, relates the dilemma some priests found themselves in when they were invited to stay in the rectory. He tells it this way,

"Will Murphy was determined that Mass at St. Margaret's Church was to be at 9:30 a.m. on Sundays. He said that was the best time for the tourists who were in the Valley. He was probably right. However, there was only one priest most of the time for four parishes, each in a different town, Cherokee, Waynesville, Canton, and Maggie. That did not seem to enter into Murphy's thinking so he and my predecessors all butted heads over the matter.

"The only solution to this dilemma was to invite priests to come for a little vacation. Clergy could stay in the rectory for any length of time 'for free' in exchange for attending to the church services on Sundays. Sometimes several clergy members came together for a vacation. Naturally, being on vacation, they stayed up late at night and slept late in the morning. Many times their morning sleep would be interrupted because Will, proud of his building accomplishments, would come around early in the morning with visitors. It was his delight to show off the church AND the rectory, UPSTAIRS INCLUDED. He wanted visitors to know that the complex was being used. He wanted them to know the church was ALIVE and WELL in Maggie Valley—even if the shepherds were still asleep!"

Father Walsh said all protestations on the part of the visiting clergy were to no avail. Privacy had to give way to evangelization and evangelization was what Mr. Murphy was all about.

CHAPTER FIVE

▼

OUR LADY OF GUADALUPE-CHEROKEE

At the same time that Will Murphy was busy cutting down the mountain and erecting an edifice on the cleared space that would become St. Margaret's, another building project was going on in North Carolina just sixteen miles west of Maggie. Another mountain was being cut down to make room for another Catholic Church.

In the spring of 1961, ground was broken in Cherokee for the erection of Our Lady of Guadalupe Church. Mr. Murphy broke ground for the Maggie Valley church in 1962. Both churches were being built at the same time but the Cherokee church was finished first because work on the church was continuous after 1965. Will Murphy did not continue construction on St. Margaret's during the tourist season.

We can surmise that Mr. Murphy kept a close eye on what was happening in Cherokee because when he first came to western North Carolina he had hoped to be able to build a church on the Indian Reservation but he could not get permission from the tribal council to build, so he concentrated his efforts elsewhere.

It was a young Glenmary priest, Father James Wilmes, then pastor of St. Francis of Assisi church in Franklin, who approached the tribal council with a petition to build. For a number of years the Glenmary priests were offering Mass in the home of Lelia Queen, a native American who had converted to Catholicism.

Father Wilmes Presents Resolution

On October 14, 1960 Father Wilmes presented the following resolution to the tribal council.

Whereas, America's principle of freedom of religion is most admirably practiced by the Cherokee Tribe, and

Whereas, Citizens of Cherokee who profess belief in the Catholic faith have no church wherein to worship their loving Lord and Savior Jesus Christ, and

Whereas, The large number of Catholic tourists to Cherokee (150-200) each service cannot be accommodated in the room (basement) now used for church services, and

Whereas, The number of tourists will increase still more each year with the completion of "Cherokee Land", and

Whereas, Many tourists do not remain in Cherokee over night because it has no Catholic Church, and

Whereas, Many Catholics attend church daily and will not vacation in an area where Catholic facilities are not available, and

Whereas, The presence of churches of all major American denominations is a sign of progress, broadmindedness, proportionate representation of Americans, and favorably impresses visitors and industries seeking a place to settle, and

Whereas, Encouragement can be given all American Catholics to vacation at Cherokee by having pictures of the Cherokee Chapel in Catholic national weeklies, and

Whereas, Mrs. Candler (Lelia) Queen, an enrolled member of the Eastern Band of Cherokee Indians, has a holding in the Cherokee community, Swain County, and

Whereas, Mrs. Queen has agreed with Bishop Vincent S. Waters, Bishop of the Catholic Diocese of Raleigh, to give the Catholic Diocese of Raleigh,

through the Eastern Cherokee Band the use of the here-in-after described prop-
erty and the possessory right which she now has,

NOW THEREFORE BE IT RESOLVED by the Eastern Band of
Cherokee Indians in annual Council assembled, that the Catholic Church be
granted permission to build a chapel.

In an article in the *Glenmary Challenge,* Spring, 1961, written by Father
Wilmes, we read the following:

"A missioner stood up to speak before the assembled Indians. A black haired,
ruddy faced Cherokee interpreter stood at his side ready to translate the English
words. The council of chiefs looked up at the missioner. The priest looked into
their faces and offered a little prayer to the great Indian chief Sequoia, the
writer of the only Indian alphabet, the bestower of many happy memories. The
white man began, 'My dear Brothers and Sisters in Christ. My thoughts go
back this morning to a great chief of your tribe.'

"This did not happen 400 years ago, nor were the Indians wrapped in
blankets smoking a peace pipe, nor was the missioner in a black robe with a
crucifix in one hand. Yet these were full-blooded Cherokees and a missioner
was asking for a favor."

Father Wilmes preceded his presentation of the resolution by trying to
clear up some of the misconceptions the Cherokee had regarding the
Catholic beliefs, misconceptions that were quite common in the Bible belt.

He told the Cherokee Council members, *"Your great chief, Sequoia,*
died a Catholic and was buried in a Catholic Church in Mexico. Your chief
Sequoia was a most learned man and would not accept any faith which was
foolish. Catholics do not worship Mary. Catholics use the Bible every
day…Every Catholic preacher prays the Psalms for an hour every day for
Christians of all denominations, for you. No priest can pray anyone's sins
away. All religions differ a bit, and our beloved country allows freedom of
religion…If you give us permission to build a church, God will bless all your
families…He shall bless you all by an increase of tourists who will be more
willing to come if they know there is a church here. Many people write to
inquire about a Catholic Church and don't come because we have none. The

main reason we ask for a church is that the Jesus you love and the same Jesus I love will have another resting place here for those souls who believe that the Catholic faith is His teaching, and wish to worship in this way because He gave, not gold and silver, but his Precious Blood for them."

After Father Wilmes presented his "Whereas" petition one of the council members stood up and asked, "Do you Catholics believe that all either go to heaven or hell when they die?" "Yes," answered Father Wilmes. That cleared the matter for the inquirer who responded, "Well, you set my thinking straight."

Because all the land on the Cherokee reservation is held in trust for the native Americans by the United States Government, no land can be sold to a person who is not a native American. The Diocese of Raleigh could not buy land for the church. It was necessary that some one who owned property, like Lelia Queen, a convert to Catholicism, lease property to the Diocese of Raleigh.

Lelia Queen's sister, Myrtle Jenkins, was a member of the Tribal Council. She had been asked by the Council to do some research on how many people would benefit by having a Catholic Church on the reservation. She gave her answer, "About 1%, but remember what the Bible says about the one lost sheep. Let the Catholics save the lost sheep."

After some discussion on the Council floor the members voted on the resolution presented by Father Wilmes. The vote on the resolution was six in favor, three not in favor.

Around the year 1540, long before Father Wilmes made his presentation to the Tribal Council, some Catholics walked on native American soil. Friars had accompanied DeSoto on his expedition into the native American territory. While they tried to introduce Christianity to the Indians their success was minimal. The native Americans were already devoted to the "Great Spirit" and did not convert easily to Christianity.

Our Lady of Guadalupe Reflects Cherokee Culture

Bishop Waters wanted to make a connection between Native American spirituality and Catholicism by introducing the Cherokee to "Our Lady of Guadalupe" who had appeared to an Aztec Indian in Mexico. He also wanted the church that would be built on the reservation to be representative of the Cherokee nation. There are seven clans within the Cherokee tribe. The tribes' ancient and sacred council house was seven-sided so it was only fitting that the Catholic Church, which would be built in Cherokee would also be seven-sided. Each side represents one of the clans. The symbol of each clan is artistically designed in mosaic in the floor in front of each of the seven sections of pews, the work of the talented Cherokee artisan, G.B. Chiltoski.

Mr. Chiltoski also carved the symbols of the seven sacraments and had these symbols mounted in the railing that surrounded the seven-sided platform upon which the altar stood. G. B.'s real name was "Going Back." His father called him "G.B." or "Going Back" when, after the infamous Trail of Tears that took the Cherokee into Oklahoma, he was determined that some day the family would be "Going Back" to the reservation in North Carolina.

Bishop Waters asked Franz Van Bergen, a noted artist originally from Holland but living in Statesville, North Carolina, at the time of the Bishop's request, to design a window that would encompass one entire side of the building, the north side. The window was to tell the story of "Our Lady of Guadalupe" as the "patroness of captive nations." The window would feature Juan Diego, the Aztec Indian to whom Our Lady of Guadalupe revealed herself and Mexican decor on one side of Our Lady.

Our Lady of Guadalupe Church window in Cherokee

The other side would depict Sequoia, the Cherokee Indian who gave the Cherokee their first written alphabet, a replica of a seven-sided council house, and fauna and flora native to Cherokee. It took Van Bergen two and a half years to complete the window which has nearly 5,000 individual pieces of stained glass in it.

Dedication of the Church

Our Lady of Guadalupe Church was dedicated by Bishop Waters on August 15, 1966. The Rev. Joseph Bumann, pastor of St. John's of Waynesville and Rev. John Barry, pastor of St. Mary's in Sylva, assisted Bishop Waters. Monsignor Larry Newman, former pastor of Waynesville parish, delivered the sermon.

Two years later, on August 15, 1968, St. Margaret's Church in Maggie Valley would be dedicated.

When Sister Roberta McKinnon and I were first missioned to work on the reservation and after we had made friends with some of the Cherokee people we were told that while the church was being built one of the Baptist ministers kept warning the natives to stay away from the building site because the "Catholics are building a temple to the devil."

Cherokee–Mission of St. John's, Waynesville

Our Lady of Guadalupe parish became a mission of St. John's in Waynesville. The pastor, Rev. Ron McLaughlin, had four parishes to care for, St. John's in Waynesville, Immaculate Conception in Canton, St. Margaret's in Maggie Valley, and Our Lady of Guadalupe in Cherokee. One of the native Americans remarked one day to Father McLaughlin, "You can't make us believe that the Catholic Church really cares about us Indians. They built a church here and then forgot about us. Nobody's ever at the church." Because Father McLaughlin realized there was some truth to the statement in so far as he was able to come to Cherokee only once a week, he asked some of us who were making a retreat at St. Margaret's in Maggie Valley to return the following summer to assist him with the liturgies and to be a "Catholic presence" on the reservation.

When Father McLaughlin made his request he told Sister Roberta McKinnon , a musician, that she should learn how to sing from "shaped notes." We had never heard of shaped-note singing so after our retreat in Maggie we picked up a hymnal from one of the Baptist churches in Cherokee and took it back to Ohio with us. There Sister Roberta unlocked the secret. She discovered for herself what most of the Cherokee already knew.

Sr. Roberta discovered that DO is always a triangle, RE is always in the shape of a basket, MI is in the shape of a diamond, FA is shaped like a pennant, SOL is round, LA is a rectangle, and TI looks like an ice cream cone. Equipped with this information she anxiously returned to the reservation just in time to help out in one of the Baptist churches that needed someone to train the choir members. Twice a week, we went out at night to one of the Baptist churches twelve miles down a lonely road. When one of the parishioners from Our Lady of Guadalupe church learned that we were out at night in that particular neighborhood he told us it had a reputation for violence and warned us to be very, very careful. We didn't get frightened. We figured that if it was a safe enough area for those good folks to come for practice it was safe enough for us.

A year after Sister Roberta and I arrived in Cherokee we had a nice conversation with Ron Arch of Cherokee descent, who lived on the reservation. Ron's grandmother sent him to St. John's Catholic School in Waynesville, because she thought he would get a good education there. Eventually, Ron became a Catholic.

Being Accepted On The Reservation

Ron was very friendly and very accepting of us. After we were on the reservation for a year he shared with us his misgivings about our coming to Cherokee in the first place. Ron was a member of Our Lady of Guadalupe parish. Father Don Levernier, Glenmary, was the pastor at the time. Father Levernier told Ron and a few other persons in the parish whom he consulted that Sister Roberta and I would be coming to work on the reservation. Ron said his reaction to this information was somewhat negative because he was afraid we would be hurt. He feared that we would not be accepted for a number of reasons. Strike one–we were "white" and Cherokee was the red man's territory. Strike two–we were from the North and Yankees are not too welcome in the South. Strike three–we were Catholic and Cherokee was Baptist territory. Not only were we Catholic but we were NUNS! That had its own danger points.

Not too long after we arrived the tribe held its annual fall festival. We attended as much as we could in order to learn more about the people among whom we were working and in order to show them we cared about their customs. One night we attended the performances given on the Cherokee fairground. A part of the performance that particular night was a very lively dance put on by a group of children. In the dance they were chased by a black clad "witch" who grabbed and snatched at them. We thought it was a rather lively performance but it lacked the usual hooting calls made by slapping the hands against the mouth that, as children, we had come to associate with the Indian circle dance. We wondered if this was a typical Indian dance.

A few days later we were talking to an Episcopalian lady who had lived on the reservation for quite a few years. She had married the native Cherokee artist, G.B.

Chiltoski, who carved out the symbols of the Sacraments for Our Lady of Guadalupe church. She told us that the black "witch" was supposed to be a "nun" and that the dance represented how the nuns grabbed up the kids and put them in orphanages. When we heard that interpretation of the dance we knew we would have to work hard to overcome the image that the native Americans had of nuns.

However, we were glad to report, when speaking to Ron Arch, that from the very beginning of our stay in Cherokee we felt very much accepted by these Native Americans. We did whatever we could to help them endure their "captive" situation. Sister Roberta gave music lessons not only in the local high school but also in our little apartment that was attached to the church building. It seemed to be the aim of all the musically talented folks to learn enough music to play the piano in their churches. Naturally, we participated in "shaped note" singing, which is what the natives know best. Father Les Schmidt, one of the Glenmary priests who stopped in to see us, said we were accepted on the reservation because we did not come with pre-packaged programs. We entered into the world of the Cherokee. We did not expect them to enter into our world.

We taught GED classes and did a lot of chauffeuring to the doctor's offices and various other places. Both of us did home visiting and helped out where we could. We volunteered our services to the Sheltered Work Shop which provided limited training for the mentally and physically handicapped native Americans. Our volunteering helped keep the Work Shop from "going under" because of the lack of federal funds. Sister Roberta taught music in the Cherokee high school. We did not try to convert the natives to Catholicism but we did try to present a positive image of what the Catholic church believes and teaches.

The Cherokee–A Truly Captive Nation

Sister Roberta and I were in Cherokee in 1974, when the government tried to make restitution for the land it "stole" from the Cherokee. Anyone who was enrolled on the reservation and could prove to be 1/16 Cherokee was entitled to receive some recompense. Each received $144.12. The government was making restitution to the extent of paying the Indians $1.29 per acre for the land stolen from them. While in a certain sense this meager recompense was an insult to the Cherokees, they received the funds graciously and gratefully.

We were also in Cherokee when the Smoky Mountain Park celebrated the fortieth anniversary of its establishment. The Park was established by an act of Congress on June 15, 1934. Headlines in the Cherokee paper during that anniversary year of 1974 read, *"Remember When The President Of The USA Called Us Savages?"*

Although the Park was established in 1934, it was not dedicated until September 8, 1940. The park is situated in two states–North Carolina and Tennessee. For the dedication a platform was erected at Newfound Gap at a spot where the two states intersect. President Franklin Delano Roosevelt stood with one foot in each state while he told those attending the dedication, "Look around you at this beautiful land. The savages have had this land for thousands of years and have done nothing with it. Look what we have done in just a few years."

"Look what we have done." WHAT HAVE WE DONE?? Freeman Owle, a native Cherokees, an educator and a renowned licensed lecturer, answers the question.

"While we so-called 'savages' had the forests there were no mountain slides. We didn't dig or blast. Trees didn't die from disease and pollution. Trees were not uprooted. Animals were free to roam the forests. Native Americans loved their land and they loved the creatures that lived side by side with them. The wild flowers bloomed for them. Medicinal plants grew for them. We'll soon have the 'Rockies in the East' because a lot of pollution is coming in, killing the trees and the plants. Insects and diseases are killing the natural growth of the forests. The acidity from the rain is so high neither fish nor plants can long survive."

Not only did the Cherokee not appreciate being called "savages" but they also resented the way they were driven from their homes to make the Smoky Mountain National Park a reality. They experienced much injustice at the hands of the people of the United States.

The Cherokee also did not forget that they did not get the right to vote until 1946. During the 1976 anniversary year commemorating American Independence from Great Britain there were billboards that, as visitors approached the village notified them that **"The Cherokee did not get the right to vote until 1946."** The Cherokee had to fight in two World Wars before they were even considered citizens with the right to vote.

Already as early as 1920, the Cherokee had sought citizenship. All those early efforts seemed to be in vain. World War I brought the plight of the Cherokee Indians to the attention of the people. Could they be drafted to serve in the army if they were not citizens? This was the question. It never really was answered at that time, but some Cherokee men were drafted to serve in that war.

In May of 1924, the US District Court decreed that the Cherokee actually were not citizens but were "federal wards." Because they were "wards" and not "citizens" they were not allowed to vote.

The following month Congress passed the Indian Citizenship Act declaring all Indians born in the United States to be citizens but added that being citizens did not automatically give them the right to vote. They had to know how to read and write the English language. They also had to know how to interpret the law of the state in which they resided.

It took another World War to once again bring the plight of the American Indians to the attention of the nation. In May 1946, after the war was over, veterans of the war tried to register to vote in the primary election but they were denied the privilege.

Having fought in their second World War for freedom for others, the native Americans were now more than ever conscious of freedom for themselves. At the October 1946 annual Cherokee tribal fair volunteers passed out several thousand handbills describing the Indians' grievances. Those handbills got the attention that was needed. Officers of the American Legion began to lobby with the state political leaders. The Cherokee themselves began to challenge their county registrars. Finally, in late 1946, the Cherokee were given the right to register for voting.

Ron's Doubts Disappear

At the end of our first full year on the Cherokee reservation, Ron Arch told us that we had done remarkably well and that he no longer had doubts about our being accepted on the reservation, even though we were "white," "Yankee," and "Catholic." We felt that we were able to be the "Catholic presence" that had been missing.

Father Murphy visited us frequently in Cherokee and gave us donations to use in our work. We, in turn, visited him almost weekly in Maggie Valley, and tried to help him wherever and whenever we could. We brought youth groups from Cherokee to Maggie Valley to present religious musicals in the church. We also brought children, teen-agers, and adults to Maggie for retreats that were held in the rectory and the church.

CHAPTER SIX

▼

NEW PRIEST-NEW DIOCESE

Murphy Finds A Priest For Maggie Valley

"I guess I knew from the time I was 3 and picking berries that I wanted to be a priest. But I just never got around to it until I was 80."

In the interview that Father Murphy gave to Jim Cinque and Fred Woodall he answered the question, "When was the first time you realized that your destiny was to be a priest?" by saying, "We had great devotion in our home because we lived a long way from the church. On Good Friday, from twelve until three, we all knelt down and prayed, because that's when the good Lord was dying. My mother told us that whatever a child would ask for during those three hours, the Lord would grant, if it pleased him. One of the things I asked for was that I would be a priest. I was three years old. Another thing was that I would get a gold watch."

Father Jack McNearney, Glenmary, recalls that while St. Margaret's was being built, "Mr. Murphy looked for a priest to serve at Maggie Valley. He and I talked about the possibility of Glenmary providing that priest but I told him I doubted if Glenmary would agree to do so as we usually operated from county seats and Maggie was not the county seat of Haywood County. Also it seemed as if Maggie was merely a tourist town with little or no hope of growing."

How right! How wrong! And it was Mr. Murphy who helped make the difference. Maggie did grow. Murphy attracted others, particularly Catholics, to the area. At the time of the dedication of St. Margaret's church there were only three Catholics belonging to the parish. Presently, the parish records show that there are 172 regular families and an additional 76 seasonal families enrolled. St. Margaret's is increasing membership because Maggie did grow and is still growing. However, Maggie does remain a tourist town and the people like it that way. And because it grew it was all the more necessary to get a priest for St. Margaret's.

The final nudge for Mr. Murphy to become Father Murphy came from a young Mercy sister–Sister Carolyn Coll from Belmont. She spent time with the elderly gentleman who came to pray in the church that he had built. She came to love and respect him.

Father Murphy with Sister Carolyn Mary Coll, RSM

Sister Carolyn Coll, RSM, writes:

"I met Mr. Murphy the summer of my first profession during my retreat in Maggie Valley in June of 1970. My novice director, Sister Jeanne Marie Kienest RSM, brought all of us preparing for vows, both first and final vows, to Maggie Valley. Bishop Waters had given permission for us to stay in the Rectory. Both the church and the living quarters were beautiful. At that time there was no priest living in the rectory and due to the lack of Catholics in the area there were no immediate plans to send a priest to St. Margaret's. Father Thomas Walsh who was pastor in Waynesville provided us with liturgy and spiritual guidance. With him that summer was a seminarian, Tim O'Conner. Father O'Conner is now with the diocese of Raleigh, which, in 1970 was the only diocese in North Carolina.

"Mr. Murphy, as he was called then, would come each day to the church to pray and many times when we would have Mass or pray our office he would be there. He sat in the very back, far from us, and would pray quietly with us. When he came he was always dressed the same. He always wore a long sleeve white shirt with the cuffs turned up twice, black pants, a brown hat, and black shoes with white socks. He had two Cadillacs. One was his everyday car and the other his special occasion car. Mostly, however, Mr. Murphy walked. Several times a day he would walk up from his motel to the church to pray. It was a steep hill but it didn't really seem to bother him. He loved the church and he loved his God.

"It was several days after our arrival that I invited him to sit with us when we said office before the evening Mass. His response was, 'no,' and his reason was, 'I am not worthy to sit with you.' I was struck by the sincerity of his words and found myself feeling as if it might be the other way around. I remember getting my book and sitting next to him. That was the beginning of a beautiful friendship.

"Soon, we took walks up and down the mountain praying the rosary and he sharing his story of how he came to build the church in Maggie. He told of his dreams and how he saw his mother Margaret telling him to build the church. He told how in one dream he could see the Eucharist coming from the distance towards him, being brought by the Mother of God, and how he knew then that he had to build the church. At times, I must admit he scared me, but as time went on I truly came to believe this man to be holy, if not a real mystic. He spoke of how, on many trips from Detroit to Florida with his mother, he had passed near Maggie Valley, and how he felt called to come back to stay in Maggie and build a church there after his mother died.

"During one of our walks, he shared with me how he always wanted to be a priest but caring for his mother had been important to him. Now, this builder of churches was being invited by Bishop Waters to become a deacon. He didn't want to become a deacon. He dreamed of the priest-hood, even in his seventies. We talked about his faith and the role his mother had played in shaping it, all the while knowing how deep was his desire to serve in the priesthood. I remember telling him that if God want-ed him to be a priest he would be one.

"Our time together passed quickly but our walks and times of prayer were blessed and his stories of growing up were bountiful. I was always amazed at how much I enjoyed his presence. Once when I went by his liv-ing quarters, the second floor of a store front building that had also served as the Catholic chapel in the valley, I saw just how simply this man of means lived. It seemed the more I learned about him the less I really knew. He loved to laugh, and he enjoyed the mountains and would often say, 'Sister, isn't it beautiful? I don't believe there is any grander place on earth.'

"When I left that summer, I invited him to attend my first profession on July 19, 1970, in Belmont, a two to three hour drive from Maggie. He said he would come, and come he did in his special occasion Cadillac with his grandniece, Anne, his pastor, Father Walsh, and the seminarian, Tim. I was very happy to have them there and I enjoyed visiting with Mr. Murphy after the service.

"Bishop Waters had presided at the ceremony and it was here, before Mr. Murphy left, that the Bishop invited him again to go to the seminary. I remember the day very vividly because in my youthfulness and naiveté, I spoke to Bishop Waters and asked him point-blank why Mr. Murphy couldn't be a priest since he didn't want to be a deacon. The Bishop wasn't really responsive to me except to tell me, in very polite terms, that I needed to mind my own business. It wasn't until later that I learned that Mr. Murphy ran into the Bishop on the way out of the Motherhouse and it was then that the Bishop gave his final invitation to Mr. Murphy to go to the seminary to study for the priesthood, saying, "now or never." That profession day was to become a very special day for both of us.

"There would be more special days for us. Mr. Murphy was ordained on May 7, 1972. On August 10, 1975, I pronounced my final vows. Again I invited Father Murphy. That was truly a most memorable day for me because, not only had I reached a goal in my religious life, but there he was, Father Murphy himself, concelebrating with the Bishop and being a witness to my consecration. I had the thrill of my life. When he witnessed my first vows he was still MISTER Murphy. Now it was as FATHER Murphy that he witnessed my final vows. It was indeed a very blessed day for me. We both had reached our goals.

"Father Murphy remained a special friend of mine, a soul friend who in his own simple but profound way shared his deep love of the Catholic faith, of the Mother of God, and of the Eucharist which now, since his ordination in May, 1972, he celebrated daily. His quick wit, his hidden talent for playing his fiddle, and his quiet ways became part of the legacy that he shared with me. This simple man, whom to this day I know as a man of great faith and a mystic, touched my life in so many wonderful ways. For me he became a grandfather figure with whom, even now, I find myself sharing my thoughts and prayers, remembering all the while his great wit, his humanness, and his caring heart."

"It's Now or Never"

Father Tom Walsh tells of the first stages of Mr. Murphy's transformation into Father Murphy. In spite of the Bishop's telling Mr. Murphy, "It's

now or neve," the Bishop still thought in terms of the permanent diaconate and was giving Mr. Murphy one more chance to make up his
mind. Father Walsh describes the experience he had taking Mr. Murphy
to a meeting in Chicago on July 11, 1970.

"After Bishop Waters appointed me to be the pastor of St. John's in
Waynesville and its mission, St. Margaret's in Maggie Valley, one of the
first things he asked me to do was to take Mr. Murphy to a meeting at the
University of Chicago. The meeting centered on the subject of 'Deacons
in the Church' and was the first national meeting held on that subject.

"So off we went. Mr. Murphy drove his Cadillac. It took almost two days
to get to our destination because we could not leave until after the Sunday
Masses. It was obvious that the Bishop hoped to get Mr. Murphy interested
in becoming a Deacon. He had been a generous benefactor to the Church of
Western North Carolina. Along the way Mr. Murphy asked if a Deacon
could offer the Holy Sacrifice of the Mass. Obviously he already knew the
answer. His reluctance to becoming a Deacon was showing!

"On this trip I discovered that there was a plan B, a plan to take Mr.
Murphy to St. Meinrad's to meet Father Lynch, OSB. We stopped in
Cincinnati for the night. We arrived in Chicago at the University the next
day, registered, received the keys to our rooms, and then attended our first
conference. Because this was the first national meeting on the subject of
'Deacons in the Church,' and because Vatican II had stimulated much interest in the subject there was an atmosphere of excitement all over the place.
Speakers and attendees were full of ideas and quite talkative about the possibilities. I remember someone calling for Caesar Chavez to be ordained.

"Will Murphy was taking it all in. He wasn't saying anything, no com-
ments whatsoever. Finally he said very quietly but firmly, 'I can do all
these things now. I want to be a priest.' His mind was made up. That's
when we went into Plan B and headed for St. Meinrad's to meet with
Father Lynch, a Benedictine."

Benedictines to the Rescue

The Benedictine order began with St. Benedict, a late Fifth, early Sixth Century monk. St. Benedict felt that community was an ideal way to live one's call to Christ and a life of prayer. Though he would take material from existing orders of his time, the *Rule of St. Benedict* would become a unique model for others. While taking vows of obedience, stability of place and conversion of life, the monks commit their lives to prayer and work. Subiaco and Monte Cassino in Italy were the monasteries that Benedict personally founded.

The Benedictine order arrived in the American Midwest during the 1850's after Father Joseph Kundek approached the Swiss Abbey of Einsiedeln, asking that a monastery be founded in America. The monks of Einsiedeln were interested in a foundation in America if their three goals could be pursued there, i.e., transplant their Benedictine rule to American territory; be allowed to minister to the growing Catholic population in the Midwest; and be allowed to found a seminary for local men interested in the priesthood.

Two monks came over from Switzerland to search out the site that would have some resemblance to their mother abbey in the foothills of the Alps. The priory, beginning in 1854 as a three-room cabin on 160 acres of land in Indiana, is the St. Meinrad Archabbey today. It is one of only nine archabbeys in the world, one of two in the United States.

According to the St. Meinrad web page, in the spring of 2000, St. Meinrad's Benedictine community consisted of approximately 135 monks who follow the *Rule of St. Benedict*. Four times a day the monks gather as a community in prayer for the Liturgy of the Hours and Mass. In addition, the monks lead retreats, serve as chaplains, and give general pastoral assistance to parishes in a dozen or more dioceses. They also testify to the life and resurrection of Jesus Christ through their renowned School of Theology. They have international exposure through their noted Abbey Press.

In 1857, the monks began their teaching profession when they began their secondary education classes in the classics, philosophy, theology, as well as in commerce. Later, the monks began to focus their complete attention on preparing men for the priesthood. However, during it's first century, the School of Theology became so noted that in response to the changing needs of the Catholic Church, the School now also offers graduate-level programs for lay ministry students and extensive Continuing Education Programs for others. St. Meinrad's has more than 6,000 alumni currently serving the church in the United States and around the world.

In 1971-72, Saint Meinrad once again broke new ground. In a press release from St. Meinrad's College and School of Theology, the heading read:

80 YEAR OLD MAN TUTORED FOR PRIESTHOOD
BY MONKS AT MEINRAD ARCHABBEY
ORDINATION SET FOR MAY 11

The monks of Saint Meinrad met the invincible Michael William Murphy and put their mark on him, never to be erased, never to be forgotten.

The monastery's news release outlined the data about this wholly unique entrance into the order of Melchizedek. The release opened, "Word comes from Saint Meinrad Archabbey, St. Meinrad, Indiana, of probably one of the oldest individuals ever to be prepared for ordination to the Roman Catholic priesthood in the history of the Church. He is the Rev. Michael William Murphy, who is 80 years old."

Rt. Rev. Gabriel Verkamp, OSB, Archabbot of St. Meinrad, gave special permission for the unusual procedure of special classes. Certainly Murphy's past history of devotion, determination, and missionary zeal, had earned him the privilege of ordination. The chain of the request to enroll Will Murphy in St. Meinrad Seminary began with Bishop Waters' approach to the Apostolic Delegate, Most Rev. Luigi Raimondi, who then suggested to Rt. Rev. Verkamp that special consideration be given Mr. Murphy.

Will Was a Quick Learner

Father Lynch talks about his experiences with Will Murphy at St. Meinrad's Seminary, January 1971 until May 1972:

"One day Father Archabbot Gabriel asked me if I would have time to give instructions. I didn't know exactly what he meant, convert instructions? Or, for some odd reason, marriage instructions? I told him I could. He gave me a letter from Bishop Waters of Raleigh, North Carolina. The letter asked Archabbot Gabriel if it would be possible for someone at St. Meinrad to give instructions for ordination to 79-year old Will Murphy. He had built a church in Maggie Valley and, I believe, at Sylva and had helped with a Newman Club Center at a university in N.C. I told him that I would be happy to do so but it seemed to me that perhaps Bishop Waters was sending Will to St. Meinrad as a type of reward for the good he had done for the diocese and really might not expect him to persevere. Later Will told me that the bishop had asked him 10 years previously–age 69–about becoming a priest, and Will told Bishop Waters he thought he was too old. But at 79, Will changed his mind!

"We took Canon Law and Liturgy and some other subjects. However, I do think that he attended even that year, Father Conrad's classes on the Psalms. That is the way in which he came into contact with Father Conrad. I knew that the latter had come to Maggie Valley during Holy Week and Easter but I did not know it was for twelve years.

"Father Will was a quick learner, because he had a very sharp mind. As you possibly know, he had gone only to the 7th grade; I believe I am correct on this. I have heard of self-made men and Father Will was one. After God, his mother, Margaret, was his ideal. This is the reason why he named the church after her patron saint.

"Father Will told me that when he made his First Communion, his mother told him to always remember that day every time he received Our Lord. And he did. That is the reason why I believe he was really a mystic–or at least had tremendous union with God. After Communion (and it was not an "act") it appeared to me that he was really lost in contemplation. He folded his hands in the good old-fashioned way. It is interesting that the easterners (Moslems, etc. still do, while we have often abandoned it.) It is part of that idea of our being "buddy-buddy" with God, part of the "pseudo-informality" Cardinal Ratzinger bemoans in his theological work *FEAST OF FAITH.*

"When I asked Father Will about the changes of Vatican II, he said that he didn't think too much about it, but that the question when changes are made always is, 'Does it make the people any better?'

"In the second year at St. Meinrad's he also took Homiletics. The students in the class were amazed with his sermons–down to earth. I know that when Will first came, the seminarians said he was taking a crash course in Extreme Unction."

*Fred Dennison, Reverend Ralph Lynch, OSB, Will Murphy on the day
of their ordination as Deacons*

Had Will Murphy enrolled in the seminary for a crash course in Extreme Unction? Hardly. Although it was never said in so many words it was certainly realized that age might intervene and thwart the completion of Mr. Murphy's dream. Therefore those involved who were encouraging Father Murphy to become a priest had to think ahead. Provisions were made for a "crash course" in the necessary studies. In January 1971, Father Ralph Lynch, OSB of St. Meinrad's began the tutorial task of giving special instructions to Will Murphy although Will also attended some regular classes at the seminary. *"In spite of his age,"* the release from St. Meinrad's noted, *"the Rev. Mr. Murphy is very robust, very active, and very alert."* Indeed! Those who knew Mr. Murphy knew how very robust, active, and alert he was and could have told this to those seminarians who said he came to the seminary for a "crash course in Extreme Unction."

When speaking of his days at St. Meinrad's Father Murphy said, "When I went there I thought they wouldn't keep me for more than two weeks. The stay in the seminary wasn't too hard because all my spare time for many, many years was spent reading good literature. My mother used to say that we should never sit down without a book in our hands. Several years before she died my good holy mother said she was disappointed that she didn't have a son who was a priest, but now she has. I was ordained May 11, Ascension Thursday, 1972, twenty-two years after she died."

Ordination At Last

Tonsure and minor orders were conferred on Will Murphy by Bishop Waters in August, 1971. In March 1972, Murphy received the major orders of Subdiaconate and Diaconate at St. Meinrad's from Archbishop George Biskup, Archbishop of Indianapolis.

And finally the day Will Murphy dreamed of since that Good Friday when he was but three years old had arrived. The announcement read:

WITH SINCERE GRATITUDE TO

ALMIGHTY GOD

MICHAEL WILLIAM MURPHY

ANNOUNCES HIS ORDINATION
TO THE HOLY PRIESTHOOD
ON
ASCENSION THURSDAY—MAY 11, 1972
AT 3: 00 P.M. (E.D.T.)
IN THE CHURCH OF
ST. MARGARET
AT
MAGGIE VALLEY, NORTH CAROLINA
BY THE
MOST REVEREND VINCENT S. WATERS, D.D.
BISHOP OF RALEIGH

The ordaining prelates, all younger, led the dimunitive ordinandi into the church. The Most Rev. Vincent S. Waters, Bishop of Raleigh, who encouraged Will Murphy to prepare for the priesthood, was the ordaining prelate. Assisting in the sanctuary were Bishop Michael J. Begley of the Charlotte Diocese, Auxiliary Bishop George E. Lynch of the Raleigh Diocese, and Archabbot Gabriel Verkamp of St. Meinrad Archabbey in Indiana.

The Rev. Ron McLaughlin, then pastor of St. John's in Waynesville and of St. Margaret's in Maggie Valley, was in charge of making the arrangements for the ordination. A choir from the local high school, accompanied by musical instruments, sang during the ordination Mass. The sanctuary was filled with priests from the dioceses of Raleigh and Charlotte. The Rev. Gerald L. Lewis, Chancellor of the Raleigh Diocese, was the Master of Ceremonies. The reception was at the Maggie Valley Lodge at the lower end of the Valley.

The Lord Calls In Various Ways

Before the ordination ceremonies ever began on that eventful day there was to be a different kind of "call" to a much younger man. Brother Richard Walsh, Glenmary, who came to participate in the joyous event was called to "come on home, good and faithful servant." Little did he know when he went into the back bedroom of the rectory to vest for the services that he would not be able to participate in those services. Naturally, there was a great deal of excitement before the ordination ceremonies ever began, because the "angel of death" had come onto the premises. In one of the downstairs bedrooms in the Rectory, Brother Richard Walsh collapsed and died just as every one was lining up to proceed into the church.

Father Jack McNearney remembers it well:

"Brother Dick Walsh and I drove down from the Glenmary Headquarters in Cincinnati on May 10, 1972, to represent Glenmary at the ordination. I brought a gift for Father Murphy from Glenmary. I believe it was a golden pyx. I stayed with Father Levernier at Sylva while Brother Dick stayed with Ted and Mim Matus at Cullowhee. We arrived at St. Margaret's the next day and while vesting for the ceremony, Brother Dick dropped dead of a heart attack. I was so upset that I could not attend the service."

Instead of attending the ordination ceremony Father Jack had to see to the details of notifying Glenmary of the death, and getting the deceased Brother back to the Glenmary Headquarters for the funeral.

The confusion preceding the ordination ceremony did not end immediately after the ambulance left the premises. There was a case of **mistaken identity**. Father Tom Walsh, who had been the one to take Father Murphy to the Chicago meeting for deacons, had an unusual souvenir of the ordination—a speeding ticket.

Father Tom Walsh had been transferred from St. John's in Waynesville to St. Eugene's in Asheville. He got a late start from Asheville and was speeding toward Maggie right past Lake Junaluska when he was stopped by a patrolman and given a ticket and a fatherly admonition. He accepted both and then continued on his journey, trying desperately to arrive at St. Margaret's on time without getting another ticket. When he got near the entrance of Falling Waters Motel he heard a siren but it wasn't a police car this time. An ambulance was coming down from St. Margaret's. Father Walsh slowed down to let the speeding ambulance go past him. He came to the obvious conclusion. "This has been too much for the poor guy and he has had a heart attack–or something."

None-the-less Father Walsh rushed on in to the church and "what did I see but Will Murphy quietly processing down the aisle, on his way to being ordained!" He was shocked to see Father Murphy alive. There were others who were shocked also, not at seeing Father Murphy alive but at seeing Father Walsh alive. After the ambulance sirens stopped screaming, all that the St. John's parishioners had heard whispered was, "Walsh died." In their lives there was only one Walsh–their former pastor. But it wasn't Father Tom Walsh who died. It was Brother Richard Walsh. Same family name, different persons. Father Tom told his former parishioners that he was very much alive, "and I have a speeding ticket to prove it."

Awed By the Mystery

The Raleigh News and Observer July 1972, in an article by D.R. Lescarbeau notes the event of the ordination from the perspective of Sister Mary Dosithea and Sister Marie Angeline, Sisters of Providence, who attended the ceremony. Lescarbeau begins reflectively, "While each of American Catholicism's six holy days of obligation commemorates some great occasion or mystery of faith, for Sister Mary Dosithea and Sister Marie Angeline of the Sisters of Providence, the meaning behind the events of last Ascension Thursday in Maggie Valley, North Carolina, may well be a minor mystery."

Expecting a crowd Sisters Dosithea and Angeline arrived early and took seats near the front. From their vantage point they could readily observe as celebrants entered the church, and see the door of the rectory, which was the home for priests at St. Margaret's. It was in the midst of this zenith experience that an unexpected turn was added to the ceremony: Brother

Richard Walsh, 58, a carpenter and one of the Glenmary Home Missioners, died.

The Sisters had briefly met Brother Richard when he worked on some cabinets for them at Providence Hospital in Murphy, North Carolina. And now, just before the ordination ceremony began they were told of his sudden death. "During the processional, the organ, the trumpets and the choir seemed to be giving forth their triumphant and joyous sound for Brother Richard as well as Will Murphy, the nuns told Lescarbeau. "Everyone felt that Brother Richard now possessed what each of us is striving for. It was one of the most unusual and memorable things that has ever happened to us."

The Sisters continued their narrative. "In that beautiful setting, facing the altar, we could see the budding trees and the mountains through the clear glass wall. It's strange, but we didn't feel the normal sadness at the death of Brother Richard so much as we rejoiced in his triumph. It seemed he must have just walked into heaven because the atmosphere at St. Margaret's makes you feel closer to heaven.

"Also it did something to us to see the newly ordained but elderly priest giving his first blessing. During the ceremony Will had spoken quietly when addressed by the Bishop. He seemed frail, but after the ordination he gave his blessing in a strong clear voice loud enough for Brother Richard to hear him," said Sister Dosithea.

"Don't Get Your Shoes Dirty"

Mattie Killian remembers that ordination day very well. She said:

"Father Murphy's ordination day was a great day for him. His family and friends all came down from Detroit and elsewhere. Falling Waters Motel was reserved for his guests. There were so many people and cars that they covered the place from the main road to the church. Mr. Murphy stayed up at his place on Soco the night before the ordination. He dressed for the ceremony at his home and then drove to the motel where he parked his car. He wore his old shoes when he walked up to the church. He carried his new shoes so they would be nice and clean for the ordination."

Father Murphy's grandniece, Anne, was also present for the ceremony. She, too, noticed that Murphy had put on his old shoes. She said, "We were surprised that he didn't put on the 'brand-new' shoes that he had bought for his ordination. When we asked him about it he said, 'Oh, no! I don't want to get them dirty. I will put them on up at church.' As he was prostrating during his ordination, the sunlight danced on the new soles of his shoes, reflecting the beauty of the soul of the one being ordained."

One could almost hear Murphy's mother cautioning, "Now, Will, head up, shoulders back and stand up straight. And Will, mind you, don't get your shoes dirty before the service." Moms do talk that way, even after they are long gone from the scene.

Mattie also remembers that the day after his ordination Father Murphy came to the Motel "to see how we were doing. He was so happy. He said he wouldn't change places with the President of the United States. He said he got the two things he wished for in his life. That was a gold watch and to be a priest. He said his parents got him the gold watch. And his wish to become a priest had now come true."

It was also on the day following his ordination that Father Will had his first individual Mass. In attendance were some relatives who were able to stay in the Valley over night. It was at this Mass that he gave his great nephew his First Holy Communion.

Congregation on Ordination Day

While the clergy and the entire assembly sing the Litany of the Saints,
Will Murphy lies prostrate before the altar,
a sign of humility and a symbol of his dependence on God

*Will Murphy places his hands between those of the Bishop
and promises his obedience to the Bishop and his successors*

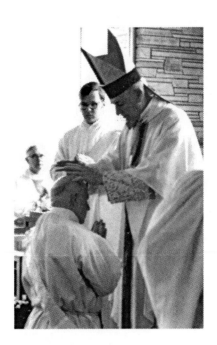

The presiding Bishop, followed by the rest of the clergy,
lays hands on the ordinand's head,
the ancient rite of conferring priestly ordination.

Father Murphy concelebrates his First Mass

News of Ordination Spreads Quickly

Tom Wells, a correspondent from the *Durham Morning Herald*, was at the ceremony and wrote the following article for the May 12, 1972, edition of the paper, capturing more than mere facts.

"Eighty-year old Michael William Murphy, one of the oldest men ever to become a Roman Catholic priest, took his vows to God yesterday in a small church deep in the Smoky Mountains of Western North Carolina.

"The retired Detroit real estate dealer spoke the centuries-old vows and then slowly prostrated himself on a blue carpet in front of the Bishop.

"For the grandson of Irish immigrants, the 90-minute Mass of Ordination was a childhood dream come true.

"It also fulfilled the wish of his late mother, who was 95 when she died. She had prayed that one of her five sons might join the priesthood.

"The ceremony took place in St. Margaret's Church, which Murphy built in honor of his mother.

"Now, with most of his life behind him and no brothers or sisters living, the stocky Murphy took an oath of obedience that will send him to a parish in Williamston, far across the state in North Carolina's flat land of tobacco and cotton farmers.

"Are you resolved with the help of the Holy Spirit to discharge, without fail, the office of priesthood and the rank of presbyter as the trusted partner of the Bishop in caring for the Lord's flock?' asked Bishop Vincent S. Waters, of the Raleigh diocese.

"(Was it really 77 years ago that he knelt on the rough, wood floor of his family's farm house, praying for a gold watch and to be a priest?)

"Are you resolved to celebrate the mystery of Christ faithfully and religiously?"

"(Was it 74 years ago that he talked his parents into letting him go to school when he was six, then made the three-mile walk home after recess because he was lonely and didn't go back for two years?)

"Are you resolved to unite yourself more closely every day to Christ...?"

"(He remembered the old homestead, a berry farm which used to lie outside Detroit, but now was eaten up by taxes and a growing city. Only the 115-year old house and one acre are left. 'It's so sad I don't think I want to go back.'

"Murphy received his first communion and was confirmed at what is now St. Mary of Redford in Detroit. His parents received special permission to erect a private chapel, dedicated to Our Lady, Queen of Heaven, in 1932.

"Mass was regularly offered at the chapel by Jesuit fathers from the University of Detroit and Benedictine fathers from St. Sylvester's monastery in Detroit.

"Murphy has run the Falling Waters Motel in Maggie about 10 years. He'll maintain ownership but will let someone else manage it.

"He will don the garb of a priest and probably rarely dress in the faded blue jacket and worn brown felt hat he wore before yesterday's ceremonies."

No, he wouldn't wear the brown felt hat anymore, nor the faded blue jacket. They were satisfactory before he was ordained. But now he must dress up–at least a little. He said that when a seminarian becomes a deacon he is permitted to wear the Roman collar, but "this I never did until one day I was required to be photographed and had to run out and buy one for the picture!" Even after ordination he wasn't fussy about wearing clerical clothes but he was too frugal to invest in any other!

The "Shed"

Father Murphy was a shrewd developer, a shrewd seminarian, a shrewd dreamer of dreams. When clergy get together on such glorious occasions as an ordination there are many things they talk about. It is a joyous time. It was on Murphy's ordination day that Father Tom Walsh and Bishop Lynch went for a short walk up the hill towards the Convent. Father Walsh tells the story:

"After the Ordination Mass, I was walking with Bishop Lynch, looking around the property. As we approached the new building up the road from the parking lot he turned to me and said, "Tom, did you ever find out what that building was for?" He laughed. He knew I had written a hasty letter to Bishop Waters explaining my part in the construction of that building. It so happened that shortly before leaving for St. Meinrad's seminary Will Murphy asked MY permission to build a 'shed' with the lumber left over from the forms he had used to erect the little bridge over the creek after the flood had ruined the first bridge. I gave permission for the shed to be built.

"One day after construction began on the 'shed' I got a call from the workmen asking me how many rooms they were to put in the house. HOUSE?? HOUSE?? Suddenly I realized I had given permission for a HOUSE. Was a 'shed' Murphy's humble name for another project, I wondered? There was no doubt about it. This Murphy was a shrewd developer from Detroit. A shed?? A house?? Didn't he know the difference? I quickly sent a letter to the Bishop explaining what had happened. Eventually that house, that 'shed,' became the Convent for the Sisters of St. Francis who staffed the Living Waters Reflection Center."

"The Shed" where the Franciscan Sisters lived

Diocese of Charlotte Created

Before Will Murphy entered the seminary, Bishop Vincent S. Waters was already working on plans for the creation of a new Diocese in North Carolina. It had become evident that one Diocese in North Carolina was not enough. On November 30, 1971, Bishop Waters of Raleigh sent this letter to the Catholics of the Carolinas:

"*My dear Brethren of the People of God,*

"*Our Holy Father, Pope Paul VI, through the Most Reverend Apostolic Delegate, has made known to us that he has in mind very soon to erect from the territory of the Diocese of Raleigh a new Diocese of Charlotte. He has chosen as the first Bishop of the prospective Diocese of Charlotte our own Reverend Monsignor Michael J. Begley, Pastor of Our Lady of Grace Parish, Greensboro, North Carolina.*

"*Rejoice with me at this good news. Be glad and realize how very good this will be for our great Southern State of North Carolina to know that a new diocese will be born very soon after the birthday of Our Blessed Lord on Christmas.*"

St. Patrick's was designated the Cathedral of the new Diocese. Archbishop Thomas Donnellan of Atlanta read from a document that placed the new Diocese of Charlotte inside the perimeters of the "divine plan," noting that it was Bishop Waters who had made the request for the creation of the new Diocese that would divide the Diocese of Raleigh in half.

"Thus, from the Diocese of Raleigh, we detach the following counties Alexander, Alleghany, Anson, Ashe, Avery, Buncombe, Burke, Cabarras, Caldwell, Catawba, Cherokee, Clay, Cleveland, Davidson, Davie, Forsyth, Graham, Guilford, Haywood, Henderson, Iredell, Lincoln, McDowell, Macon, Madison, Mecklenburg, Mitchell, Montgomery, Polk, Randolph, Richmond, Rockingham, Rowan, Rutherford, Stanley, Stokes, Surry, Swain, Transylvania, Union, Watauga, Wilkes, Yadkin, and Yancey, together with that part of the territory of Gaston County which lies outside the boundaries of the territory of the Abbey Nullius of Mary Help of Christians of Belmont. From these territories we establish a new diocese, to be called the Diocese of Charlotte from the city of that name."

On January 12, 1972, Michael J. Begley was consecrated Bishop and installed as Bishop of the new diocese. The event took place at St. Patrick's Cathedral in Charlotte. Archbishop Luigi Raimondi, D. D., Apostolic Delegate of Pope Paul VI to the United States, Bishop Vincent S. Waters of the Diocese of Raleigh, and Auxiliary Bishop George F. Lynch of the Raleigh Diocese were the co-ordaining prelates.

Sister Anna Marie Mangett, who was teaching at St. John's in Waynesville at the time of Bishop Begley's ordination, remembers that Mr. Murphy took her to Charlotte for the installation of the new Bishop. Mr. Murphy had been directed by Father Ralph Lynch from St. Meinrad to attend the installation ceremony instead of returning immediately to the seminary after the Christmas holidays. Sister Anna Marie said, "It was very foggy on the way to Charlotte. Mr. Murphy was almost 80 years old at the time but the fog didn't seem to bother him a bit. He was a very good driver. There was something special about him. He believed so firmly in God's Providence."

According to the 1972 Catholic Directory, the new Diocese of Charlotte contained 34,208 Catholics out of a total population in the state of 2, 716,044. Among the numbers were 40 diocesan priests, 21 resident religious priests and 233 Sisters. There were 50 parishes, 24 missions, 3 Catholic hospitals, 1 convalescent home, and 22 Catholic schools.

Which Diocese Would Father Murphy Belong To?

Father Ralph Lynch was concerned about what diocese Will would belong to. He remembered that Will was very attentive to classes in Canon Law. Father Lynch said that among the various items studied the first year was the distinction between "domicile" and "quasi-domicile." The former is a permanent residence while the latter is a temporary one. Will's stay at St. Meinrad's was his "quasi-domicile," while Maggie Valley was his "domicile."

Father Lynch said, "At the end of the year Will went to his place in North Carolina for Christmas. The Diocese of Charlotte was created on January 12, 1972. I told Will not to return to St. Meinrad until after the ceremonies in Charlotte. Father Will had the data on the erection of the diocese in which it stated that 'priests will belong to the Diocese in which they have a benefice (i.e., parish, etc.) and seminarians will belong to the diocese in which they have a domicile.'

"I told Will to ask Bishop Waters to which diocese he belonged since he had to obtain dismissorial letters for his ordinations at St. Meinrad. Will then said that he belonged to the Charlotte Diocese since he was a seminarian and his domicile was in Maggie Valley. I told him to write and check on it. The letter we received said that he belonged to the Diocese of Raleigh–which was not a happy answer for him."

The next ten to fifteen years were years of growth for Catholicism in western North Carolina and Will Murphy was one of the chief lay missionaries helping to bring about that growth. By the time Bishop Waters wrote the letter that told of the creation of a new Diocese, Will

Murphy was already an established businessman in the new Diocese of Charlotte and had begun his mission impact in Western North Carolina. Perhaps, he, like Francis of Assisi, heard a voice telling him "rebuild my church." Definitely he heard the voice of his own mother whose last words to him before she died were, "I want you to build a church."

At the historic installation of Bishop Begley, the Apostolic Delegate noted that a new diocese means and represents an increase of life. This increase in life implies a dynamism proper to the church. The church, the Body of Christ, is a living, growing organism and a new diocese is a manifestation of life."

CHAPTER SEVEN

▼

MURPHY'S PRIESTLY MINISTRY BEGINS

Murphy Ministers in Raleigh Diocese

The ordination ceremonies were over. While the people in the Valley hoped that his first assignment would be to St. Margaret's, that was not to be. Father Murphy himself had requested an assignment elsewhere. He said he didn't think he could handle a parish right away. He needed some practice. Bishop Waters asked him to minister as an assistant pastor in Our Lady of Lourdes Parish, which was located across the state in Raleigh.

After one month at that parish, he was transferred to serve in the Missionary Apostolate at St. Peters, Greenville (care of Williamston and Plymouth).

A local paper lamented the fact that Father Murphy would be leaving Maggie Valley. The writer rejoiced with Father Murphy at his ordination but "the ways of religion and the church continue to mystify us." The point was that after his many years of work and dedication in the Valley "as soon as he is ordained, his bishop plucks him from the mountains he loves and sends him to a parish in Williamston" and then he added, "The people of Maggie Valley must be sorry to see him go. Williamston, we hope, will be just as glad to have him there."

That his ministry now would be in the flat lands as opposed to the mountains may not have been attractive to Father Murphy, but he had expressed his lack of confidence in his ability to run a parish without some practice elsewhere, and the flat lands was the place his Bishop chose to send him.

Father Murphy's heart was still in the mountains. It wasn't long before he felt ready to return to Maggie Valley, but he had to figure out how, within the perimeters of holy obedience, he could get back to St. Margaret's. One way would be to retire from the Raleigh Diocese and join the Charlotte Diocese. St. Margaret's was in the Charlotte Diocese.

Time to Retire?

The story has it that after being stationed in the Raleigh Diocese for less than a year, Father Murphy approached Bishop Waters and asked, "What is the retirement age in this diocese?" The Bishop answered that it was 75. Father Murphy answered, "Well, I am over 80, so I would like to retire." The Bishop, less shocked than surprised that Father Murphy now had confidence in himself, answered, "Why, you have just been ordained." Fact or fiction, shortly thereafter Father Murphy was back in Maggie Valley.

The story must have been fact rather than fiction because Father Murphy, after being back in Maggie Valley, often laughingly told the story himself. His coming back so soon to the Valley explains why, as Father Lynch says in his testimony, Will Murphy was so interested in making sure he understood the difference between a "domicile" and a "quasi-domicile." Already in his seminary days he knew that he belonged to the Raleigh Diocese. He could be "frozen" there when the new Diocese of Charlotte was created. Maggie Valley would be in the Charlotte Diocese.

While he knew he promised obedience to the Bishop of Raleigh who ordained him because he was a seminarian from that Diocese, he also knew that, according to what he learned in Father Lynch's class, his rightful Diocese just might be the Charlotte Diocese. That's where his "domicile" was. He had it all figured out. He would retire from the Raleigh Diocese and return to the Charlotte Diocese, return to his "domicile." While he would be forever grateful to Bishop Waters for allowing him to go to the Seminary, and then ordaining him and giving him some experience in parish work, he would be more comfortable serving God's people in the mountains.

Murphy–First Pastor of St. Margaret's

Bishop Waters could read between the lines. He knew why Father Murphy wanted to retire. Thus it was that on April 25, 1973, Father Murphy was officially retired from the Diocese of Raleigh. On May 1, 1973, almost a year after his ordination, he moved back to Maggie Valley but he did not go directly to the Rectory. He did not think of himself as having been appointed to be pastor of St. Margaret's. He did not even think of himself as being the priest–in residence. When he came back to the Valley, he went right back into the apartment he had always lived in. He thought the Rectory would be put to better use if it would continue as it was–a place for people to come to pray or simply to relax.

When Bishop Begley realized that Father Murphy was not living in the rectory he told him he should live in the rectory and take care of the people of Maggie Valley and especially he should care for the tourists.

Up to this time St. Margaret's was a mission of St. John's in Waynesville. St. Margaret's did not become a parish until Father Murphy was installed as the pastor, the first pastor of the church he had built, the first pastor of the church in which he was ordained at the age of 80. He became the pastor on June 20, 1973, when Father Don Levernier, Glenmary, pastor of St. Mary's in Sylva and Dean of the Smoky Mountain Vicariate, installed him as pastor. St. Margaret's no longer needed to rely upon a visiting priest. The Reverend

Michael William Murphy was officially the pastor, probably the only pastor of a church he had built as a layman and was ordained in at a "ripe old age."

Homilies

As the pastor it was Father Murphy's privilege to offer a homily at every Mass. He occasionally referred to the feast at the week day Mass; he often asked for prayers for certain intentions, but preaching the Word with words was never one of his gifts. He liked to listen to homilies but he did not like to give them.

However, we do have a copy of a simple sermon he gave on May 3,1981. A friend of his had died and he felt the need to share his memories with the congregation. To make sure he said everything he wanted to say he wrote down his sermon. This is what he wrote:

"This is the beautiful month of May, the month dedicated to the Blessed Virgin Mary, the Mother of Our Lord and Savior Jesus Christ. Let us all try to assist at the Holy Sacrifice of the Mass each weekday at 5:30 p.m. and offer up the special prayers, asking her protection and guidance to live and work for the honor and glory of God and the edification of our neighbor. Let us pray for the greatest need of the Church, an increase in the number of Priests and Sisters. There is only one Priest for every 14,000 people. May each family pray the holy Rosary after the evening meal.

"April 17, Sister Marie Eugene, a Sister of the Immaculate Heart of Mary, died at the Convent in Monroe, Michigan. She was nearly ninety years old and led a life of holiness and service. She taught me how to serve the Priest at the Holy Sacrifice of the Mass at St. Mary's Parish Church in Redford, Michigan, when I was about 40 years old. At that time, it was all in Latin. She belonged to a family that was holy indeed and what a blessing would come to the world if other families would follow their example. Her father, Michael Hackette, the son of poor Irish parents, had five children. He earned a living by working and repairing railroad tracks. He was the father of a Priest, two Immaculate Heart of

Mary sisters, and two well-known and highly respected doctors. The Holy Sacrifice of the Mass was offered up to God in this Church for the happy repose of her soul the day of her funeral. May she rest in peace. May her soul and all the souls of the faithful departed through the mercy of God rest in peace. Amen.

"It is a holy and wholesome thought to pray for the dead that they may be loosed from their sins. 2 Maccabees 12:43." Rev. Michael William Murphy A note was attached to the sermon saying that he had sent a copy to the Immaculate Heart of Mary Sisters in Monroe.

Father Murphy Administers the Sacrament of Baptism

Shortly after Father Murphy came to St. Margaret's he was scheduled to baptize little Lorne Lucree after the 5:30 evening Mass. I was present for that Mass. Father Murphy didn't have much practice baptizing babies so when the Mass was over I hurried to the sacristy to help him get ready for the baptism. He was standing there in a daze. He looked at me, puzzled and said, "You were up there at the altar standing right next to me during the Mass. How could that be?" When I said it couldn't be because I was kneeling in the third pew, he insisted, "Yes, it was you. You were standing right next to me. I couldn't see your face, but it was YOU!" He appeared to be in a trance, so certain was he that I was in the sanctuary with him.

I put some things out for the baptism and then returned to the sacristy. He was still standing there, mystified. He couldn't let go of the "mystery." "It was YOU. You were there, standing right next to me at the altar." The builder who was accustomed to figuring measurements and materials without the use of paper and pencil was faced with a mystery he couldn't solve. He was "stumped." I was "stumped," too, but the baptism had to go on. I tried to make a joke out of it by saying, "Father Murphy, that was a sign from God that some day women will stand next to priests at the altar. They also will offer the holy sacrifice." That pulled him out of his trance in a hurry.

Father Murphy Assists at the Sacrament of Matrimony

On the day of the dedication the church was filled. The reporter remarked that "Mike Murphy will probably never see the church filled again." Mr. Murphy told the Extension Reporter, and others, that he "built for the future." After he became the pastor of St. Margaret's Father Murphy saw the church filled many times, especially when a wedding was taking place.

Almost immediately after the church was built young couples, and even the not-so young couples, who were planning to be married sought out the little church on the mountain as the ideal place where they would exchange vows. St. Margaret's became the church of choice for weddings.

One day early in October 1976, there was an unusual amount of activity around St. Margaret's. Often tourists would gather at the church but these people didn't seem to be tourists. They were in uniform. The place had the appearance of being invaded by law officers. Later on we learned that the Director of the FBI, Clarence Kelley, was getting married in the church. He was marrying Shirley Ann Dyckes from Waynesville. Father Tom Burke, then pastor of St. John's in Waynesville, performed the ceremony. This was Kelley's second marriage. His wife had died a year previous to the ceremony. There was a reason for FBI agents surrounding the place, although it was doubtful that any one in Maggie would come in to cause a commotion. No one was allowed on the parking lot without a pass.

Father Murphy had been forbidden to tell anyone about the ceremony that was to be performed in the church that particular morning. When it was over he "gloated" over the fact that he was entrusted with a secret that he positively did not dare to share with anyone. Father Murphy had no special love for government officials, but he was delighted that one of them chose his little church in the valley in which to get married. He seemed particularly delighted that he was able to keep a secret from everyone.

Another wedding, that of Daniel Wilson and Julie Gallagher from Western Carolina University in Cullowhee, interested Father Murphy very much because there were so many people involved in the ceremony and they were all decked out in bridal array–eight young couples plus the bride and groom. Never before had Father Murphy witnessed such an elaborate wedding ceremony. Never before had there been such an elegant wedding in "his" church. Franklin Graham, Billy's son, was the commentator for the ceremony. Father Murphy had a special reverence for Billy Graham because he was such a good evangelist. He was, therefore, delighted to meet Billy's son, Franklin.

Father James Kelly, Glenmary pastor of the church in Sylva, the church that Father Murphy built, performed the marriage ceremony and celebrated the Mass at the Wilson-Gallagher wedding. That was just fine with Father Murphy. Weddings weren't his specialty.

It wasn't exactly the ceremony, nor even the elegant style of the Wilson-Gallagher wedding that made a lasting impression on Father Murphy. It was the four-piece band that performed at the luncheon that gave him the most delight. The band was playing his favorite tunes, the ones he, himself, used to play at weddings. He felt right at home at this wedding. The fact that the bride and groom were from Cullowhee where he had donated the Newman Center added to his enjoyment. Any one from Cullowhee deserved the best!

War and Peace

Though he was "letting go" of more and more, business was still in the Murphy bones. At one point in time before his ordination this business side of Murphy caused some friction with the parish of St. John's in Waynesville. Maggie Valley did not have a fire station and the insurance rates were consequently quite high. The Chancery was sending the insurance bill for the church and the rectory to St. John's because St. Margaret's was considered a mission of St. John's and did not have sufficient funds to pay the insurance.

Father Tom Walsh says, "The burden became a really sore spot for St. John's as it had a small Catholic school that was a drain on the budget." Walsh took the issue to the Bishop who subsequently sent him to talk the matter over with Murphy, and see if, in addition to donating the buildings, he might consider picking up the insurance on them.

"I dutifully went to see him, " Walsh says, and "We talked and talked and talked–about many things. It seemed like hours. However, all the while we were talking Murphy was preparing his response. Finally he said, 'I think the insurance is the OWNERS responsibility!'" Just that simple. That was that!! After all, the buildings were no longer Murphy's. They now belonged to the Diocese. Murphy had other things in mind. He'd rather spend his money on creating something new than continuing to pay for something that was no longer his.

An entry which Father Murphy made in his ledger for November 18, 1975, indicates that he was giving the Motel to the Diocese as he had promised. He was a priest now and wasn't supposed to be running a business. An entry recorded in his ledger on that day in November read, "Deeded Motel in Maggie Valley, NC, to Bishop of Charlotte for Diocese. $300,000 value." But whether a manager of a motel or a donor of buildings, or a priest, Murphy always kept his feet on the ground and his head in the air. He was keeping his promise to his mother, the promise to walk tall and stand erect.

Now that he was pastor, Father Murphy would have to see to the paying of all the bills for the church and the rectory. He paid those bills out of his own pocket, never using the Sunday offerings or other donations to the church to pay bills. He invested all income for the church in a savings account for the church, letting the money accumulate for future expenses when he would no longer be able to take care of the bills. He continued to pay the bills from his personal funds until a parish council was formed. He then turned over all the financial transactions to the council.

Murphy Retires a Second Time

Eventually, on June 7, 1982, Father Murphy also retired from the Charlotte Diocese. He enjoyed telling people he was probably the only priest ever to be retired from two Dioceses at the same time. Upon his retirement he became "pastor emeritus" and continued to live in the Rectory. Rev. James O'Malley, Redemptorist, pastor of St. John's in Waynesville, became the pastor also of St. Margaret's.

Even after his retirement, as much as before, Father Murphy took center stage. He was often featured in newspapers and magazines. He even made *The National Enquirer* where the story of his life was told, excitedly but respectfully, in contrast to many of the other articles in that paper.

Rick Sluder, in the June 3, 1984, edition of the *Raleigh News and Observer* opened his article with a story about some visitors from England who were subject to the usual condition of canine trepidation. Above the fearsome sound of the dog's barking, Father Murphy called through the door, "It's all right. He's a real barker but he won't hurt you." Then Murphy gently told the dog, "Be quiet, now. There are nice people on the other side of this door."

Father Murphy and Sugar

Father Murphy told Rick Sluder that there were always nice people on the other side of the door, and that both he and Sugar were always pleased to have guests. During those years, Father Murphy developed a sort of ritual with visitors, whether they came to satisfy spiritual needs or their curiosity. He inquired about where they were from, where they were going, why they didn't settle in beautiful Maggie Valley. and then showed them the view from his window. He took the Bishop's orders seriously, i.e., "Take care of the people of Maggie Valley and the tourists." Murphy told Sluder that there were people stopping by from all over the world, even Great Britain. He had recently had a visit with some people from England and that visit was still fresh in his mind.

We presume these British folks were welcomed with the same warmth and hospitality that was the aged priest's trademark, though privately and decidedly, England was not Murphy's favorite country. England had been cruel to Ireland. Some of the bitterness of Father Murphy's ancestors rubbed off on him. He always said, "We have to love everybody but some are easier to love than others."

Someone in the parish thought it would be a good idea to have a sign erected by the driveway indicating the time of the Mass and the name of the pastor. Inadvertently the pastor's name was spelled "Murphey." As soon as he saw that sign Father Murphy took his pocket knife and went down to the sign and scratched out the 'e'. When asked who scratched out the 'e' he admitted that he had done it because, "The English spell their Murpheys with an 'e'. We Irish don't have the 'e.'" For years that mutilated sign was visible evidence of the unfriendly feelings between the two nationalities.

The ancient Irish grief, the memory of what England had done to Ireland, would sometimes lead Murphy into spontaneous "Brit-bashing." Once when he was watching TV with the Sisters, a commentator was talking about Queen Victoria and various aspects of British History. Father Murphy's Irish showed up like a little Erin demon. "Do you hear all that British stuff?" he asked. One of the Sisters answered, "Do you want me to change the channel?" His quick IRA response was, "No! Just blow it up!" He wasn't perfect but he was now and would be forevermore a "Murphy."

Murphy Continues His Ministry

Father Murphy continued his ministry from his chosen place—St. Margaret's. He was always "at home" for others. Many guests came to see him. Many retreatants went to him for inspiration. He was always concerned with evangelization. He always extended his hand in welcome when someone came to see him. He always had an ear for listening and, because he felt inadequate in giving spiritual direction, he was lavish with his pamphlets. No one left without a pamphlet as a souvenir.

Jean Battlo had many exchanges with Father Murphy when she came to Living Waters for spiritual renewal. She paints a truer picture of him than what we can get from any newspaper or magazine article. She tells us that those seeking spiritual guidance were never given direct guidance. Everyone had to read between the lines, had to look for some deeper meaning. Everyone had to come to the realization that, "It's not what we say that makes the difference, or what we do, but who we are." It was WHO Father Murphy was that inspired, not his words. While he dealt all of his life with material things, it was his spirit that spoke the loudest.

Jean Battlo describes her experience:

"Will Murphy never married. Beyond the businessman was a singular personality whose life's centrality revolved around a trinity, his mother, his church, and his God. I never knew Father Murphy as a businessman, and it was hard for me to imagine him as a businessman. I got to know him only after he was a priest. I had made him a personal guru for my own gerrymandering spiritual trip, but if I had told him he was a guru he would have said, "I'm just a poor sinner like everyone else." On retreats, whenever I was near him, bundles of questions would bubble into my mind about the man. Already a living icon to so many, the newspaper articles, the visitors that JUST HAD TO see Father Murphy, the interviews–all fell away under a spell of amazing simplicity.

"One day I was walking with the 96-year-old Father Murphy up the steep incline from the Living Waters cafeteria to the rectory where he lived. As we plodded up the hill Father Murphy would stop from time to time. When he needed to stop his shuffling up the hill he showed no embarrassment. He knew he was living in God's good time, that he was in his nineties, and that now was the time to pause. He would turn at such a time and, like a connoisseur savoring a vintage wine, he would look over unto the hills and drink in the scenery.

"At other times his contemplative pause would contain reveries or memories. As I made this trip more and more often over the six years I knew him, I was at first startled to realize that he really didn't know who I was. By the time I met Father Murphy in 1983, two months before my own mother died, he was already being met and 'viewed' by numerous friends, and even tourists. He was fast becoming one of the Smokies' attractions.

"While I was a little surprised that he could not remember even frequent visitors to the Center like me, I was more surprised that it did not upset or hurt me. Cursed and blessed with the exaggerated stigma of sensitivities that are the common baggage of writers, I am generally a little crushed at non-recognition which, without the blink of an eye, I can translate into rejection. Enigmatically, I did not experience this rejection when I was with Father Murphy.

"The Living Waters Reflection Center had become for me in those years, as for hundreds of others, a real retreat, in every sense and possible meaning of that word. The stillness that was present in the very bustle of activity there, the silence in the first hearing of a Taize chant, or a friend's call and laughter by the gurgling waters, the sense of 'home' more soothing even than one's own, had become commonplace for me at Living Waters. Additionally, I knew it to be the same for many others. And I knew that, though the Spirit's thrust must have been present, this sacred ground itself, was in part, the work of human hands.

"So how was it that my minute little personal anguishes did not erupt on the occasions when he did not recall my name? As usual, the living waters gurgled an explanation. It was the joy and love with which he greeted me each time he saw me that made the difference. Somehow my subjective mythologies transformed that near anonymity into a dismissal of my flaws, warts, and wrinkles. His acceptance of me had the flavor of unconditional love, the same love that mirrors the Creator's acceptance of His own. It had the feeling of the returned prodigal, still truly loved, respected, and most importantly, wholly welcomed back. It was a curious anomaly for me, but I often sensed the Creator's love when I was in the presence of this holy man. And I sensed the leprechaun.

"So in love with the Irish was I as a child that I often told my mother, 'If we weren't Italian, I'd want to be Irish.' The aging priest embodied the

Irish spirit as he made the journey up the hill, paused a moment, took a deep breath, looked to the hills and then, in a sudden reverie, broke forth into a verse from a remembered Irish melody. Enthralled, I'd listen to the sibylline sound of the whispy voice in song like a siren's recall of other days, other ways where work and time were graced. The broken, yet noticeable lilt in his Irish voice caused this neophyte, whose faith is often blighted with contemporary bludgeoning rationality, a throat-tightening lust or longing for the things past. Often when I was with Father Murphy I wished that I could encapsulate my life, as he always did, in the single simple encapsulation of constant self-definition, 'I'm just a poor sinner and a child of God.'

"And that was the summation of the man in any season. Any probe, any contemporary delving analysis, any study or search through his life for biographical notes of explanations as to how a man came to make, then give away, thousands and thousands of dollars for the propagation of his faith, must ever be reduced to that magnificent and singularly simple self-vision.

"For those of us who seriously struggle at self-correction and at winning in some self-created spiritual Olympics, it will be readily understood that this 'gift to be simple' takes a lifetime to develop. Yet, presumably, that admission, 'I'm just a poor sinner and a child of God' was the seat of the soul of the busy businessman, Will Murphy, as he amassed the fortunes he shared so generously.

"One day in 1988 after I knocked on the rectory door, Father Murphy answered with his usual greeting and assurance, 'Come in, come in and don't worry about Sugar. She won't hurt you.'

"Sugar, the dog, was a constant companion for the priest, and she seldom missed Mass. Generally, in my years with Murphy, she would lie quietly at the foot of the altar, one of those curious animal sentinels in our lives that cause us sometimes to wonder if they have souls. I greeted Father Murphy and Sugar. I thought we might play a game of checkers, which occasionally I won to Father's overt chagrin. I sometimes said to him, 'Now don't just let me win.' I was happier when his masterly strategy was successful and he won.

Most of the time he won. He was a 'master' at checkers. It was in this game as it was in his life that he knew all the right moves.

"This time my visit proved to be very different. Stuffed with spiritual study and still seeking, I had often wished that this priest, a seeming mystic, would suggest some reading matter to enlighten my dark mind. He never did. But on this particular day Father Murphy closed the door and, with a gleam in his smiling Irish eyes, said jubilantly, 'I have something you just HAVE TO read.' A literary imperative indeed. This was just what I was waiting for. I all but ran to the table where he indicated this life-quenching-theology-in-print awaited me.

"My mind raced through the list of the theological verities he thought I had to read. Was it a new insightful tome by Hans Kung, acceptable to the Pope that would revolutionize Catholic thought for the millennium? Or a rational study that gave proof of the Holy Spirit? Perhaps, a new discovery, again rational, that in some miraculous way gave concrete proof of the Resurrection, the afterlife, and the communion of saints? My hopes were high.

"Sugar and I got to the table first and waited as Father shuffled in stocking feet toward his seat where a warm colorful, cuddly afghan promoted the idea of spiritual comforts to come. As Father Murphy bent to get my reading material, I prepared for my literary Damascus experience. IF he though I HAD TO read it, then surely the dust of doubt was going to be shaken from my dusty mind like heaven's housekeeper beating out the soil of ages.

"With a smile and a look I interpreted as his knowing how much I needed answers to my multitude of questions, Father plucked a pamphlet from what was a pile of a hundred or more, and handed it to me. I looked at the title,

The Need for Priests
What you, the layman, can do to increase vocations

"I almost laughed out loud, feeling I had fallen for a joke God was making and that I was tumbling back to the 1950's. I took the pamphlet with me, but I never gave a report back to Father Murphy. However, because of the man, I still read his literary choices though twelve years after this introduction to pamphlets I'm not sure what I have learned."

Murphy's Sacred Space

Spiritual writers tell us that it is good to have a certain place set aside for prayer. Father Murphy had that special place. It was his easy chair, which was lined with an afghan made by Sister Helena Blinzler, one of the first Franciscans to assist him. A window and a lamp provided ample lighting. A coffee table gave him a nice place to put his reading material. Father Murphy, even in his very late years, never went to bed for a nap. He just took it right there in his chair. But most of all, that chair was his prayer chair. One of those persons, Mary Jo Holmes who came to see Father Murphy every year during Holy week, took a picture of Father Murphy in that chair.

Father Murphy's sacred space

Mary Jo describes:

"One of my favorite memories of Father Murphy is seeing him praying his psalms while sitting in his lounge chair near the wood-burning stove. The lovely crocheted afghan that covered his chair was the perfect background for a picture of him seated there while at prayer. I took that picture, had it enlarged, framed, and then presented it to him on the evening of his ninetieth birthday. Father Murphy thanked me for the gift and said it was 'nice.' The next morning when we came in for services he was laughing. He said he looked at the picture and thought to himself, 'That man has the same kind of af-a-ghan (his pronunciation) that I have. And a lamp just like the one I have!' Then he looked at the figure in the picture and finally realized he was the person in the picture. He laughed heartily when telling how, by the process of identifying everything else in the picture, he finally stumbled upon himself."

Tears and Fears

While Sister Roberta McKinnon and I were missioned in Cherokee, we went over to see Father Murphy at least once a week, usually on a Friday. We cooked him a hot meal and cleaned his house for him. We found that the kitchen demanded the most attention, especially the stove.

On one of these visits the stove was an exceptional "mess," a mess that defied description. We were puzzled so we asked Father Murphy what happened. He got up out of his easy chair and came to the kitchen to see what it was that we were making such a fuss about. Mostly, we couldn't figure out how he could have managed to get that mess way up on the stove lights under the hood.

When he saw what we were puzzled about he said, "Oh, that stuff, that's just eggs. I was boiling eggs. I looked out the window and there were rabbits in the yard. They were playing and jumping one over the other. I forgot I had eggs on the stove. They just exploded. That's what that stuff is. Just eggs. My breakfast." With that explanation he went to his chair to resume his reading.

Another time we went to clean the stove and found a piece of metal the size of a half-dollar. We took that to him and said, "What is this, Father Murphy? Do you have so much money that you are melting it?" He took it in his hand, patted the metal piece, examined it carefully and looked puzzled. Suddenly he knew. He said, "Why, this is my teakettle! It melted." It didn't look like a teakettle to us, but evidently he was watching the bunnies again and the teakettle went dry, melting part of the bottom.

He solved the egg problem. After those eggs exploded, he dined on peanut butter on toast along with a cup of hot tea for breakfast. Not wanting to risk any more explosions, he never had eggs for breakfast unless we fixed them for him. He solved the tea kettle problem by getting a whistling teakettle.

After one of our early morning Mass-and-breakfast trips, Father Murphy told us about an episode in his life that, he said, changed him forever. One day he and his brother Elliot were working on the roof of a barn. He stood on the very peak with his arms outstretched, holding on to nothing, as he had done earlier in his youth when he climbed the telephone poles to show off before some of his nieces and nephews.

As he was standing there something happened to him. He told us, "I'll never, never tell anyone what happened on that roof but it changed my life forever." He became very, very serious as he spoke about the incident, almost crying, but he never did tell us what happened that day. We knew better than to pry any further into his soul-shaking experience. Secretly, though, we hoped he would someday reveal the mystery, but he never did.

Father Murphy had a way of putting his hands together as if saying, "Dominus Vobiscum" whenever he was talking with people but particularly when he was in chapel talking to the Lord and thought no one was around. We often entered the church just in time to see him walking up the aisle while muttering prayers. He would sigh aloud, "My Jesus, my Jesus." He would take a breath and then start in all over again. He put his whole heart and soul into those muttered prayers, but when he became aware that someone else was in the church with him he stopped.

We often attended Father Murphy's Mass at St. Margaret's. One day he became visibly overcome with emotion when praying, "Take this, all of you, and drink from it, this is the cup of my blood, the blood of the new and everlasting covenant. It will be shed for you and for all so that sins may be forgiven. Do this in memory of me." It was obvious that he had a deep insight into the mystery of transubstantiation as well as the recognition of his own sinfulness. Sister Roberta and I looked at each other and later on shared our thoughts, "Is Father Murphy getting childish?" We prepared breakfast for him and did not refer to the incident. Neither did he.

Then the next time we came for Mass it was the same thing. And the next time. And the next time. It happened again and again. Then one day as we were fixing breakfast for him he came into the kitchen to apologize. He said, "I'm so sorry. I'm so sorry. I don't know why I cry like that. I try not to. But it just happens. And it happens only when you are here."

That may have been true for a while but it wasn't long before it was happening every time he said the words of consecration. Soon the whole congregation became aware of this phenomena. Some thought he was getting senile; some thought he was a mystic. Some didn't know what to think and would make inquiries from us about him.

At one of the Masses offered during the Charismatic Conference Father Murphy was going through the hand motions, the "Dominus Vobiscum" motions, and he added a few foot motions with it, just a little shuffle. After the Mass he told one of the participants, "I just loved it when everyone was dancing. I really liked that. Oh my, oh my, oh my. It was wonderful!"

No one had the heart to tell Father Murphy he was the only one "dancing!" I didn't realize that he was unaware his "shuffle-dancing" was a solo performance. Murphy loved music; he loved dancing. He played the violin for barn dances. He did the calls. The charismatic expression of delight in the Lord was icing-on-the-cake for him.

Father Murphy and his violin

We could understand and appreciate Father Murphy's deep spirituality, his profound faith, and his way of expressing his love for the Lord. What we did not understand was his fears. It became more and more evident to Sister Roberta and me on our many trips from Cherokee to St. Margaret's that something was bothering Father Murphy. He would beg us to stay overnight. Sometimes we did; most of the times we did not.

He had an old Cadillac that he kept parked out in front of the church. It was unsightly and in the way for visitors who wanted to take a picture of the church. When we suggested that he get rid of the eye-sore he said, "Oh, no! That's there so when someone comes here they'll think I have company." It was becoming clear. He was afraid to be alone. We told him it was quite unlikely anyone would think he had company because all four tires on the car were flat. So he got rid of the antique.

The next time we saw Father Murphy he told us the cause of his fears. When Falling Waters had more guests than it could handle, he told the manager of the motel to send the overflow up to the Rectory. Any money received from these guests he deposited in St. Margaret's Savings Account. Those were the days when the person making a deposit needed to show a small savings book where the clerk stamped in the date and the amount of the deposit. Father Murphy kept his own personal money in a number of different banks.

One day after some tourist-guests had been staying overnight in the rectory, Father Murphy went to look for his personal savings books. They had disappeared. He was convinced one of the tourists had taken them. He immediately notified the banks so that no withdrawals could be made on his accounts. And then he lived in fear that someone, knowing how much money he had in the bank, would kidnap him and hold him for ransom. Not a very pleasant thought! Several years previous to his coming to St. Margaret's some priest had been robbed, tied to his bed where he died of a heart attack. Father Murphy never forgot that. He was frightened that the same thing might happen to him. He was afraid to be alone.

Starting a Parish Council

A few months after Father Murphy was installed as pastor of St. Margaret's, some members of the parish thought it was time to organize a parish council. It was time to get a finance committee started so that St. Margaret's could pay its own bills. No one had any idea what expenses were being paid by Father Murphy. Everyone wondered what would happen to St. Margaret's if Father Murphy suddenly died. Could the parish support itself? Father Murphy did not like the idea of a parish council. He said, "This isn't a parish. I built St. Margaret's for all the people."

It wasn't easy to get him to see that, like it or not, a parish was being born. We reminded him that he had been installed as the pastor and that meant there was a parish he had to take care of. It wasn't his memory that had gone bad. It was his own distrust of his ability to run a parish. He had gone to a parish in Williamston to learn how to be a pastor. Having served almost a year in Williamston, he still did not trust himself in the role of pastor. He preferred thinking the Bishop intended him to take care of visitors, not the regulars. But more and more "regulars" were settling in Maggie Valley. Viola Henry was no longer the ONLY Catholic in the area as she was before St. Margaret's was built.

After the parish council was formed the group decided that before conducting any parish business the members of the council should make a retreat together to get to know each other and to make sure all were united on the goals for the parish. The retreat was conducted by Father Joe McCloskey, SJ, from Hot Springs. Its theme was "On Fire." The idea was that the members of the council could not set parishioners "on fire" for the work of the Lord if they, themselves, were not "on fire."

Each member was given time for prayer and then the group got together for sharing. Every one shared the way they felt about the presence of the Holy Spirit in their lives. When it came time for Father Murphy to share he said simply, "Try to smooth it over. Something happened in a short time to change my life forever but I can't tell you what it was." Ever penitent about errors known only to himself and his heavenly Father, he added, "I hope other people do better than I did."

No one knew exactly what he meant by his remarks. My thinking was that he was referring to the incident he had told Sister Roberta and me about when we were preparing breakfast for him. That incident involved his standing on the top of the barn and having an experience that changed his life–the experience that he said he would never reveal to anyone and apparently never did.

CHAPTER EIGHT

▼

THE HOUSE OF PRAYER

House of Prayer under construction, early 1976

It was on November 4, 1974, that Sister Roberta and I stopped in again to see Father Murphy, and of all our Friday experiences this one remains most vivid in our minds. This would be a day we would never forget because it had such an impact on our own individual futures.

Father Murphy met us as we entered the kitchen and before we could get anywhere near the stove to see if there were any more egg explosions or teakettles that had melted he said, "Come with me. Outside. I want to show you something." He looked excited. We followed him out the door. We looked at each other as he kept on walking. He never looked back to see if we were following. We were. He led us up the hill. We still didn't know why we were going up there. We puffed our way up but he walked with determination. He got there first and was surveying the area admiringly when we arrived. There, in the midst of a jungle of trees and bushes was a clearing. He said, "This is where I'm going to put the building. This is where it's going to be. This is just the right spot."

The Vision Dream

We said, "Father Murphy, why are you putting up a building way up here on the hill? What's this one for?" He explained that he had had a vision of people, a whole procession of people holding candles, praying, and singing as they were descending the hill. "It was like a Eucharistic procession," he said. And then he asked, "Have you ever been to Lourdes? It was like that."

Neither one of us had been to Lourdes, but we knew about the Eucharistic processions there. After a moment of silence on his part, and on ours, he explained further, "I want to put a building up here so people who used to come to the rectory can come back again. Since I've been living here nobody comes to stay anymore. The Sisters of Mercy used to come, but they don't come any more either."

Before Father Murphy moved into the Rectory the Sisters of Mercy from Belmont were among those who "used to come" and now were not coming anymore. Sister Jeanne Marie Keinast, RSM tells what happened.

"Sometime in the spring of 1968, the same year the church was dedicated, a couple of us had the opportunity to spend a night in St. Margaret's rectory which was vacant at the time. On that occasion Mr.

Murphy (as he was then called) said he would like priests and sisters to feel free to use the rectory. About the same time the newest document on Sister Formation was recommending a month apart for sisters preparing for vows. As Director of Formation it occurred to me, because I had already been there, that St. Margaret's Rectory would be an ideal spot for such an experience.

"After the Major Superior had given a sort of half-hearted approval ('we've never done that before') I presented the idea to Mr. Murphy. He was thrilled that there would be sisters in the rectory for three weeks. The fourth week of the four weeks set aside for formation would be reserved for a retreat at the Motherhouse.

"Father Tom Walsh was pastor of St. John's in Waynesville at the time and St. Margaret's in Maggie Valley was his mission parish. He agreed to come each day for Mass, much to Mr. Murphy's delight. A seminarian was with Father Walsh for the summer and both would stay for supper with us after Mass. We prayed Office in the Church in the mornings and evenings and often Mr. Murphy would pray with us.

"During those weeks of formation Sister Carolyn Mary and Mr. Murphy became friends, probably because she took the time to talk to him and to pray the rosary with him. In August, when the sisters made their vows, Mr. Murphy was invited to be present for the ceremony in the Motherhouse Chapel of the Mercy Sisters in Belmont. Sometime after the ceremony Sister Carolyn Mary, one of the newly professed, took Mr.Murphy to Bishop Waters and said, 'This man should be a priest.' The Bishop said 'Make up your mind. It's now or never.'

"We came to the rectory for three summers. After Mr. Murphy went to the seminary we did not feel the same way about using the facility. So we stopped coming. Being in the beautiful valley was a time of grace for all of us and Living Waters now holds a special place in our hearts."

Bishop Begley had come to St. Margaret's on the Sunday before our visit. Here was Father Murphy's chance. He explained how he felt about having the whole place to himself and asked permission to build another place where others could come. The Bishop said "Yes." That's all Father Murphy needed to hear. He received permission on Sunday. He had the site cleared of the trees and debris by Wednesday. And on Friday of that same week, when Sister Roberta and I came to see him, what he showed us up on the hill was the foundation, the "footers" for this new building. We were mystified. Puzzled. We had known Father Murphy for quite some time but we had not yet fathomed the depth of his deep faith, his charity, and his expertise with construction details.

He was very happy about this new project. He was himself again, a builder. He had been a builder for so many years that, even though he was now ordained, he couldn't get the wood and nails out of his system. He was in the process of making another dream a reality. He was making it possible for people to hold candles, and pray, and sing as they moved about on the hill that was so close to heaven.

As we were going back down the hill I turned to him and said, "Father Murphy, do you have an architect engaged for this new enterprise of yours, and a construction company?" I'll never forget the look he gave me. He stopped dead in his tracks and so, naturally, did I. He looked me straight in the eye and said firmly, "I am MY OWN ARCHITECT and I am MY OWN CONSTRUCTION COMPANY." He may as well have added, "How stupid can you be?" because his looks were saying that. But he didn't say anything more. We proceeded down the hill, he with a satisfied grin on his face and Sister Roberta and I with quizzical expressions on ours.

We marveled at Father Murphy's sincerity. When he said he had a vision we knew he meant it. Sometime after his death we found the following account of a dream among his notes.

"One year ago today I had my lovely dream about a procession of the Blessed Sacrament at St. Margaret Church. The procession marched down the mountain, north side of the church. It was as far as eye could see, a row of people on each side and angels in the center. The people wore clothes like we wear but the angels wore clothes like petals of white lilies.

Two angels leading the procession carried the Most Blessed Sacrament between them."

He made that entry on October 3, 1968, a few months after the dedication of St. Margaret's and a year after he had had the vision-dream.

After St. Margaret's was built there was no need for the home chapel anymore. Before it was dismantled Sister Roberta and I came from Cherokee to take Father Murphy down to his "old place" so he, himself, could offer Mass in his former residence. He had invited so many visiting priests to offer Mass there. Now he was the "visiting" priest. It was his first Mass in this, his first little chapel. It was also the last Mass offered in that chapel and he had the privilege of offering it.

No longer used for Catholic services, the chapel was used by members of other denominations. One preacher installed a sound system in the chapel. When Father Murphy heard about it he thought the installation was superfluous. He said the preacher could be heard for miles around without it. Father Murphy always respected and enjoyed the clergy of other faiths and often invited them to visit him in the rectory. Many did.

Shortly after he offered his first and only Mass in his former home the chapel was dismantled. The lovely wormy-chestnut pews were given to the Catholic Church in Hayesville. The very small statues of the Sacred Heart and the Blessed Virgin Mary that had been in his own home first and then in the little chapel, were taken to St. Margaret's Rectory. The tabernacle was given to the Diocese.

Now that he had put closure to one project in the Valley, the small chapel, and had completed the building of the memorial church to his mother, Father Murphy was not resting on his laurels. We had known him as a lay person; we knew him as a priest. Now we were getting a look at Murphy, the builder.

We knew that he had been a land developer in Detroit. He had told us that some businessmen from Detroit came out to the Murphys to see if they could buy their berry farm. When the Murphys found out that the businessmen wanted to develop the land they decided they could be land developers, too, instead of berry farmers.

At one time, according to Father Murphy, he and his brother had several hundred projects on the go. He did most of the bookwork. Naturally, then, after his mother's death and after he left Detroit, it was difficult for him to give up building. So when he came on his first trip to western North Carolina in September, 1950, he looked around to see what he could do about the lack of Catholic churches in the south. He and his mother had always been interested in the "no priest lands" of the South. By this time, he had already built two churches and a motel, but he wasn't finished yet.

Father Murphy began the construction of the House of Prayer in November 1974. One morning when Sister Roberta and I stopped in to see the progress being made on the new House of Prayer he told us that he had changed his mind about the material for the outer structure of the building. He said he woke up at 4:00 a.m. that morning. That's when he decided to use stone instead of wood. While still in bed, and without the use of paper and pencil, he began to figure out how much stone it would take for the exterior of that building.

Because he had used some of the same stone in St. Margaret's he was also able to figure out about how much it would cost him. He knew the size of the building; he deducted for windows and doors, and then, knowing exactly what to order he waited for dawn to come. He said, "I could hardly wait for the office to open so I could call to put in the order for stone." Builder Murphy, not Father Murphy, was back in business and enjoying it. Excitement oozed out of him. Oh Happy Day! He couldn't wait for us to come in from Cherokee so he could share his change of plans with us. He did an almost perfect job of figuring out how much stone to order.

A Director for the House of Prayer

At first Father Murphy did not want anyone to be in charge of the House of Prayer he was building. He thought that people would just come, stay for a while to pray, and then would go again, leaving the building in perfect order. We had to convince him that that wouldn't work. Someone had to oversee the place. We reminded him that before he came to live in the Rectory, it was the staff of Falling Waters Motel, Lelia Rathbone, Mattie Killian, and Iva Lee Phillips, who cleaned the rectory and the church.. While those good workers might be able to continue the cleaning of the church and the motel they could hardly be asked to take on the care of another building. Neither could that staff be expected to "drum up" business for the House of Prayer. The place would need an administrator and a program director.

Don Levernier, Glenmarian, was the pastor of Our Lady of Guadalupe parish in Cherokee at the time and head of the Smoky Mountain Vicariate. Bishop Begley of the Charlotte Diocese asked him to arrange a meeting at which the future of this House of Prayer would be discussed. Father Levernier invited Jack Strong, a business man from Waynesville, Dr. Maurice Morrill, Dean of the Graduate School of Cullowhee University, Sister Roberta, and me to meet with him, with Father Murphy, and with the Bishop. It would be a meeting of the minds regarding how this new project of Father Murphy's would be handled.

We met in the Rectory and at this meeting I volunteered to move from Cherokee to Maggie Valley to take care of the House of Prayer on the condition that "I won't have to worry about money." I wanted the Bishop to know that if he accepted this gift of a House of Prayer he would have to be prepared to subsidize it because no foundation like that can be self-sufficient for at least five years after its opening. It takes time to advertise, to become known, to iron out the wrinkles.

When we had our next meeting Father Murphy said, "I know what I will do so that there will be some income for the House of Prayer. I will give Falling Waters Motel to the Diocese. Any revenue coming from the motel can be used for the House of Prayer."

After Father Murphy made his generous offer of giving the motel to the Diocese, the Bishop asked about how much revenue could be expected from the business. Because Father Murphy had all his bookwork done by a CPA in Waynesville, he could not tell us how much revenue the Motel might generate in one year. The Bishop then asked Jack Strong to stop in to see the accountant and to bring a report of the motel's income and expenses to the next meeting.

When we arrived at the next meeting Jack apologized for not having the information, which the Bishop had requested. He had stopped at the accountant's office the day before, telling the accountant that he would be back on the following day to pick up the details regarding the financial condition of Falling Waters. When Jack went to the accountant's office the next morning he learned that the night before the accountant had set his office on fire and then shot himself. No records were to be had. We stopped our meeting long enough to say a prayer for the poor accountant who must have felt that the entire Holy Roman Catholic Church was coming after him! What he had to hide, if anything, we would not know then, but some later events gave us a clue that the accountant had not always been totally honest with Father Murphy.

On November 18, 1975, Father Murphy deeded Falling Waters to the Bishop of the Diocese as he promised. Construction on the House of Prayer had already started a year earlier and progress was evident. Sister Roberta and I continued to follow the progress of the new building that was being erected.

One of the things we learned about Murphy, the builder, was that he would get so excited about starting something new that he didn't always put the finishing touches on the job at hand. That may have worked in Detroit when he had a multitude of workers to complete a multitude of projects, but not in Maggie Valley where skilled labor was hard to come by. We saw the unfinished areas in the rectory when we went there to clean the place for Father Murphy. So naturally we kept an eye on this new building that was gradually taking shape.

Father Murphy was so accustomed to having more than one building project going on simultaneously he just couldn't sit still. The House of Prayer was nearing completion so what next? Why not a new laundry for the motel? Badly needed. Construction work lit the fire in him. He became an "eager beaver" just as soon as he made up his mind that there was a construction need somewhere. Just as he couldn't wait until the sun came up to order the stone for the House of Prayer, neither could he wait until the current project was completed before beginning another one, a new laundry.

Several weeks before we were scheduled to open up the new building for retreatants I stopped in to check the progress. Again it was a Friday. Claude Phillips, the builder Father Murphy had hired for the new construction, told me that on Monday he was going to start building a new laundry at the motel. There was still a lot of unfinished work in the kitchen and the office of the House of Prayer. No cupboards were in place. I did not want to open for business until every detail was taken care of. I knew it would be "now or never."But that wasn't exactly the way Father Murphy was thinking. Claude took his orders from Father Murphy and if "Mr. Murphy," as Claude always called him, said "Start the new laundry on Monday" that's what Claude would do.

When I found that out I went directly to Father Murphy and told him I was very unhappy about his decision to have Claude start the new laundry before finishing the building he was now working on. I told him we couldn't possibly open on schedule because there were no cupboards in the kitchen and in the office.

When I came back on Monday Claude was busy at work on the cupboards. He greeted me with the comment. "I didn't know you were a priest."

A priest? I assured him I was not a priest. I asked him, "Where did you ever get the idea I might be a priest?"

He replied, "Father Murphy said you were a priest."

I said, "He did? Why did he say that?"

Claude explained, "When I came to work this morning Mr. Murphy told me I should finish the cupboards in here because the 'High Priest has spoken.' So I thought you were a priest."

Claude was working on the cupboards. We could open on schedule.

Murphy Loved Benedictines

Murphy loved Benedictines. St. Meinrad's was good to him so naturally Benedictines had a special place in his life. That was fine except that he extended favors to them beyond "policy." A group of Benedictine Sisters came to the Valley for renewal. Because the new facilities were not yet ready, because the motel was being remodeled, and because Father Murphy seemed to appreciate having someone staying in the rectory with him, we assigned those Benedictines to the rooms in the Rectory.

After they left I went upstairs to check the rooms to make sure they were ready for the next visitors. I discovered the beds had not been remade with clean linen. I called downstairs, "Father Murphy, did you tell the Sisters to make up their beds before they left?"

He said, "No"

I said, "NO?? Why not??"

He said, "Because they were Benedictines. "

I said, "So what? We're Franciscans and we make our own beds."

He was surprised when I threw the soiled linens down the stairway and they plopped at his feet. He looked up at me with a slight smile to let me know he knew I was a bit irked with him. I had a sneaky suspicion he must have told them NOT to remake their beds because we would take care of them. He continued reading his book, very satisfied with himself, and seemingly pleased that I was annoyed with him.

House of Prayer Opens

I moved from Cherokee to Maggie Valley on June 1, 1976. The cupboards actually were finished on time. Sister Helena Blinzler and Sister Maurice Kleman, both Tiffin Franciscans, came in from Ohio to assist with the work.

We had requested that the House of Prayer be called "St. Michael's Oratory" after Father Murphy and Bishop Begley's patron saint. No luck. The Bishop thought the word "Oratory" would be confusing because the title "Oratory" belongs to the Oratorians who have houses of prayer all over the world, including a house in Rock Hill, South Carolina, just a few hours drive from Maggie Valley. Father Levernier then suggested the name "Catholic Center" because there are so few "Catholic" places in the area and one of Father Murphy's deep desires was to make people aware that the Catholic Church had something to offer to the South.

So the place was briefly called "the Catholic Center." Our good Bible Belt neighbors would now know that the Catholic Church was alive and active in the Valley. First St. Margaret's Catholic Church and now the Catholic Center. However, the name usually used for the new project was "House of Prayer." The title "Catholic Center" was too easily confused with the office in Charlotte by that same name.

Shortly after my arrival in Maggie Valley, I began to help Father Murphy with his bookwork. Unfortunately just as I started taking care of his payroll and making his reports to the state and the Diocese, he began receiving notices from the IRS that he had not paid his taxes for several years. He kept ignoring these notices, claiming that indeed he had paid all his taxes and that he didn't owe anything. He was VERY sure that if there was a mistake it wasn't his. And then it came, the final letter from the IRS threatening him with a stiff monetary penalty and possibly even a jail term if he didn't pay up. But he still insisted he paid all his taxes.

That's when our relationship took a tumble. Father Murphy told someone that he had no trouble with the IRS until I started taking care of his books. When I heard what he had said I immediately went to see him. I returned his financial records to him and said, "Father Murphy, if you think I'm responsible for your problem with the IRS you will have to do your own payroll from now on." And then I added, "All I was trying to do was to keep you out of jail, but if you want to go to jail that's OK with me. I can already see the headlines. '*Catholic priest in jail; refuses to pay his taxes.*' What a scandal! " And with that I walked out of the Rectory–in tears. I think it was the tears plus the idea of "scandal" that got to him. He loved the priesthood too much to want to cause scandal. And he was too gentle to want to hurt my feelings. After I left he took out his checkbook and paid the IRS what he owed, still not at all convinced that he owed it.

He knew I was offended by his accusation so the next day, as a peace offering, he went out and bought a very expensive television and radio for the Convent. I had been asking for a TV but he wasn't about to buy one until he needed it for a "peace offering." He never said he was sorry. He didn't have to. The TV said it for him. I had never asked for a radio. He threw that in for good measure.

As we were working through the "mess," trying to figure out what had gone wrong, what it was that caused the IRS to get on his case, I asked Father Murphy how he paid his taxes and other bills while he was in the seminary. He said that whenever he had to pay a bill, taxes included, he sent BLANK checks to his accountant. I asked, "Did you sign them?" He said, "Of course!" That was THE mistake he lived to regret. And that was probably one of the reasons his accountant chose suicide as a way out. He never used Father Murphy's checks to pay the IRS what Murphy owed.

When the mystery was solved he said, "My mother always said I was too trusting. She was right." Of course, I wasn't going to let him get away with that, even if it meant saying his mother, whom he idolized, was wrong. "Too trusting? Why then didn't you trust me?" I asked. He looked surprised. He never answered questions like that. Ever afterwards when I turned on the TV I remembered that it was a peace offering.

Naturally, I went back to taking care of his payroll again and preparing the financial statements for the state and the Diocese. He not only paid all the payroll expenses out of his personal checking account but he also paid all the other bills for St. Margaret's. All collections, all revenues received from whatever source, all went into St. Margaret's Savings Account. He never claimed a salary or used any church funds for his own personal expenses.

Later on, when the decision was made to add on to the Motel in order to provide a dining room and kitchen for the Reflection Center he asked the Diocese if he could withdraw $30,000 from the church savings account to donate to the Diocese for building the new addition to Falling Waters Motel. He figured this was about the amount of money he earned while being the pastor of the church and serving without a salary or receiving any other compensation. The Chancery approved.

The House of Prayer Fulfills Its Purpose

Again, as it was true for St. Margaret's, so it was true for the House of Prayer, "Build it and they will come." Individuals and groups came to use the House of Prayer. It was becoming known.

In October 1976, Sister Bessie McCarthy, RSM, brought a busload of senior citizens from St. Patrick's Cathedral parish, Charlotte, to pray and to enjoy the beauty of the "color" season. Because we did not have enough rooms for all those participating in the senior citizens' program, Father Murphy opened his rectory bedrooms for our use. That was the beginning of our using rectory rooms for the overflow.

The House of Prayer, designed similarly to Falling Waters Motel, had eighteen bedrooms, each with two beds and a private bath. The building had an ample dining area that also served as a conference area.

The Glenmarys, with Father Jack McNearney as the advisor, brought a large group of their seminarians, students, and priests to the Center for a renewal program at Thanksgiving time. Their renewal program culminated with the ordination of two seminarians to the ministry. It was one of the nicest Thanksgivings we ever had. Father Murphy had a great deal of respect for the Glenmarys because of their dedication to priestless areas. He was delighted to celebrate Thanksgiving with them in his "dream" house. It was one of the few times that Father Murphy did not eat the holiday meal at the home of his good Methodist friend, Ernestine Upchurch.

Just before Christmas an Episcopalian priest from the area arranged to have a "Broken Door" renewal for people with addictions. One individual from Charlotte with an alcohol problem registered for the retreat but did not show up for the opening conference. The next afternoon she called me from a local motel where she had registered. She wanted me to come to get her. I said, "If you got this far why can't you come the rest of the way?" She said, "Because I'm drunk; I can't see to drive."

So I went down to get her and brought her to our place for the retreat. She wouldn't look at me. She said that was a part of her problem, that she could never look anyone eye to eye, and when she was drinking she couldn't see anything anyway. She was worried about her car. It was still parked down at the Motel where she had registered. I didn't realize she had registered there or I would have checked her out of the Motel when I picked her up. I thought she was just parking there because she couldn't drive any further.

I was about to experience one of the most embarrassing moments of my life. When the intoxicated lady began to sober up a bit she became anxiety-ridden because her car was down at the motel and she had things in there she was worried about. So we arranged that when the priest conducting the retreat went back to Waynesville he would drop me off at the motel and I would bring her car back to our place.

It was midnight when he dropped me off. She had given me the keys to her car. I got into her car and began to back out when I heard a CRUNCH! I was backing into the motel owner's station wagon. He came out to see what was going on. It wasn't easy to explain that I was a nun, that the owner of the car had called me to get her from his motel because she was too drunk to drive any further, and that now she wanted her car to be where she was.

The motel manager began to ask me all kinds of questions regarding the car, the insurance, and what not. I couldn't tell him anything. I couldn't answer any of his questions. I wasn't even sure of the name of the lady to whom the car belonged. He looked at me with a mixture of disbelief and shock. He didn't really believe I was who I said I was. I could only tell him that I had the keys to this lady's car and was supposed to transport the car to the House of Prayer. The next day I called the Diocesan office in Charlotte. I needed to report the accident. I was skimpy in giving the details and was still embarrassed.

The lady who caused my problem wanted to stay over the holidays. Knowing she had a problem I was reluctant to have her stay in the House of Prayer all by herself so I invited her to stay in the Convent with me. Sisters Maurice and Helena had gone to Ohio for the holidays. I was all by myself. I had plenty of room. Besides that, I could keep an eye on her. All went well. After a few days with me she was getting "antsy" and wanted to leave. Convent life disturbed her style. She was ready to turn over a new leaf. That's what she said. The brief retreat was just what she needed. After praising her for the good retreat she made and for the changes she planned for her life, I gave her back the keys to her car and gave her my blessing. I sent her on her way.

About two hours after she left, I received a call from a gas station in Morganton, North Carolina. My good retreatant had run into the gas pump! She was drunk again. She had given my name for reference.

I then began to wonder if she had been drinking while with me in the Convent. That would be against all the rules! I examined her room. Under the mattress I found several almost empty bottles of "spirits." She either had more of the stuff stored away in her car or she found a place to buy liquor before she ever left the Valley. She must have started drinking just as soon as she was out of my sight.

After this episode Father Joe Kelleher helped to bring me back to the task at hand. He brought a group of students from Annunciation Parish, Albemarle, for a few days of retreat. That was early in January 1977. Father Murphy enjoyed the young folks but he was a bit embarrassed when Father Kelleher told the students to kiss the hands of a "very holy man." Of course Father Murphy would not allow it.

We were delighted that the Rev. George Wheatley, Western Carolina University Campus Minister, together with a group of students and alumni from Cullowhee wished to reserve the weekend of February 4 for spiritual renewal. Reverend Walter Rathbone, one of Father Murphy's Methodist friends, had encouraged him to buy the property upon which the House of Prayer was built. It was members of that same denomination who witnessed the disaster that happened that weekend.

Fire Destroys the House of Prayer

Whenever there was anyone in the House of Prayer, I did not worry about the building. But when there wasn't any one there, I became a bit anxious. The place could be burning long before we would know it because there wouldn't be anyone in the building to hear the fire alarm. Often at night, I would look out of my Convent bedroom window and, with my eyes on the Center, I'd ask the Blessed Virgin to put her mantle over the building to protect it from all harm. I had an uneasy feeling that some day it would go up in flames.

It was a cold, blizzardy day on February 2, 1977, when my brother Cletus and his wife Florence came from Florida to visit me. They were on their way back to Michigan where they lived. They went through some terrible weather and saw many accidents along the way. They made it to Maggie Valley but only as far as Falling Waters Motel. They carried their suitcases all the way up the steep hill to the House of Prayer. I was very glad to see them. They wanted to be helpful, so the next day I had them vacuum the entire place. We moved all the furniture. That was the first time some of that heavy furniture had been moved since we opened the place. We felt good about our clean house. Little did we know we were preparing a "clean offering unto the Lord."

On February 4, Cletus and Florence carried their suitcases back down the hill. The highway had been cleared and travelers could move. I bid my company "Goodbye" and because I needed to get some supplies for the retreat that was beginning that evening I followed them out to the snow-plowed road. A Wesleyan group from Cullowhee University was having a homecoming retreat for some of their members. They wanted to do their own cooking, but there were some supplies we had to furnish.

I don't know if I was tired from all the cleaning the day before, or if I had a premonition of what was to come and didn't want to face it. I just dragged myself along behind the shopping cart. It took me several hours to do what usually would take thirty minutes. Finally, I was finished shopping and headed back to the House of Prayer. When I got out of the car I could hear a beeping noise as I neared the building. I put my groceries down by the door and went back to check the car to see if I had left the key in the ignition or the lights on. I had not. The car was OK but I still kept on hearing a sound that I could not identify.

When I went to the entry door I noticed some loose wires were hanging from the doorbell. We had been experiencing some problems with the electrical wiring. When I locked the building at night I would turn off all the lights. When I would look around to check to make sure I had all the lights off, the front bedroom light would be on. I would go back into the building, turn the hall light on and the bedroom light would go off. I thought someone was in the building, playing tricks on me. I even looked under the bed to make sure nobody was in the room. This went on for some time. I couldn't win! When I saw the wires hanging loose around the doorbell that cold morning I thought we had another electrical problem and that the cold weather was causing the doorbell to ring. I examined the wires. The doorbell wasn't the problem. What was?

I had wasted time trying to solve the problem before setting foot inside the building. Finally when I unlocked the door I realized that what I was hearing was the FIRE ALARM. I immediately went to the telephone to call the fire department. There was no 911 number in Maggie those days and I didn't know the fire department's number so I called the operator. I told her to please call the fire department. She wanted to know WHERE the fire was. I tried to tell her but she couldn't understand me. Fire was already eating at the wires.

I left the phone off the hook so I would not have to redial and started to run to the Convent. I met Sister Helena on the way. She was carrying an armful of blankets that she had washed while I was shopping. I told her to drop the blankets and to run back into the convent to tell Sister Maurice that the Center was on fire and that she should call the fire department because I couldn't get through.

Then I remembered that I had left the phone off the hook and that Sister Maurice wouldn't be able to dial out as long as I was still connected. I hurried back into the burning building and tried talking to the operator again. No luck. Fire was burning the line and she couldn't make out what I was saying. I put the phone back on the hook. Alas, the Convent was on the same phone line that the Center was on. Sister Maurice could not get through to the operator either.

While I was standing there thinking what to do next I could hear a lot of explosions coming from the storage room. We had lots of canned goods stored there and some cleaning fluids. I suddenly realized the room I was in had filled with smoke and that I could no longer see the door to get out. I had no choice except to crawl along the floor and trust I would find the door, or go to my office and climb out through the window. Climbing out seemed better than crawling out so I went into the office.

The office door had been closed; the office was not yet filled with smoke. But when I opened the door that room, too, filled with smoke. I stood at the window, looked around the office and said to myself "What shall I take out through the window with me?" At that moment nothing seemed important. Everything could be replaced. Nothing in that room was worth saving. NOTHING! Bills paid; bills to be paid; retreatants coming; retreatants here and gone; retreat notes; camera; tape player that belonged to my mother. It's strange how, when faced with an ultimatum, things of this world are so insignificant. NOTHING was important to me at that moment except, "How do I get out of here?" Later I regretted that I didn't throw out the checkbook before leaping. That would have been a big help in preparing an inventory for the insurance company.

As soon as I got to the window, I grabbed the desk chair, intending to smash the window. Then I had a better idea. Why not climb on the chair, unlock the window, and crawl out? I scrambled up onto the chair, perched on the windowsill and looked down the steep incline below the window, which was about eight or ten feet above the ground. If I lost my footing I might not just fall, I would roll all the way down the hill. I dropped to the ground and escaped with only a few scratches. I was coughing and gasping, and relieved to be out of the burning building. The fire chief told me later that if I had remained in the building thirty seconds longer I would not have survived. The lack of oxygen and toxic fumes would have suffocated me.

After dropping to the ground and gaining my composure I ran to the car, which was still parked in front of the burning building. I was going to park it in the carport up at the Convent. Then I realized we could be in danger up there, too. I went to the Convent, picked up Sisters Maurice and Helena and went on down to the church. Father Murphy was standing by the church door, looking aghast at what he was seeing.

By this time, the fire fighters were arriving. Father Murphy moved to the lawn in front of the church. We joined him there. We talked about how our dream was going up in smoke. Of course, we called it "holy smoke." Father Murphy said he would never rebuild that house of prayer. NEVER! He just kept shaking his head in disbelief. The retreatants for the Wesleyan weekend were arriving from far and wide. They were shocked when they saw what was happening up on the hill in the House of Prayer where they had already brought their food and had planned to spend the weekend.

I'll never forget the one lad who came up to Father Murphy and the rest of us watching the fire. He asked, "Have you had anything to eat yet?" It sounded like a quote from the Bible, like the Lord himself. It was getting late. We said, "No." Without another word he left and came back later with a bucket of Kentucky fried chicken. It was delicious because it came from a youth with a loving, thoughtful heart. That night Father Thomas Burke from Waynesville came over to assist Father Murphy in offering a Mass of Thanksgiving that no one was hurt in the fire. He stayed all night so that Father Murphy would not be alone.

We never did get the call through to the fire department. Years later, I met a man who told me he was driving by, saw the flames coming out of the roof of the building, and reported the fire. Fire fighters from Waynesville, Sylva, and Maggie fought the fire. It was difficult because the roads were still icy and the firemen had to keep going down to the creek to fill their tanks with water. There was no water hydrant nearby. It took a while to fill the tanks with water, but the fire fighters never gave up, even though they soon realized they could not save the building.

After the fire was contained, the fire fighters stayed on the job all night to make sure there would not be a flare-up. Firefighters and helicopters sprayed the wooded area above the House of Prayer so that Ghost Town would not catch fire. They also kept spraying the Convent because sparks were flying all over it. Years later we discovered lots of burned shingles on the Convent and had to replace the roof.

We went back into the Convent, got ready to go to bed when, looking out of the east bedroom window, I saw a huge log, all red with fire, burning way down in the wooded area. Just one log, but I figured it could set all the surrounding area on fire. That possibility convinced me that we all should accept Sister Lucy Comer's and Sister Judith Pask's invitation to spend the night in their apartment. We felt safe there, away from the glowing embers.

Later that year, when we were in that wooded area picking blackberries, I came across that log lying there all by itself in the woods, all charred. Something tugged at me and I thanked the log for not spreading the fire by being totally consumed and setting the dried grass aflame. There were no ashes–just a twelve foot long piece of charred wood. In a way it was a beautiful sight. I can still see it when I close my eyes. A fallen tree being consumed but not totally? The sight had spiritual overtones. It represented the prayer and the love of all those who came to our aid that scary day, that scary night.

The next day Monsignor Joseph Showfety, Chancellor of the Diocese, came to St. Margaret's not to access the loss, but to be there for Father Murphy and us. He said to Father Murphy, "Father, I'm so sorry about the fire." Father Murphy replied, "Every day is a good day but some days are better than others." When I told Monsignor Showfety that we could not save the tabernacle and the Blessed Sacrament he said, "Don't worry about that." Monsignor Showfety offered the morning Mass for us. The Gospel reading for the day was appropriate and Monsignor's homily very touching. Suddenly I found myself crying–non-stop!

"I'll Never" Turns Into "I Will"

While we stood there on the church grounds watching the fire, Father Murphy shook his head and said firmly, "I will NEVER rebuild." Bob and Betty Prier came over the night after the fire to be with us. They had been doing volunteer work at the House of Prayer and were very much a part of the place. When Father Murphy saw Bob he said, "You know how to draw, don't you? Can you make a drawing for a new building?" Gone already was that resolution not to rebuild. Father Murphy liked Bob. He knew Bob was a well-educated man who surely must know how to draw.

The next day after Mass we all sat down at the table in Father Murphy's living room and began to reconstruct the House of Prayer. Bob drew and erased and drew and erased as we kept telling him what the IDEAL House of Prayer would be like. This was our chance for some input, our chance to make improvements on the original building, our chance to rectify what wasn't totally satisfactory in the building that burned. After several days, the drawings were finished and sent in to the Chancery. That was the first "inkling" the Chancery had that Father Murphy wanted to rebuild.

The lines of communication were opening but the Chancery was not in a hurry to make building decisions. When the insurance representative showed up with Monsignor Showfety, the two of them had some kind of bet going on. One bet that there were no blue prints for the building that burned, The other said there had to be blue prints somewhere. Both were right. There were no blue prints on paper. But there were blue prints–right in Murphy's head! And that's the only place they were.

The location for rebuilding became the #1 problem. The Diocese decided that the House of Prayer should not be rebuilt on the same spot where it was. We all agreed. There simply was not enough parking space available there. We considered alternative locations. Moreover, the Diocese was not sure it wanted a House of Prayer in Maggie Valley because it was not centrally located in the Diocese. A questionnaire went out to all the priests of the Diocese regarding whether or not to rebuild and, if so, where? A number of priests preferred the Morganton area because Morganton is pretty much the center of the Diocese. When Father Murphy heard that Morganton was the preferred location he said, "If the Diocese wants to build in Morganton that's OK with me. But then let the Diocese pay for it." As the saying goes, "Murphy wasn't born yesterday!"

It was on the feast of the Transfiguration, August 6, 1977, that Bishop Begley came to St. Margaret's and announced that the House of Prayer would be rebuilt and that it would be rebuilt in Maggie Valley somewhere on the property Father Murphy had given to the Diocese. That was good news indeed! Work began in earnest to find a suitable site on the premises. There were a number of possibilities; each was examined carefully, each had its drawbacks. It would be a few years before a final decision on the location would be made.

In the meanwhile, we continued our retreat ministry the best way we could by using the motel for rooms, the rectory for meals, and the church for conferences. One of the groups we accommodated was from Germany. About fifteen young college students came to the United States to participate in a charismatic conference. We thought we would give them a real treat, one that would make them feel at home in America. We went to the market and bought some fresh corn. We served the corn on the cob and were amazed when not even one ear was eaten. We could hear a lot of laughing going on at the table but because we couldn't understand German we did not know what the joke was.

All the corn on the cob came back. We figured those young folks did not want to mess with the cobs so we cut the corn off the cob and served some delicious creamed corn the next day. Again, the same laughter. And again no corn was eaten. After that meal one of the young students who could speak some English came to the kitchen to tell us it wasn't our cooking that they were laughing at. It was the corn. She said, "In Germany only pigs eat corn." That was news to us. We didn't realize that corn was an American vegetable. The next day we served them kraut. They ate that.

Another Fire–Another Move

A young entrepreneur rented the former pancake house, which was at the entrance to Falling Waters Motel. It belonged to Father Murphy. The renter opened a restaurant there and he called his new enterprise the "Huggy Bear Restaurant." That business lasted several years until one day the kitchen caught fire.

It was October 9, 1979, and again the Diocesan Clergy were arriving for their annual retreat. I slipped away for a brief visit with friends, Sister Barbara Westrick and Martha Moore, at the Holiday Inn located at the entrance to Maggie Valley. We heard the sirens of the fire engines and saw the police go by but did not give much thought as to where they were going. When I returned to the Falling Waters, I saw the site surrounded by fire trucks and police cars.

DEJA VU! Not again! This time, it was the restaurant on fire and not the retreat facilities. A few of the priests who arrived earlier had eaten their evening meal at the restaurant before getting the keys to their rooms. Every now and then we meet a priest who tells us that he was the last person to be served in that restaurant. A dubious honor!

Since that restaurant building still belonged to Father Murphy, he had to make a decision regarding its future. It already had had several lifetimes. Some of us wanted him to tear it down and make a parking lot out of that space. But because the damage was mostly interior and because he had a lot of confidence in Claude, his carpenter, Father Murphy decided to salvage what could be salvaged.

Then when the renovation of the restaurant was finished, we moved our food operation from the rectory into the former restaurant, which we now began to call the "White House" because it was painted white. We couldn't think of a better name!

When the White House became a parish hall there was some talk about naming it "Murphy Hall." Father Murphy didn't like the idea. He said, "It's not even a hall. A hall is something you walk down when you go to your bed room." Finally the White House was to be given a more dignified, less political name. It would be called "Murphy-Garland Hall" in memory of Father Murphy's parents. He did not object to that. Anything to honor his parents was OK with him.

"Falling Waters" Becomes "Living Waters"

Just when it seemed that we were getting nowhere with finding the proper site for the new construction, Father Murphy had an idea. He and Claude Philips, the man who built the original House of Prayer, stepped off the area adjoining the Falling Waters Motel to see if there would be room to put up a building that would connect with the motel. Father Murphy always "stepped off" an area before building on it. No need to get a surveyor involved if there wasn't enough room for what he had in mind.

Living Waters

Father Murphy and Claude thought there would be enough space in the area for a dining room, a kitchen, a meeting room, and a chapel once the trees were down and the hill excavated. There would even be space for more bedrooms above the dining room and kitchen. The Falling Waters Motel could continue to be used for bedrooms for those who wanted to come for prayer and quiet time. Father John McSweeney, pastor of St. John's in Waynesville, and Msgr. Joe Kerin, chancellor of the Diocese, came down to talk over plans. Now, finally, after years of "make do" we were getting somewhere.

Emory Jackson from Hendersonville, an architect who had done some work for the Diocese earlier, was hired to design the new addition. In August 1980, bids were received for the new construction and the contract was awarded to the Coxe Construction Company of Asheville. After the plans for the new construction were accepted, there was still one problem. What should we do about the pool? If we were no longer going to operate as a motel did we need a pool? The pool either had to undergo extensive renovation or it had to be removed. We looked into the cost of renovation versus the cost of removal.

Many of us wanted to keep the swimming pool. We saw it as an asset, a drawing card. It would help attract retreatants. It was Father John McSweeney, who was enthusiastically involved with the plans for the addition about to be constructed, who helped make the final decision. He asked the head of the construction company how much it would cost to renovate the pool versus how much it would cost to remove it. Since the pool was very deep many loads of dirt would have to be hauled in to fill it. That would be an expensive project. I saw Father McSweeney wink at the construction manager as together they came to the conclusion that it would be far more expensive to remove the pool than to renovate it.

In the spring of 1980, while the architect was busy working on the plans for the new construction, we began to remodel Falling Waters Motel, making two rooms out of one. We were not open that summer, not for retreatants, nor for tourists. Charles Blanchard, a member of St. Margaret's parish, oversaw the renovation and put in many hours of hard labor. Father Murphy wasn't too happy to see the motel being tampered with but because he had a great admiration and love for Charlie, and because he realized the importance of the retreat ministry we were involved in, he OK'd the project. The remodeling work was finished just in time for the Charlotte Diocesan Clergy retreat that October.

When Father Murphy deeded the motel to the Diocese, the motel was incorporated as a separate business entity within the Diocese of Charlotte under the title "Pax Christi." When the remodeling was finished, the former motel ceased to be a business enterprise. On November 7, 1980, "Pax Christi" received an insurance refund. The motel was no longer a motel. Now it was tax exempt and was known as "Living Waters Catholic Reflection Center."

It was Sister Jean Linder, OSF, who suggested that we change the name to "Living Waters" to reflect the new mission of the former motel. "Living Waters" was a bit more biblical than "Falling Waters." The name change did not affect Father Murphy in the least. He would continue to think of the place as "Falling Waters." Why not?

Sister Judith Pask, SFCC, designed the logo for Living Waters using a large jagged orange sun as the focus point with the words, "To Reflect the Son, deep in the heart of a mountain" emanating from it.

Home, Home, At Last!

The House of Prayer had burned on February 4, 1977. Finally, on October 4, 1981, (almost five years later) we were able to move into the new addition to Falling Waters Motel, now called "Living Waters."

We had fed the retreatants first in the new, well-equipped dining room of the House of Prayer. When that burned, we started all over again, setting up tables in the Rectory, buying new tableware, pots and pans, and using the Rectory's four-burner, one-oven stove to prepare the meals.

We could not have fed 50-75 retreatants in the Rectory without the assistance of many volunteers from St. Margaret's. Parishioners brought in their hotplates and fried bacon and pancakes for the guests who lined up to receive their food hot from the grill. The volunteers heated water wherever they could find an electrical outlet, even in the adjoining bedroom so that we could wash the dishes and reset the tables. We placed a 4' by 8' board on the bed and lined up each day's dessert for easy distribution. Everything had to be done quietly because of the conferences taking place in the church adjoining the makeshift dining room. Keeping the workers subdued in the cramped quarters was the most difficult task of all!

When the White House became available we moved our equipment there and, rain or shine, fed the hungry. We no longer had to keep quiet. We now had room to move around and bang the pots and pans without disturbing the retreatants. It was a big improvement over using the Rectory.

Sister Georgiana Agerter, a Tiffin Franciscan, who had come in from Ohio to help design the kitchen and dining room for the new addition under construction, was the food manager. Despite the inconveniences, she managed very well in the improvised eating facilities. On October 4, 1981, (Feast of St. Francis) she was able to use her culinary skills in a facility that was ideal, a facility she helped to design. The transition was smooth even though it was a "nail-biting" experience. The stoves in the new kitchen were not in place and ready for operation until 6:00 p.m. the night the annual diocesan clergy retreat was to begin!

Sister Thomas Kill arrived for a sabbatical after many years of teaching music in Ohio. During her sabbatical year she assisted Sister Georgiana in the kitchen and dining room. She took care of all the liturgies for the retreats. When her sabbatical year was over she was assigned to assist with our ministry in Maggie Valley. She also gave music lessons at Living Waters. She set up her studio right next to the conference room so there would be a large area for recitals. Her reputation as a music teacher became well known and students came from all over to take lessons from her. She made a difference in the lives of many people. If we didn't know it before we knew it now—music is an excellent means of evangelization.

Even with the rooms gained by the remodeling of the motel and by the new addition to it, we did not have enough rooms to accommodate everyone. As we had been doing since October 1977, when the first Charlotte Diocesan Clergy retreat was held in Maggie Valley, we continued to rent rooms in the neighboring motels for those retreatants we could not accommodate at our motel. Our retreatants were "spread around." That was not only good for the area economically; it was also good for the Catholic Church. It was good for our neighbors to know that so many people, most of them Catholic, would spend so many days together, gathered in one place for prayer.

Aerial View of Living Waters Catholic Reflection Center

We were home, HOME, and now we could initiate programs and accommodate the many people who wanted to "Reflect the Son, deep in the heart of the mountains."

Living Waters Catholic Reflection Center was formally dedicated on the feast of the Sacred Heart, June 1982. Bishop Michael J. Begley came from Charlotte to preside over the dedication. At that time, the retreat facility was placed under the patronage of the Sacred Heart of Jesus.

CHAPTER NINE

▼

DOING THE LORD'S WORK

Sister Agnes Comes to the Valley

In 1981, because of the construction work going on, we were limited in the number of retreats we could offer at Living Waters and the number of retreatants we could accommodate. We did not do much advertising. By 1982, we were in "full swing" at the Center. We had done extensive advertising and were becoming very busy. It became more and more evident that we no longer could give Father Murphy the care he needed and deserved. Parishioners helped out all they could but it was necessary to have someone assist Father Murphy full time.

We consulted with Bishop Begley and leading members of the parish and then decided to ask Sister Agnes Collet, OSF, to come to Maggie Valley to assist in the care of Father Murphy.

Sister Agnes arrived on September 1, 1982. No longer would Father Murphy be alone at night. No longer would he have only peanut butter toast for breakfast. He could again have his eggs. And he didn't have to listen to the whistling teakettle anymore to know when his tea was ready. She called him. He wasn't accustomed to taking his medicine on time, and he sometimes got the dosages mixed up. Sister Agnes, a former teacher, was now fast becoming a nurse-practitioner. Father Murphy was extremely grateful to have someone to take care of his needs. He was lavish with his "thank you, thank you, thank you" expressions of gratitude.

Because Sister Agnes was an out-going person and always in good humor she was a delightful companion for Father Murphy. She became a "mother figure" to him. She not only tolerated a dog in the house, but encouraged it. She played checkers with Father Murphy and read to him. She procured videos to show him and watched TV with him. She went out walking with him almost every day. She prayed with him.

But she never got him a canary to listen to, nor fish to watch in an aquarium because we told her we had tried that once. It didn't work. A bird in a cage and tiny fish in a small aquarium didn't interest Father Murphy. When he was younger he enjoyed going fishing. Those were the real fish, not these little miniatures that didn't seem to want to grow up. And as he got older the birds in the air and at his bird feeder intrigued him, but not a bird in a cage. He didn't think much of our efforts to distract him from reading and napping all day long when he didn't have visitors. We told Sister Agnes what happened when all of us had to be away for a week.

We put the birdseed on one windowsill and the fish food on another and asked Father Murphy to feed these little creatures every day. We showed him where we put the food. When we returned the fish were swimming in and out of the grass in their aquarium.

We couldn't figure out the grass in the aquarium. It was two to three inches tall. We asked Father Murphy about the grass. He said he fed the fish every day but he never put any grass in the aquarium. He did not know how the grass got there. It was as much a mystery to him as it was to us. So we checked out the food supply.

The supply of seed for the bird was almost entirely gone, but there was lots of fish food left. We finally figured out he had been feeding bird seed to the fish, as well as to the bird. Because of the warm light over the aquarium, which he forgot to turn off at night, the seed had sprouted. We laughed. We were amused at the sight of the fish having such a good time in the grass that had sprung up in their aquarium. We thanked Father Murphy for his efforts and told him the fish would probably have preferred fish food. He agreed but he didn't see anything amusing in the situation.

Praying, reading, and visiting were Father Murphy's favorite pastimes in his later years. And talking. He had an excellent memory for what "used to be." He didn't care much for games–except for Pedro and checkers. He almost always won the game when he played checkers. As for Pedro, anyone who knew how to play Pedro was on his list of favorite people. And anyone who did not know how to play Pedro was expected to learn. So we all learned, and as often as we could we engaged Father Murphy in a game. When he was leading he would ask, "What's the score now?" When he was losing he never asked about the score.

One Sunday, Sister Agnes noticed that Father Murphy wasn't feeling good. She thought maybe a game of Pedro would cheer him up. So she called me and suggested that I invite him down to the Center to play. I called Father Murphy to see if he thought that was a good idea. He mumbled a bit and then, suddenly awakening, said, "OH YES!" It had just dawned on him that I was suggesting cards, not a doctor. When he got down to the Center and we were beginning to play he said, "If you had called and said there was a prayer meeting going on down here, I would have said I was too sick to come." And then he laughed. No guilt feelings at all!

Sister Agnes enjoyed cooking. Father Murphy enjoyed eating and was taught by his mother to eat everything placed before him. It wasn't long before he had to tell Sister Agnes to go easy on the food. He called her over one morning as he was tugging away at his socks and said, "You have to get me some better socks. These take me 15 minutes to put on. Every time I stoop over to pull them on–I'm getting too fat–I cut off my breath and have to come up for air." It wasn't all Sister Agnes' fault that Father Murphy began to put on weight. It was also the fault of many of the parishioners who invited them to their homes for some very elegant meals. Everyone in the neighborhood knew that they both loved good food.

A Crisis Moment

Sugar, the dog, seemed to understand and love this shuffling elderly priest. Although Sugar was a friendly dog she did present a problem. She was a German Shepherd. She had to go!

Sister Agnes would often call Esther and Tom Quirk to take her and Father Murphy into Waynesville to do various things. Esther tells about the frantic call she received one day.

"Sister Agnes called us. She was very upset. She said the insurance company had asked the Diocese to not allow any Pit Bulls, German Shepherds, or Dobermans in any of the rectories. These dogs were considered dangerous. The insurance company would not pay for any damages done by these dogs. Someone from the Diocesan offices called and said Father Murphy's faithful dog "Sugar," a mile-tempered German Shepherd, would have to go. Father Murphy loved having that dog around. It reminded him of his life on the farm. And it alerted him to visitors in the church.

"Sister Agnes wanted me to take her and Sugar to the vet in order to have the dog put to sleep. She was crying. I panicked and jumped into the car and sped to the Rectory. On the way up there I decided that there had to be another way out. We just could not put Father Murphy's dog to sleep.

"I picked up Sister Agnes and Sugar but I couldn't leave the church parking lot without telling her how I felt. Upon hearing me out she agreed that we would have to find a way to save the dog. We contacted Shirley Pinto and she said we could leave Sugar at her home until other plans could be made for the dog. So we did that. We allowed others to think that Sugar had gone to "Doggie Heaven," but Father Murphy knew better because we took him regularly to see his dog at Shirley's house. He loved that!

"An elderly couple staying in the campground next to Shirley's place fell in love with the dog. Shirley made arrangements with them to take the dog out West when they left the campground. They were happy to adopt Sugar. The dog lived with them until her already present hip dysphasia became worse and she finally had to be put to rest–one and a half years after she escaped the death chambers in the Waynesville vet's office.

After Sister Agnes' arrival we were able to concentrate on our ministry at Living Waters. We were very happy with the response we were getting to the programs we were offering. We felt confident that we were doing the Lord's work. And then came the test. Would we lay down our lives for what we believed in? We just might have to.

The Threat

The threat came early one morning about 3:00 a.m. Sister Georgiana appeared at my bedroom door with a frightening message, "Someone is going to kill us." Naturally that got my attention. I had heard the phone ring. It had an ominous sound. Any phone ringing at 3:00 a.m. has an ominous sound. When Sister Georgiana answered the phone, the voice on the other end of the line informed her that Satan had appeared to him and told him to kill the nuns. He said he didn't know there were any nuns in the area until he looked in the telephone book and found that some Sisters of St. Francis lived in Maggie Valley.

The caller explained that he wanted to become a Knight in the Service of Satan but before he could become one he was told he had to kill someone. He said it wasn't until Satan appeared to him during a Halloween ritual that he knew whom he had to kill. Halloween was fast approaching. He said he would call back.

When the phone rang again I picked up the extension line. The three of us carried on quite a conversation. His voice was raspy. It was very difficult to make out what he was saying. There was something fiendish in his voice. At least it seemed that way to us. He sounded like an old, old lady. It was only after we asked his name, which he would not give to us, that we found out he was a seventeen-year-old boy living with his grandmother. He didn't want to wake her so he was speaking in a very low, whispery, raspy voice. There was some goodness in him. He had some respect for his grandmother.

When we asked, "When are you going to do this evil deed?" he said, "I won't tell you when or you won't be home when we come. We're going to have some fun with you first, and then we're going to kill you."

Then I asked him if he ever prayed. He said, "No, oh no!" So I invited him to listen while we prayed. Sister Georgiana and I prayed the Our Father and the Hail Mary out loud over the phone. He didn't join in but when we were finished he said, "Thank you" and hung up. His "thank you" was another sign of some respect, some civility, some mellowing. How could someone be a killer who was considerate of his grandmother and who said "thank you" for prayers offered?

Our next move was to call the sheriff. Whoever took our call dismissed the episode as a prank at first, but later on a law officer did come up to the Convent to collect some details and left with a promise to look into the matter.

Later in the morning, Father O'Malley, pastor of St. John's in Waynesville, called us. He had heard about our mysterious call and he said he had a strange call, too. His call was strange but not threatening. We had prayed the Hail Mary. That must have got that young man thinking. So he called Father O'Malley at around 3:45 a.m. and asked him if he believed in the Blessed Virgin Mary. Naturally Father O'Malley said he did and offered to send the young man some literature if the boy would give his name and address. The boy gave his name and address, not a very smart move for a would-be murderer. Was it our Hail Mary that softened him? Was our Blessed Lady taking charge?

We didn't sleep in the Convent that next evening. When we told Father Murphy about the call he admitted that he, too, had had an unusual early morning call. He said the caller didn't make any sense so, "I hung up and went back to sleep." It wasn't too hard to convince Father Murphy that he should not sleep in the Rectory until the case was solved. He still remembered that a priest of another Diocese was murdered in his rectory not too many years before this incident. To be murdered was bad enough but to be sacrificed to the devil? None of us could stomach the thought!

With the information that Father O'Malley gave us and with the help of a food delivery salesman who, when hearing of the threat, gave us the name of a possible suspect the case was solved. The suspect was a young man who was working in a grocery store where the salesman made deliveries. An SBI agent for our area apprehended the suspect within 48 hours and turned him over to the local sheriff.

When the culprit was caught, the sheriff made him apologize to us for the scare he had given us. On the way to the place where we were to meet for the apology, the young man told the sheriff that it didn't work this time but that he still wanted to be a knight in the service of Satan. He had caused problems at home and at school and was living with his grandmother. He had gone to the public library to find a book on Satanism.

The young man was brought before the judge. We had to go to court to testify. When he appeared in court he had dyed his hair orange. That did not impress the judge who had already concluded that the boy had deep psychological problems. He ordered the court to see that the boy received counseling and that he remained on probation for an extended period of time.

However, because he had admitted that he still wanted to become a "knight" and because by this time we were also convinced that there was something wrong with the fellow, we were a bit uneasy for a while, a bit jumpy when the telephone rang. And jumpy when it didn't ring. And jumpy when it was a dark, stormy night with the winds howling. And when it was a moonlight night and Halloween was in the air.

While we were working our way through this confusion, we kept telling each other, "We must be doing something right or the devil wouldn't be trying to interfere with our work."

After the murder threat, all was quiet for a while on the campus. Father Murphy, at 95, still insisted on walking from Living Waters up the hill to

St. Margaret's. But he was showing signs of wearing out. So was Sister Agnes who was celebrating an 80th birthday.

Our next move was to ask Sister Francine Sartor, a Tiffin Franciscan with lots of experience in the care of the aging at St. Francis Home, to come to assist Sister Agnes. Sister Francine arrived in Maggie Valley on September 9, 1988. She learned to drive so that she could take Father Murphy wherever he wanted to go. Bruce Carden, a Baptist, agreed to be her instructor.

Bruce later said, "I have one claim to fame. Many people still refer to me as the driving instructor who taught Sister Francine Sartor, a 60-year-old Catholic nun, to drive so that she could take Father Murphy out to see the beautiful sights in the Smokies." And then he added, "However, it was she who was the teacher and I her grateful pupil. She taught me faith, hope, and love–and especially the greatest of these, LOVE."

Come to the Water

Our Lord said to the Samaritan woman at the well in John's Gospel, "Whoever drinks this water will thirst again but whoever drinks the water I shall give will never thirst. The water I shall give will become in him a spring of water welling up to eternal life."

Many years after Father Murphy first conceived the idea of a "House of Prayer," and many years after he gave Falling Waters Motel to the Diocese of Charlotte, and many years after the Motel became "Living Waters Catholic Reflection Center" people thirsting for spiritual renewal continue to come to drink of the "Living Water." Alive with mystery, with new life, these retreatants leave, refreshed and energized in the Spirit. Jonathan Creek, which tumbles over rocks in front of the Center is a favorite spot for reflection. One retreatant, before leaving Living Waters, wrote:

Reflections on A Creek
Babbling, bubbling,
Swishing, swirling,

Rushing, rippling,
Ripples racing,
Frisky, foaming,
Freely flowing,
Fresh and clear,
Frolicking, cleansing,
Refreshing, renewing:
Living Waters,
From deep within,
the heart of the Mountain,
Impelled by a Force
Strong and sure,
Reflecting the Son
Springing from the Father,
Impelled by their Spirit
Of life strong and sure.
Stream of life,
Flow through me.

Sister Nora Ng RGS

In 1982, the 800th anniversary of the birth of St. Francis, Living Waters initiated its first "nature" retreat called, appropriately "The Canticle of the Creatures." Sister Carol Hauser and Sister Mary Ann Jansen, Brown County Ursulines from Ohio, spearheaded this retreat which was developed around the four elements: air, water, fire, and earth. In his Canticle St. Francis gives praise to God for Brother Wind, Sister Water, Brother Fire, Mother Earth and all creation. His Canticle is a fitting prayer for the nature retreats.

The Rev. Ed Wahl, Oratorian from Rock Hill, SC, often came to Living Waters to help with the retreats. One of his specialties was "The Spirituality and Interpretation of Dreams." Father Wahl did a lot of hiking in the Smokies. He gave Living Waters its first set of directions for walking the trails.

Because Native American spirituality is based upon all creation in union with the Great Spirit, Freeman Owle, a Native American from Cherokee, has been a contributing director of these retreats. After one of his explanations of the Native American custom of standing in the water and throwing some of it over one's shoulders to get rid of the evils that torment one's spirit, a retreatant who had experienced the refreshing, healing waters of Collins Creek, wrote the following:

Cleansing at Collins Creek

Seven times I caught the ice-cold stream
and threw it overhead;
With each new catch I prayed and laid
a gnawing care to bed.
I caught the water as it flowed,
and threw it to the sky
Seven times I said a heartfelt prayer,
and watched my cares flow by.
And then I heard the silent words,
so steeped in mystery;
"Living Water is my name!
Go now for you are free."

Sister Cecilia Murphy, RSM.

It is customary during these nature retreats to walk the nature trails in the Great Smokies. Even though the trails are in the national park we have been able to offer the Eucharist on the trails without interference. Only once did we run into a problem.

An imposing Franciscan Friar, decked out in his brown robes on top of which he wore the usual Mass vestments, was offering the Eucharist along the banks of the Oconaluftee River in the park. He was surrounded by a large group of retreatants. A forest Ranger was observing him, noticing his peculiar dress, his strange motions, and the reaction of the group around him. The Ranger concluded that the Franciscan was the leader of a cult, which the management was trying to keep out of the public park because of the nuisance the cult had created in previous years when they left enormous amounts of trash.

After that experience we tried to inform the Rangers in advance regarding who we were and what the group was doing on the trails. The Rangers were very cooperative. They had no objections to our using the national park for religious services.

A Near Tragedy

Year after year Living Waters was expanding the programs it was offering to those who wanted to "Reflect the Son deep in the heart of a mountain." The offerings included guided retreats. These retreats are silent retreats, peaceful, calm retreats, with much inner reflection. During these retreats the Lord often writes straight with crooked lines.

It was during a guided retreat that we were again threatened by fire. All the retreatants were gathered in the Conference Room. We were singing the final hymn at the conclusion of the Mass when we heard sirens and saw fire engines rushing to Phil's grocery store and gas station right across the street from Living Waters. There are three fuel tanks there, all above ground. Fumes from one of the tanks that was being filled by the supplier caught on fire.

Businesses were evacuated and traffic blocked on either side of the store as emergency workers prepared for a possible explosion. We were told not to leave the building, not even to go on to the porch for a better view. We watched from the windows in the conference room. We watched and we prayed. Firefighters from Maggie Valley, Jonathan Creek, and Lake Junaluska hosed down the tanks and put out the fire before it could spread to the adjacent fuel tanks. Emergency management personnel estimated an explosion could blast seven to nine city blocks in each direction. Living Waters was less than a block from the fire. We were directly across the road. We prayed silently and out loud but we didn't panic. Somehow we seemed to know a miracle would happen. Within a few minutes "Brother Fire" was no longer a threat.

St. Francis, in his Canticle prayed, "Praised be You, my Lord, through Brother Fire, through whom you light the night and he is beautiful and playful and robust and strong." St. Francis was a romantic dreamer. He saw only beauty in all of God's creation. It took a lot of faith on our part that morning to praise God for "fire," to see fire as "beautiful and playful and robust and strong." We did praise God for putting the fire out before something catastrophic happened to all of us.

How Great Thou Art

Each morning during the nature retreats sponsored by the Center the retreatants greet the day by singing, with uplifted arms, the much-favored hymn, "How Great Thou Art."

However, it was not during a nature retreat that we were forcefully reminded of the line of that hymn that says, "Thy power throughout the universe displayed." The reminder came at the end of the annual diocesan clergy retreat during the wee hours of the morning, beginning at four a.m., when all of nature seemed to be on a rampage.

We didn't see the stars that the hymn refers to, but we did see lightning and lots of it. We didn't hear the "rolling thunder" but we heard cracking, explosive thunder instead. We heard the mighty rush of wind and the agonizing groan of trees as they were uprooted and piled on top of each other just a few feet away from our convent bedroom windows. We heard the explosion when the transformer was struck, leaving us without power. It seemed we were being attacked by demons. We had heard the news reports the night before so we knew that it was hurricane Opal lashing her tail as she came all the way from the Carolina coast inland to unleash her power in the Valley.

Sister Jean Linder, a member of the staff who was on night duty at the Center, describes the chaotic chain of events:

"I was asleep in my private quarters in the Reflection Center. I was awakened by violent thunder and flashing lightning. I jumped out of bed. The electricity was off. I fumbled around trying to get to the bathroom but ended up in the hallway where I knocked over a plant, adding to the confusion. Finally I found my flashlight and dressed quickly. Then I started down the steps and saw a strong flashlight beam coming toward me. Father Jim Byer had found his way to his car and located his much stronger light.

"We both started down the porch to check on things and saw ahead of us a tree limb on fire. It was still attached to the tree and burning high above the driveway at the curve where the drive goes down to the parish center. I quickly returned to the office to call 911. I finally got the call through and gave the operator my message. However, the fire engine never did arrive because there were so many calls to 911 that morning.

"I went back to be with Jim and found that a live wire which had fallen on the tree branch caused the fire. As we stood there the branch fell to the driveway and burned itself out. I then went on to the kitchen to see about breakfast. With the help of several priests, Sister Francine and I put breakfast on the table. We could serve only cold cereal, milk, and fruit because we had no power. It was a breakfast without coffee but everyone seemed to understand. We lit candles from the sacristy and put them on every table so that there would be at least a little light in the dining room."

It took days to clean up the debris but we survived Opal, as we had survived all the other catastrophes that we encountered in our efforts to "Reflect the Son deep in the heart of a mountain." We began to realize that fires and tornadoes and demonic threats are simply par for the course. When the going got rough we just kept on singing, "How Great Thou Art."

Traveling with Father Murphy

Most people have read *Travels with a Donkey* and have seen the movie, *Driving Miss Daisy.* Some day I'd like to make a movie called, *"Traveling with Murphy."*

After traveling side by side with Father Murphy for fourteen years, it would seem nothing would surprise me along the way. But many things did. However, no more "peace offerings" were necessary. Father Murphy learned to trust me! His mother was right! He could trust.

Knowing that he loved to pray the rosary, I used to pray it with him when we went traveling. One time, on our way back from Asheville, when we finished praying the rosary, he turned to me (I was driving) and said, "You know, when I stopped praying for a while I stopped because the Sacred Heart was there and we were talking." I didn't have the audacity to ask him what they talked about. Neither did I have the courage to tell him he had no need to apologize because there was no long pause in the rosary. There wasn't even a short pause. No interruption whatsoever in the flow of our praying. I had no idea something unusual was happening. Evidently apparitions are timeless. Somehow, though, by the time we arrived back at the rectory I knew I was singularly blessed.

I felt more blessed on that occasion than I did on another when I was taking Father Murphy somewhere. His Cadillac was aging just as he was, just as we all were. The car was sputtering along. I was afraid of an over-heated engine. I told Father Murphy about the "engine hot" sign. He took the occasion to relate a story of a time when he had been stranded in Tennessee with some similar bout of Cadillac gout, complicated by being captive in a traffic jam. Father Murphy then told the Blessed Mother to get him out of the problems he was having. She did. The traffic eased up and the car got over its gout.

I thought if his prayers worked that time they should work in the present situation just as well. So now I asked him to pray to the Blessed

Mother to cool off his car as it was beginning to steam a little. He said, "No, you pray. You're driving it." So I prayed. We got home safely.

On one of our trips to the bank, Father Murphy was admiring the beautiful blue sky with white puffy clouds floating around. He looked at the sky and the clouds and said, "You know, I often thought it would have been nice if when Our Lord was taken up into heaven and disappeared behind the clouds that there wouldn't have been any clouds so we could have seen where he was heading."

At another time we went to the bank in Clyde. He had not been accustomed to going to a drive-in bank. He thought not having to get out of the car was a neat idea. After we made our deposit he said, "Let's go back and do that all over again." I asked him if he had any more money to deposit. He said, "No. Let's go home."

Though largely uneducated in the ways the world holds degrees, Father Murphy maintained a love for knowledge as well as an apparent respect for learning. One day when we were on our way to a conference at Sacred Heart College in Belmont Father Murphy suddenly remembered that he did not have a note pad with him. As we approached Gastonia he said, "Stop here. I have to get a tablet. I forgot to bring one. I have to take notes."

On the return trip he shared the few notes he had taken. It was a matter of principle with him, more than anything else, and a carry-over from his seminary days. If a person goes to a conference or attends a class, that person ought to be very attentive and try to remember at least a few things.

He also never gave up on his interest in things mechanical. He was long years away from his days of tinkering with the radio when he stopped in Cherokee and asked Sister Roberta McKinnon and me to go with him to see Fontana Dam. He had been there before but he wanted to go back. He was intrigued with the way dams work, and wanted us to share the experience with him.

We rode the incline train into the "belly" of the dam. Father Murphy asked many intelligent questions of the guide. He was all eyes and ears. It was quite an experience for all of us since we had no idea of the immense task it must have been to build that dam. Secretly, though, we were a bit scared. We prayed so that none of the water flowing over our heads would cause the dam to collapse. If Father Murphy could have found a reason to build a dam on Jonathan Creek, he probably would have tried it. Instead, he had to be content with the little waterfall that was behind Murphy Garland Hall. He said that one of the hardest things for him to give up when he gave the property to the Diocese was that little waterfall. He compensated by building his own near the motel.

One day, Father Murphy called and asked when we were going to Ohio. He wanted to go along. I told him we wouldn't be going until June. He said he wanted to go to Michigan to check up on some of his property there, and to see his relatives whom he hadn't seen for quite a few years. He didn't want to wait until June. When I asked him when he wanted to go he said, "Tomorrow!" He was the type of person who, once his mind was made up, needed to go into action immediately.

I told him I would drive the Center's car. He didn't want that. He wanted me to drive his Cadillac. Franciscans don't drive Cadillacs very well. I told him "OK" but we would first have to get some new tires before we could start on our journey. Because he always got his tires in Asheville at the Cadillac dealer we would have to wait until the following day to start out for Michigan. He reluctantly waited one more day.

On the way to Michigan we stopped at the Shrine of Our Lady of Consolation in Carey, Ohio. Father Murphy wanted to stay there a long time because he remembered having visited that shrine with his mother. His nostalgic visit to the past was already beginning at that shrine in Carey, but it wouldn't end there. On our journey he pointed out many places of historic interest to him. He was remembering days long gone by.

It was a fun trip, especially when we reached the outskirts of Detroit and he would say, "Now at the next corner there will be a grocery store. Turn there." We'd get to the spot and there was no grocery store there. Then he would be confused regarding where we should turn. So many things had changed since he had last been to Detroit twelve years earlier.

The last time he had seen some of his relatives was at his ordination eight years before when they all came to Maggie Valley. He seemed very happy on the way to Detroit. We shared stories coming and going.

When we passed a hog farm, I told him of the time when my brother said to my sister and to me, "Let's play pig." We had been playing in the area where my father was cleaning out the breeding pens. My brother, Nathan, was five; I was three-and-one half; my sister Alvina was two. We played together a lot, but we never had such a golden opportunity as this one. The pigs were all out in the pasture and these smelly breeding pens became our play castles for a short time, a very short time.

Each pen had its own front yard space and its own feeding area linked by a door. My brother knew all the rules for playing "pig." "First thing we gotta do is we hafta take off our clothes cause pigs don't wear clothes." Playing in our birthday suits certainly wasn't our usual way of playing but we dutifully took off all our clothes, got down on all fours, stuck our little rear ends in the air as high as we could get them—a substitute for tails.

We crawled through the open doors in and out of the feeding area, oinking and snorting all the time until we finally reached the pen where my father was finishing his work. The pens were clean because my father had just scrubbed them but they were sloppy wet.

When we got to where my father was we "oinked" louder and louder until we got his attention. We stopped in our tracks and looked up at him to see if he would recognize his "three little pigs." He did! These three dirty pigs had familiar faces, which by this time bore a close resemblance to the ones out in the pasture. I don't remember if he smiled, but I'm sure he did. I do remember that he told us to get our clothes back on right away or we'd get sick with all that dampness around. Of course we had to "oink" all the way back to where our clothes were, but we were happy. "Pop," as we called him, recognized us. We still belonged to him and there is no sweeter joy, even to a dirty little pig, than belonging to somebody.

Later, I heard him tell my Mom what we had done. She told my brother he should have had better sense than to play pig in those wet pens.

And "don't play games where you have to take off your clothes." She did not scold my little sister; she didn't scold me; she really didn't scold my brother either, but she let him know that he was never to tell us to take off our clothes again.

I shared this story from my early childhood with Father Murphy and he matched it with some of his own. It was a good form of entertainment on that long journey to Detroit and back again to Maggie Valley. My only regret was that I didn't have a tape recorder in the car with me.

Because my story included my little sister, Father Murphy was reminded about the time his father left a tool in the field and asked him to go back to the field to get it. When he went out to the field his little sister followed him. On the way back to the house she said to him, "Take hold of my dear little hand." He laughed as he told it. As a child he must not have been accustomed to holding his little sister's "dear little hand" because her request made such an impression on him that he told it over and over again through the years.

He also told how, when he was a youngster and still couldn't read very well, he got all excited because the Murphys had a mailbox near their farm. The city had not reached them and there had been no rural mail delivery yet where he lived. He commented, "My that was a wonderful thing when they began rural mail delivery. I went home and said, 'We have a mailbox, too. It is just for US. It even says 'US' on it.'" He added, "I had no idea that US meant "U.S.Mail."

Father Murphy knew the route to Detroit through Tennessee, Kentucky, Ohio, and into Michigan very well. He did not need a map. He had made the trip often when he was still able to drive. He laughingly told me about the time he did need a map. He was traveling with his mother and sister. They rode in the back seat of the car. He and his brother were in the front seat. The ladies had the maps. When Will Murphy stopped to get gas his mother and sister got out of the car to go to the restroom. He filled his gas tank, paid his bill, and then got back into the car, started chatting with his brother, and drove off. He drove for an hour before he realized the ladies were not with him. He had been hearing papers rustling in the back seat, and so he presumed the women folk were looking at the maps.

Finally he asked a question regarding some place on the map. There was no response from the back seat, so he glanced back to see why they weren't answering his questions. No wonder! There was no one in the back seat. No one! It was the maps rustling in the wind that he had been hearing. He went back (an hour's drive) and found the ladies. They were not at all pleased to have been forgotten.

On the way to Michigan, we prayed one rosary in Tennessee, one in Kentucky, and one in Ohio. The next day, we prayed the three rosaries while traveling from one relative's place to another. But that was the last of that. The third day he announced before we started that he already had prayed three rosaries and was not interested in praying any more. Thereafter he always had his rosaries prayed before we got into the car. He much preferred to chat and look around and point out to me the many places of interest that he found along the way. Likewise, he couldn't be praying when it was time to give me, his private chauffeur, directions.

Margaret Murphy's headstone

James Murphy's headstone

One of the places he wanted me to take him was to the cemetery. He wanted to visit his parents' graves. But he had another agenda that I didn't know about. He wanted to offer Mass on his mother's grave. He was prepared. Those were the days when Mass was often offered in the home. He had offered the Mass the day before at his niece's home in Wall Lake where we stayed overnight. So he had all the essentials with him.

I was glad I did not know at the time that there was some church regulation that does not allow for using a grave marker for an altar. His mother always wanted a priest in the family. It was as if he now wanted to show her that she had her priest-son. It was a very emotional experience for him and I'm glad that I didn't know it was more or less "illegal" or I might have tried to prevent him from doing what I now believe was his main purpose for wanting to go back to Michigan. It wasn't so much to see his relatives or to check up on his property as it was to pay this very special visit to his parents' graves.

CHAPTER TEN

▼

THE FINAL HOURS

The Last Sorrowful Mystery

"The Crucifixion and Death of Our Lord"

Father Murphy's last days were very sad. Sister Agnes and Sister Francine, his faithful caretakers, were finding it increasingly difficult to care for Father Murphy. The Rectory was not equipped for the type of care he needed. The Sisters were recalled to the Motherhouse in Tiffin, Ohio with the understanding that they would bring Father Murphy with them. They could continue to care for him at St. Francis Home, a retirement home, which is located on the Motherhouse grounds, a home well equipped for elderly patients.

It would have been so easy for the two Sisters to continue to give Father Murphy the kind of care at the Home that he had been accustomed to receiving from them. But that was not to be. His nephews felt that Father Murphy would prefer staying in the Valley he loved so well. The Sisters' plan for Father Murphy's continued care failed, and they had to depart without him. The care of Father Murphy was then turned over to his family.

Sister Agnes and Sister Francine left Maggie Valley on March 1. John and Grace Schneider, who were always so faithful to Father Murphy and the Sisters, loaded the suitcases into the Center's station wagon, gave the Sisters time to give Father Murphy a tearful and final "Goodbye" and took them directly to the Motherhouse in Tiffin, Ohio.

Father Murphy saw their suitcases were packed. He thought they were his. The next day he asked, "When am I going? They took my suitcases yesterday." We had to tell him he was not going, that his family preferred that he stay in Maggie. He was confused but too disturbed to really comprehend what was happening. He sat down in his easy chair and woefully asked, "Who's going to take care of me now?"

His nephews had arranged for a nursing service to come in to care for him but from that time on he went downhill even faster than before. He seemed to be giving up. In less than two months he would no longer need the nursing service.

Shirley Pinto was the only person from the parish allowed to help care for Father Murphy. The family knew she was trustworthy and loved Father Murphy very much. The nephews had their reasons for restricting visitors. They knew that one of Father Murphy's trusted friends had betrayed him. They were being cautious for his sake. He was their only surviving uncle, their father's last living brother, and they wanted to do what was the best for him.

Shirley describes those last days:

"To experience Father Murphy's final hours on this earth was a touching, emotional feeling that struck all the senses of my spiritual being. To explain these feelings I must go back and reminisce about the years that I spent with Father Murphy. My first meeting with Mr. Murphy, as he was then called, was in our new restaurant that my husband Al and I had just opened in June 1970. The restaurant was called "Alfredo's."

"Mr. Murphy was one of our first customers, and we would talk for many hours about how he came to Maggie Valley and built Saint Margaret's Church that was dedicated in 1968. One day he said to me,

'Do you know how when you plan something in your mind to build and it doesn't come out exactly to your expectations? Well, St. Margaret's was above and beyond all my expectations.' I said to him, 'Mr. Murphy, St. Margaret's is one of the most beautiful churches I have ever seen. My favorite thing is that all the windows look out at the beautiful mountains.' He said, 'Yes, I told the architects that we did not need stained glass windows when God had given us his own stained glass windows with the beautiful mountains of Maggie.'

"At that time Al, myself, and our daughter, Therese, were the eighth, ninth, and tenth members of St. Margaret's Church. There was Mrs. Viola Henry, Mrs. Julia Moody and her son, Leonard, and Jim Cryan and his three boys, Jimmy, David, and Pete, the altar boys of St. Margaret's Church. I said to Mr. Murphy one day in the restaurant, 'Mr. Murphy, the church has seating for 250 people and there are only ten of us and you that are parishioners of St. Margaret's Church. Why did you build such a large church?'

"He answered me, 'Because of the beautiful mountains, the good water, the pure air, and the wonderful people, I know that people will come to live here, and anyway I did not build the church for the Catholic people only. I built the church for the people who will come to Maggie who are not Catholic and will get to know us and experience the Holy Sacrifice of the Mass.'

"Mr. Murphy's whole world was the Eucharist, and each day I learned that more and more. Many times Mr. Murphy would call me up at the restaurant and say, 'Mrs. Alfredo, can you and David come to the church? There is a priest here to say Mass.' So, no matter how busy we were, David Cryan, my dishwasher and I would go up to the church for Mass. David was the altar boy. Mr. Murphy and I were worshipers.

"Then on July 19, 1970, God's providence took charge and set into motion the change of Mr. Michael William Murphy to Father Michael William Murphy. I will let him tell you the story in his own words as he related it to me when I interviewed him for St. Margaret's Cookbook, *LITTLE BITS OF HEAVEN.*

'One day while I was living at the first place I purchased in Maggie Valley, good Bishop Waters came to visit here. After we talked awhile, he said he wanted me to be a priest. My answer was that I was only a poor sinner and did not have much education. Each time he came to visit here when the church was being erected, he would joke about my being a priest.

'After the church was dedicated, some Sisters from Belmont, North Carolina, made a retreat here. Two of them had not yet made final vows so we prayed together for direction. One of the Sisters invited Anne, my niece, and me to attend the ceremonies on July 19, 1970. We did. Before the ceremony, one of the Sisters who was going to pronounce her vows, talked to Bishop Waters and told him to insist on my studying for the priesthood. Her name was Sister Carolyn Mary Coll. After Bishop Waters talked to her, he came over to me and said it was either go to the seminary or forget about it.

'Bishop Waters always said that it would be worthwhile to ordain me if I offered the Holy Sacrifice of the Mass only one time. I have offered it daily for over eighteen years now! Time will not be long enough to thank God for this wonderful blessing.'

"When I was talking with Sister Carolyn Mary about that day with Father Murphy, she said to me, 'I was like him. I wasn't sure about becoming a nun. In talking with him and encouraging him, he encouraged me.' So I said to him, 'If you'll do it, I'll do it.' The holiness in this gentle, little man was so inspiring. He touched me so greatly that I have never regretted becoming a nun.'

"I knew what she meant. I had the great privilege and honor to be at Father Michael William Murphy's ordination at St. Margaret's Church and I have to say I heard the angels sing. It was such a great day, beautiful weather, and the church was full of all of Father Murphy's family and the International Press.

"Father Murphy was a little frightened at first to be the parish priest at St. Margaret's Church by himself, so he requested to be stationed in another parish where he could get some practice. He was sent to Williamston, North

Carolina, and in 1973, he came home to Maggie Valley and became pastor of St. Margaret's Church. And the rest is history.

"In assisting Father Murphy and St. Margaret's Church through the years, I have felt and sensed St. Margaret's becoming "Holy Ground" because of Father Murphy's tireless and unending compassion and prayers. I have watched through the years as person after person who came into contact with Father Murphy and St. Margaret's Church, would be inspired and changed. There is a sense of presence in St. Margaret's that remains to this day—a sense of Father Murphy's reverence for the Holy Sacrifice of the Mass. Even now that he isn't here bodily, the presence remains.

"One day, Father and I were standing outside the church overlooking Maggie Valley and he said to me. 'I always want to do what God wants me to do,' and I said to him, Father, I believe that you have been doing what God wants you to do ever since the day you were born. For the cookbook, I asked Father to make a statement regarding what he would like to say to the people of the world. And he said, 'To live for the honor and glory of God and the benefit of the people.'

"Now, his final hours on this earth had come.

"During Father Murphy's final hours, he had three lovely young ladies from Canton to take care of him, Louise, Kim, and Mary, all Baptists. And when I would go to the rectory to see to his needs, the girls would ask me if there was something they could do to make him more comfortable. I would say the Rosary with Father and the girls asked me one day if I would teach them the Rosary so that they could say it for him when I was not there because it seemed to put him at such peace. Therefore I explained the rosary to them and they saw a new side to the Catholic faith. Thus, Father Murphy, in an indirect way, was demonstrating his Catholic faith to the people of the world.

"Around 7:00 in the evening Louise called me and said that Father was having a very restless day and seemed to be under great stress and could I come up. When I arrived I could see that Father, though he could not tell us in words, was going through a great spiritual struggle, so I read some

Scripture to him and said a decade of the Rosary. He was still struggling, so I read to him from a small prayer booklet called *The Pieta* which had many of the old prayers that his mother used to read to him. I sensed that Father was struggling about leaving this earth. I told him that it was all right and that his mother and father, whom he loved so dearly, were waiting for him with our Lord.

"In *The Pieta,* a little prayer book I always carry with me, I found a small reading about a Pope who was struggling in his final hours. I decided to read this to Father Murphy. It seems that the Pope wasn't sure he was worthy enough to go to heaven. He said to the Cardinals and Bishops, 'My dear friends! What comfort can you give me now that I must die and am not worthy of heaven?' No one answered him. One of the curates named John, finally said, 'Father, why do you doubt the mercy of God?' The Pope replied, 'What comfort can you give me now that I must die. I'll be damned for my sins?' John replied, 'I'll read three prayers over you. I hope you'll be comforted and that you'll obtain mercy from God.' The pope was unable to say more. The curate and all those present knelt and said an 'Our Father.' Then the curate recited the prayers.

"The story continues to say that the Pope died in peace and later appeared to John, the curate, and his countenance was as brilliant as the sun and his clothes as white as snow and he said, 'My dear brother! Whereas I was supposed to be a child of damnation I've become a child of happiness. As you recited the first prayer my sins fell from me as rain from heaven, and the second prayer I was purified as a goldsmith purifies gold in a hot fire, and as you recited the third prayer I was purified even more. Then I saw heaven open and the Lord Jesus standing on the right hand of God the Father Who said to me, 'Come, all thy sins are forgiven thee, you'll be and reign in the realm of my Father forever. Amen'.

"After I read the prayers, Father Murphy became calm and peaceful. It was 3 a.m. I told the girls that I would go home and rest and if they needed me to just call and I would come back in the morning. Louise called and said that he had rested all night.

"In the morning I went up to see how Father was doing. He looked so peaceful. I told the girls that there was going to be a Mass soon. From his bed he could look out and see the altar in the church, so I told them to let him watch the Mass, and if they needed me I would be at home.

"When the organ began to play and the retreatants began to sing, Father Murphy perked up for a moment and then slumped back in his bed. He had heard the angels singing. Retreatants who went to confession to him used to tell us that Father would tell them, 'Just do the best you can. Even the angels can't do any better.' He often spoke of the angels as intimate friends. When he heard angels singing in the church, it was a good time to die! And so he did.

"That was April 25, 1990. An hour later Louise called and said that Father had just passed away. When I arrived at the church the ambulance had just taken Father to Garrett's Funeral Home. The girls ran up and hugged me and started to cry in a joyful manner and said, 'It was exactly how you explained it to us! When the music of the Mass started Father seemed to go into a peaceful trance, then as the Mass started it seemed like he was not in the bed anymore but in church, and when the Priest was giving the final blessing Father peacefully passed away.'

"I went down to the funeral home with Father Bill Evans to help make the arrangements for the funeral. We requested that Father Murphy lie in state at St. Margaret's Church. That afternoon Father Gray offered a Mass for Father Murphy and we signed up people to stay with Father Murphy for the 24-hour period while he lay in state. Father Gray asked me to tell the congregation about Father Murphy's final hours. Parishioners of St. Margaret's and residents of Maggie Valley came and prayed all night."

A Soliloquy

Father Murphy, I want you to know those were among the saddest days of my life. I went to see you in the hospital but the nurse would not let me into your room. There was a sign on your door, NO VISITORS. I tried to tell the nurse who I was and that I just wanted to let you know that I, and all your parishioners, were praying for you, that we cared about you, that we were feeling your pain. But that was not to be. I turned away from your hospital door without being able to say, "Goodbye." I turned away, never to see you alive again even though you came back to the Rectory to spend your last days.

After having walked daily with you for fourteen years, after having assisted at your inspiring Eucharists every day, after hearing you sigh out, "JESUS, JESUS" so frequently, I had every reason to hope and expect to be with you in those final moments. But I couldn't. No one could except for Shirley. For two weeks I waited in the church, in the Convent, in the Center, hoping that the restrictions would be lifted. But we could not get to your bedside as you lay dying.

Father Murphy, I wanted to be there to repeat the words of your favorite prayer, I wanted to repeat it a "thousand times" because you could no longer speak the Sacred Name yourself. I wanted to be there to hold your hand and to say, "It's OK now. I'll take you to the Doctor even if you haven't changed your clothes."

I wanted to say, "Thanks for the $20 you lent me in the grocery store," and when I wanted to pay you back you refused my money saying almost tearfully, as if you had often been taken advantage of, "Nobody ever pays me back the money I give them."

I wanted to be there to assure you that we would not be putting a soldering iron in the coffin with you, like your brother teasingly predicted. Instead, we would be vesting you in your priestly robes and we would place your well-worn rosary in your hands.

I wanted to be there to tell you that I understood the discomfort you were in when you were in the hospital several months earlier. You wanted me to take down the bars from your bed. You wanted me to take out the intravenous. You wanted me to take you "where I belong." When I asked, "Where's that"? You said, "I don't know but I want you to take me there."

I would not take down the bars, nor remove the intravenous, nor take you where you wanted to go, nor do any of the other things you wanted me to do against the doctors orders. When I left the room and the new nurse on duty came in you told her, "She's no saint." Because somehow, somewhere along the line you thought you were my boss, I just wanted you to know you never were my boss, just a very loving, kind, considerate friend.

I wanted to be there to tell you it was Spring now and the rabbits were playing leap-frog again in the yard, and the birds and the squirrels were around the feeder again.

I wanted to tell you that the clouds were parting and that if this were Ascension Thursday you would be granted your wish of seeing "where He was heading."

I wanted to tell you that you were the kindest man I ever met, and the most generous. I wanted to tell you that I understood why you didn't trust me with your payroll accounts.

And I wanted to remind you that if you needed a Pedro partner, sure-ly, well almost surely, you would find more than one. I would have warned you that you were about to meet your match because my brother Cletus, who used to play Pedro with you, had gone to heaven before you and he was a real "card shark."

There were so many things I wanted to say to you but most of all it was the Sacred Name. A thousand times a day. A thousand times. JESUS! JESUS! I knew how much it meant to you. It was your mother's favorite prayer. It was your favorite prayer. It has become my favorite prayer. It has become the favorite prayer of your parishioners.

I wanted to be there when the angels "who could do no better" came to take you home. But no one was allowed to be with you except Shirley, and the caretakers who did not know you and whose voices were not familiar to you, but who cared deeply for you, cared enough to learn to pray the rosary so you could live out the "the agony in the garden" all the way through to the "resurrection" and the "coronation of Mary," the lady who meant so much to you. And while they were praying the rosary the

Sacred Heart, with whom you conversed when I said the rosary with you, came with the angels to accompany you to eternal life.

I wanted to let you know that all your parishioners were also on the other side of the door. They, too, wanted to be at your side. Somehow, it seemed to all of us that even though you were in your favorite bed, in your favorite room, in your favorite valley, you were dying alone, alone in a foreign land like some of the patriarchs before you.

The Wake

Father Murphy, you returned to St. Margaret's on April 30, 1990. Father Bill Evans, pastor of St. Margaret's, prepared a beautiful Vesper Service for you. Those of us who had been with you for so many years, Sisters Agnes, Francine, Maurice, and I, were privileged to place the pall on your casket and to take part in the Vesper services.

Franciscan Sisters follow the casket into church for the Vesper services for Father Murphy, April 30, 1990.

It was getting dark. While the organ played soft music we followed you down the aisle of St. Margaret's church for the last time. We could almost hear you within your casket sighing over and over again, "My Jesus , My

Jesus." You were home. You were home in so many different ways. You were in the church you built before you became a priest. You were again lying near the altar just as you did on you ordination day–prostrate before the Lord. You were with the people whom you shepherded for many years. It was a comforting thought to know that at long last you were with the family you loved so much, your beloved mother and father, sisters and brothers.

While I knelt there I had time to remember how much you wanted to live to be 100. On your 95th birthday there was a celebration with a concelebrated Mass at St. Margaret's for you. Bishop Donoghue came from Charlotte to preside. Father Joe Kelleher, the man who always called you "Uncle Bill," came to give the homily. The parish arranged for a marvelous birthday party for you at the Stompin' Ground. The Irish dancers came to add just the right touch to the celebration.

At that party, Ernestine Upchurch, your long time Methodist friend, spoke eloquently of you. Your grandniece, Anne, was there with her family. Father Conrad Lewis, your mentor, presented you with a tee shirt that carried the logo, "It's a miracle." And when anyone greeted you with a "Happy Birthday" you told each one, "All I want for a birthday present is to live long enough to celebrate my 100th."

Father Murphy, do you remember this conversation you had with Sister Jean Linder? She taped it. You were ONLY 95 years old at the time. Sister Agnes was present and some times she had to help you to remember.

SJ— Father Murphy, do you have any brothers or sisters living now?

FM— Oh, no, everybody's dead. Nobody at all. There were eight in our family and they're all gone.

SJ— And you weren't even the oldest, nor the youngest, were you?

FM— No, there were two younger than I.

SJ— Did you think you would be the longest living member of your family?

FM— No, I never thought of that. Margaret was younger and then Elliott was the youngest.

SA— You were sickly when you were young, weren't you?

FM— Oh, well, I was kind of delicate. Yes, I guess I was.

SA— You heard them talking about you one day when you were sick. Do you remember what that was that you heard your mother and your older sisters talking about when you were sick?

FM— Oh, yes! I remember. I had been asleep on one of the chairs, I guess, and when I was awake they didn't know it and they were talking about that they didn't think I would live very long. And now I lived so much longer than any of the rest.

SJ— How did that make you feel when you heard they didn't expect you to live long? Did that scare you?

FM— I don't believe it scared me.

SJ— You thought, "I'll show them. I'll fool them," didn't you?

FM— I can remember them saying that they didn't think I would live long. I was delicate. Oh, gosh, I was raised poor. We had a lot of land, but we were in debt on it, too, and the farmers had to raise potatoes and a few things like that so they could sell them. And pickles, too. But afterwards when we got to raising berries–we had nineteen acres of berries–the biggest berry farm in Michigan!

SJ— I'll bet Murphy berries were known all around the state.

FM— My father would take a big load of berries every day except Sunday, to the market. And I remember one day he got $500 for the load. Five hundred dollars then would be like...

SJ— You thought you were a millionaire, then, didn't you?

FM— Oh, my! Five hundred dollars was so much in those days!

SA— You know, he talks about the West Market that they went to. It was close to their home. The East Market was on the other side of town.

FM— My father'd go there most of the time. It was a bigger one. I think the Italians would buy the berries and then they'd go around through the streets selling them, you see. Great big market. Oh, my that market–longer than from here to the road, I guess.

SJ— Those were hard years, weren't they?

FM— But we got along fine. Once we got in the berry business we got out of debt then and we were two thousand dollars in debt on the farm. It was hard for my people to make the interest even. For years. And then when we got that, the first year we paid off four hundred dollars. The next year we paid eight hundred dollars, that would be twelve and the next year we paid the rest and had money left.

SJ— Oh, that's when you really felt like you came up above water!

FM— Oh, yes! The berry business, you see, we had a big berry farm. Well, we'd get $500 for a load, you know. That counted up. Not all loads, of course, but $200, $300, $400 a load. We could get all the pickers we wanted at that time. The Polish people were just coming to Detroit and they were very poor and they were glad to have their children, their boys, have a chance to earn a little money picking the berries, you know. We had all the pickers we needed. Everything was grand! Now you wouldn't be allowed to have them picking, I don't think.

SJ— Thank you very much for the interview, Father Murphy.

Father Murphy, you may have been a delicate child but you certainly didn't let that keep you from living life fully for nearly a century. Everyone enjoyed visiting you because you were so "quick on the ball," as they would say, so alert, so Irish with your spontaneous responses. You made people laugh. You had an answer for everything. Yes, you surprised everyone, even yourself, by living so long, but you didn't quite make it to that one hundred mark.

No, you didn't quite make it. No touchdown this time. That hundredth birthday was probably one of the few goals that eluded you. You had already accomplished so much. You did not need that extra year. You fought the good fight and you won. By the grace of God, you lived much longer than even your mother expected you to live.

Word of your death spread quickly. The Raleigh *News and Observer* reported, "The man on the mountain is dead. The grief felt by the people in the town below envelops the valley like the cool gray morning mist resting on the mountaintops. Tourist season won't be the same this year, or any year, now that their best attraction is gone. Even the visitors will feel the loss. The mountain fog will lift as the day moves on, and so will the people's grief. There is joy, too, in the valley, for not a soul in town doubts that Father Michael William Murphy is in the one place he thought just might be more beautiful than the valley." The Raleigh paper had it correct. Indeed, no one doubts that you are in the one place that just might be more beautiful than the valley.

Father Murphy, you made Catholics feel welcome in the valley with your winning ways, your gentleness, your generosity. Viola Henry remembers very well the fear the mountain people had of Catholics in the early days. She was the first Catholic in the valley when she and her husband moved here in 1947. She said, "When we first moved here, I was the only Catholic, and the people didn't understand what our religion was all about. Some even peeked in our windows at night to see what a Catholic looked like. Maybe they expected horns. My husband and I found out much later that they thought I was sent here by the Pope to convert the Baptists or kill them. But Will Murphy's influence helped change that image and dispel the myths about Catholicism."

Father Murphy, you did do a great deal to make Catholics more respected in the area but there is still a lot to do. Several years ago someone said to one of your friends, "You seem to be such a spiritual person. I'm surprised you are still a Catholic." There are still people in the area who wonder about us Catholics. Not too many years ago, Viola Henry was given an award for all the work she had done in the civic community. The presenter of the award ended her litany of praise for Viola by saying, "And she was able to do all of this in spite of the fact that she's Catholic."

So you see, Father Murphy, you'll have to keep right on blessing our beloved friends and neighbors so that the good work you did while you were here will continue now that you no longer can be physically in our midst.

Viola continued her praise of you: "When Murphy moved here, people were worried. He was from the North. He had never married, but his compassion and sense of humor won the people over. He didn't try to convert people, but brought them a long way in understanding what the Catholic faith meant. Up until the mid-1970's Mr. Murphy used to call me on the phone and say, 'Mrs. Henry, the Bishop's here and he'd like to offer the Holy Sacrifice of the Mass. Could you come on over?' And I always went," she said with a laugh.

But now it's over. Now there are no more berries to pick. No more churches to build. No more mountains to level. No more violins to make. No more radios. No more horses to feed. Your favorite chair is empty. Your colorful afghan is still there as if waiting for you to sit down. But you won't sit there anymore. You won't pick up your prayer book. It's still on the stand by your chair. You won't put any more wood on the fire. Next to enjoying good food yourself your favorite occupation was to feed the fire. You loved to see the fire blaze forth, especially when the wood was wet. You wouldn't listen to us and put a protective cover over the wood piled near your kitchen door. You said, "Wet wood burns longer." We didn't believe you but it was your choice.

Wakes are a good time for remembering. Time passes so quickly.

Father Murphy, there is something that even at this late date, ten years after your funeral, that I would like to ask you. What really happened that night at your wake?

Were you up to some old trick of yours?

Sister Francine and I had signed up to be with you from 1:00 a.m. to 2:00 a.m. We wanted to keep vigil with you before the Blessed Sacrament. We wanted to speak our last words to you. So we knelt to pray. We knelt, and we knelt, and we knelt. Normally we would kneel for five to ten minutes and then sit down for some contemplative prayer.

Well, that night both of us experienced the same thing. We knelt for what we thought was five-ten minutes. Then we sat down. Lo and behold our vigil replacements came in to take our places. But our time wasn't up yet. At least that's what we thought. We looked at our watches. Indeed our hour was up. We were mystified. What had happened? Why didn't we sense the passing of time? Why did an hour only seem like ten minutes? Neither of us could figure out what had happened. The time had gone so fast that we believe to this day that you "suspended" time just for us. You knew we were tired after a long day of preparation for your funeral so you played a practical joke on us. We left the church puzzled. Suspension of time? Now, we believe there is such a thing.

The Funeral

Father Murphy, did you realize that it was just seventeen years after you returned to St. Margaret's from your assignment in Williamston that we gathered for your funeral? You came back to your beloved Maggie Valley on May 1, 1973. You left the valley for good on May 1, 1990. You lived for seventeen years in the rectory that you built. You offered Mass for seventeen years in the church you erected in memory of your mother. All your dreams were fulfilled. All your mother's dreams were fulfilled. Those had to be among the most precious years of your life.

Father Murphy, the church was filled for your funeral, filled with your family, your friends, your parishioners, and your fellow clergymen. It was a sad, yet glorious day for all of us.

In the beautiful Mass of the Resurrection, in the liturgy so well prepared for you by Father Bill Evans, we all sang lustily, with hearts that were aching at the same time as they were rejoicing. We sang as the procession of clerics and relatives came into the church:

> *Alleluia! Not as orphans*
> *Are we left in sorrow now;*

Alleluia! He is near us,
Faith believes, no questions now,
Though the cloud from sight received him
When the forty days were o'er
Shall our hearts forget his promise,
"I am with you ever more"

The Rev. Edward Gray, CSSR, pastor of St. John's in Waynesville, gave the homily. He was always so gentle with you. He respected you and treated you kindly as a neighbor and a friend.

At Communion time we sang *"I am the bread of life"* with its uplifting refrain,

And I will raise you up!
And I will raise you up!
And I will raise you up!
On the last day!

After the services were over we sang a recessional hymn, ever ancient, ever new, and ever appropriate for the occasion,

For all the saints who from their labors rest,
All who by faith before the world confessed
Your name, O Jesus, be forever blest,
Alleluia! Alleluia!

We followed your casket to the hearse that would take you out of your beautiful valley. It would take you back to Detroit where you lived for so many years. It would take you to the Holy Sepulchre Cemetery where you would be buried next to your father and mother. But that hearse would carry your mortal remains only. No vehicle made by man could ever carry your spirit away from the valley. You will forever look down upon us from another mountaintop and we shall forever remember you.

Father Murphy, we watched you leave. The hearse moved slowly down the hill. We watched it go. Yes, It's over. The pain of separation from your loved ones is over. Now the singing begins for real. And the dancing. The tears you shed at the Consecration of the Mass fall as gentle rain upon us who are still in this "Valley of Tears."

Having said farewell to you, those who attended your funeral filed down to the dining room at Living Waters. There we shared our memories of you. It is springtime once again for you and for all of us, but my memories go back to the day you told me how when you first came to the valley, you could not get over the beauty of autumn. You said you would get up with the sun in the morning, start out in a different direction each day, drive and drive and drive while drinking in the beauty of the fall scenery around you, and then you would return home at night, almost in tears because you couldn't see that beauty again until the next day. You did this for at least three weeks every October.

When you could no longer drive we took you to see the beauty of the fall colors. During the last years you would "oh" and "ah" at everything and then you would say, "I've never seen this before." Sometimes we would correct you by saying, "Father Murphy, just yesterday we went down this same road." You would act surprised, and then you would repeat over and over again, "Oh my, oh my, oh my. Just look at that! Did you ever see anything so grand?"

You liked that word "grand." You would sigh and repeat, "Just look at that!" And then would come the clincher, "I've never been here before." Finally, we realized you were right. You never were "here" before. Neither were we. Each day, each hour of each day, nature was changing and we were changing right along with it. When we realized how right you were, it was much more fun to go riding with you and to see the world through your eyes.

Father Murphy, remember Father Lynch, your faithful mentor at St. Meinrad's? We were sharing memories in the dining room after your funeral and he said to me, "I'm convinced that Father Murphy was a mystic."

Father Ralph Lynch, OSB and Father William Murphy

Many spiritual writers, when talking about mysticism, will say that a mystic is one who finds God in the ordinary. Father Murphy, you found God all around you. That's why you did not put stained glass windows in St. Margaret's church. You wanted every one to enjoy the view that spoke so eloquently of the Creator of all.

Father Murphy, I believe a mystic is one who sees the REAL in what seems to be unREAL, one who sees clearly the burning bush and knows the I AM WHO AM. Yes, a mystic is one who sees God in the ordinary, one who enjoys life, one who enjoys peanut butter, pure drinking water, fresh mountain air, and good loving neighbors.

So What Is Being A Mystic–Murphy-Style?

— It is going to the window, looking at the scenery and exclaiming, "Isn't it grand! Have you ever seen anything so beautiful?"

— it is an "I've never seen this before" state of mind, seeing everything anew for the very first time;

— it is never having to mention God's name because of being so deeply immersed in God's beauty, God's all prevailing presence that the WORD comes forth with every word spoken;

— it is being totally human, appreciating pure drinking water, good neighbors, wonderful climate, fresh mountain air;

— it is wanting people around even when their names are allusive and their faces aren't too clear, and their voices not too audible. PRESENCE is everything,

— it is walking up and down the aisles in church knowing Someone is there. It is wistfully sighing the name JESUS when no one except that Someone is within hearing distance;

— it is being aware of one's sinfulness and admitting it. "I am just a poor sinner. They say if we could see ourselves as others see us, we'd all jump in the river."

— it is being so aware of sinfulness that tears flow when saying the words, "This is the cup of my blood which will be shed for you and for all so that sins may be forgiven."

— it is to say, "Thank you, thank you, thank you," while clapping hands together for the least little favor;

— it is to sing off key, and with a satisfying grin, when hearing about an invitation to once more partake of a neighboring church's potluck, "I'm a Methodist, I'm a Methodist, I eat the Methodist pie. I'm a Methodist, I'm a Methodist, I'm a Methodist until I die." Where did you ever learn this little ditty?

— it is to say humbly, "I can't give a homily; you give it."

— it is accepting just as humbly the observation of many, "You are giving a homily all the time. Your life is a homily."

— it is to laugh heartily when playing cards, and saying, "A-HA! my right Pedro takes your left Pedro!"

— it is to admit, after being invited to a card game, "If you had said it was going to be a prayer meeting I would have been too sick to come."

— it is to lick the ice-cream dish CLEAN simply because ice-cream is so-o-o-o good;

— it is to worry when a young Mercy Sister is about to make final vows, "Do you think maybe they won't profess her because when we prayed I held her hand?"

— it is in knowing and exclaiming with Hopkins the Jesuit poet, that "the whole world is charged with the grandeur of God" and that "deep down lies the dearest fresh freshness of things."

— Yes, Father Murphy, you saw God in the ordinary. How do I know? How could I not know?

I am closing your ledger now. I have no more need of it. You have no more need of it. The angels have opened another ledger, one that recorded all the wonderful deeds of your life. That ledger we will keep open. We will make entries in it every day because the work you began here in Maggie Valley continues on in St. Margaret's Church and the Living Waters Catholic Reflection Center.

CHAPTER ELEVEN

▼

THE VISION REVISITED

Father Murphy, do you remember telling us about your mother's vision? You not only told us about it but you wrote about it in your ledger. Your mother tried to get you to see what she was seeing because it was so beautiful.

Your mother said to you, "Look! Look!"

You and your little brother and sister stopped your game and looked where your mother was pointing. You saw nothing, but you knew she was seeing something because she was looking up to the heavens and pointing. You looked again in the direction of her pointing. You stared and saw nothing.

"What? What is it, Mother?" you asked.

"There! There! Just above you! Don't you see? It's the Blessed Virgin Mary!"

You did not see anything but you never doubted that she saw something.

"Look, now can you see them? It is Our Lady. There are three monks with her."

You wanted to be able to tell her that you, too, could now see what she was seeing but you knew that she would not want you to say something that was not true. You still did not see.

Father Murphy, now you see, don't you? Now you see what your mother saw. Do you suppose your mother couldn't tell a Monk from a Friar? Most people can't. I can't. My guess is that you can't either, even though you are now in a place where all visions become reality, where faith is no longer needed. You were not surprised, were you, when, in September 1998, we received a letter from our Bishop, the Most Reverend William G. Curlin, with a very special announcement:

"We are very happy to announce that three Augustinian Friars have accepted Bishop Curlin's invitation to serve in the pastoral care of St. Margaret's Church and also as the directors of Living Waters Reflection Center. The Friars are experienced in both parish and retreat ministry. The Augustinian Friars are one of the oldest religious orders in the Catholic Church. Theirs is a rich history of serving the Church throughout the world. The Diocese of Charlotte is honored that the Augustinian Friars will be serving in Maggie Valley. Augustinian Friars presently serve in the pastoral care of St. John Neumann Church and as the chaplain of Charlotte Catholic High School.

"The Diocese of Charlotte is most grateful for the many years of devoted ministry provided by Sister Jane Schmenk, Sister Jean Linder and Sister Francine Sartor at the Reflection Center and for the Church in Western North Carolina."

Father Murphy, the Diocese gave us a nice farewell banquet. In an article written for the Catholic News and Herald, December 11, 1998, Joanita Nellenbach wrote:

"Guests packed the dining room in Living Waters Catholic Reflection Center on the evening of November 29, to express their gratitude and affection for three women who have made a difference.

"Sisters Jane Schmenk, Jean Linder, and Francine Sartor of the Sisters of St. Francis of Tiffin, Ohio, will be leaving Living Waters at the end of December. Fathers Terrance Hyland and Francis J. Doyle and Brother

William C. Harkin of the Order of St. Augustine, will run the reflection center as well as St. Margaret Church.

"Members of the parish, as well as sisters and priests from throughout the diocese, were on hand to pay tribute to the many years of service the three Franciscans have given to the Diocese of Charlotte.

"For me, they have strengthened the presence of Jesus in our midst," Bishop William G. Curlin said. "The love, the generosity that they have poured out, their Franciscan charisma, have been special gifts. They leave a legacy of love that can only inspire those who follow them."

Sister Jean Linder, OSF Sister Jane Schmenk, OSF Sister Francine Sartor, OSF

Father Frank now stands at the altar where you once stood. As pastor of St. Margaret's, he offers the Eucharist just as reverently as you did. However, he hasn't started dancing around like you sometimes did. He's much younger than you were when you were pastor. Maybe the dancing will happen when he gets closer to the age you were when you first two-stepped in that sanctuary, using your *"dominus vobiscum"* gestures as you looked at the congregation and welcomed them into your heart. He has the same leprechaun spirit that you had, and the same glint of mischief is in his eyes. And he is very much concerned about people, just as you were.

Father Francis J. Doyle, OSA, Father Terrance Hyland, OSA,
Brother William C. Harkin, OSA

The Augustinians believe in community living. Each Sunday bulletin carries a few words from St. Augustine's Sermon 355 that tells the parishioners, "We live here with you, we live for you; and our vow is that we may live with you forever in the presence of Christ." That's exactly what you would have said if you had thought of it first!

Just to remind you of what you already know, the Rectory is no longer a Rectory. It is now a Friary. That's over and above anything you would have dreamed up back in those days when Bishop Waters threw cold water on your "second story" project. The Friary is called "Lecceto.

Besides being the pastor of St. Margaret's, Father Frank is also the Prior of Lecceto. "Lecceto" is named after the 13th century Augustinian hermitage in the Tuscan region of Italy just outside the city of Siena. Lecceto, which takes its name from the ilex or "lecce" tree (a class of oak) surrounding the hermitage, has a glorious history in the eremitical roots of the Augustinian Order. The spirit of St. Augustine's North African monastic life flourishes at this site to this very day. Within the history of the

Augustinian Order, Lecceto's fame is well known as a place of intense contemplation where friars grew in extraordinary sanctity.

Father Terry Hyland, OSA, is the Director of the Reflection Center. He also offers the "Holy Sacrifice" at that same altar in St. Margaret's. He doesn't weep at the Consecration like you did but that could happen some day because he has your deep spirit of compassion. He is an off-the-scale extroverted feeler, an ideal temperament for one who welcomes retreatants to the Center. Even the ladybugs that have invaded the church are safe with him, like they were with you.

Father Terry likewise offers the Eucharist at Living Waters where he spends a lot of time with retreatants who want to "reflect the Son deep in the heart of a mountain." He could not be doing that if you had not been so generous in giving Falling Waters Motel to the Diocese.

Father Murphy, if the third member of this Maggie Valley Augustinian community, Brother William Harkin, OSA, had been here when you were here you could have asked him to give the homilies that you felt unable to give. He is a Deacon and puts into words the thoughts that you never expressed verbally but lived out visibly.

You could also have asked Brother Bill to take care of your finances so the IRS would leave you alone because taking care of money matters is one of his jobs as Pastoral Associate of St. Margaret's and Assistant Director of Living Waters. He has your spirit of generosity, always eager to be of help, always willing to listen. If he saw the ledger you kept he would be amazed at your generosity as well as the simplicity with which you kept your records.

And if you saw him do his bookkeeping, not using a ledger but using a computer, you would exclaim in amazement, "Oh my, oh my, oh my! Just look at that! How does it work?" In your youth you figured out how to make radios and violins. If you were young again you would not only give Brother Bill a "run for the money," but you would also challenge another Bill, Bill Gates, the multi-billionaire computer expert, by inventing a computer that even Sugar, your dog, could work, getting what he wanted with just a few barks.

Also living in the Friary, but not directly connected with St. Margaret's or Living Waters, are Dennis McGowan, OSA and Christopher Nowak, OSA. Father Dennis is the pastor of St. John's in Waynesville and Father Chris is the Parochial Vicar of that Parish.

They also sometimes stand at the altar where you stood when they substitute for Father Frank or Father Terry. Because you built such a large rectory Maggie Valley now has a Friary and the three monks your mother saw have now turned into five Friars.

Yes, Father Murphy, your spirit is still very much alive here in the Valley. These Friars carry your spirit within them and they share it with all they meet. Visitors who come to St. Margaret's and retreatants who spend time at Living Waters all say that they sense something very special about this place. They sense your SPIRIT, and it is your SPIRIT that has made St. Margaret's, Living Waters, and the Friary–HOLY GROUND.

This is Holy Ground.
We're standing on Holy Ground,
For God is present
And where God is, is holy!

▼

CHAPTER TWELVE

MEMORIES

Father Murphy not only found God "in the ordinary" and in the beauty of nature. He also found God in the people. He was completely dedicated to the "good people" of the Valley, and the "good people" who came to visit him. Some of those people have responded to my request to write down their memories.

After Father Murphy died, Sister Agnes jotted down some of her favorite memories. Sister Agnes died on July 7, 1994, a little more than four years after Father Murphy's death. She had been caring for him for eight years and was much impressed with him as the following jottings reveal.

"On our walk up and down the mountain, we would stop to inspect a new flower, listen to a bird's song or just notice the birds in the sky.

"I often stooped to pick a tiny flower along the path but Father Murphy would object. 'Don't pick it. God put it there for all to enjoy,' he would say.

"While I'd be cooking dinner, I'd hear 'Come quickly! The sky is so beautiful; it's changing so fast.'

"Until about six months ago, Father Murphy knelt on the floor to say his morning and night prayers. When this became a real effort I'd sit on the side of his bed to say his morning prayers with him. When ten o'clock came I'd sit on the side of his bed and say his night prayers with him."

"We never went to bed with an unresolved problem. We'd each acknowledge our part and say a prayer together. 'Let not the sun go down upon your anger' was a way of life with him.

"No meal was just an ordinary meal. Father Murphy noticed a pretty plate of food and thanked the one who prepared it. 'Thank you for a good meal,' or 'Oh, how pretty! It's too nice to spoil'—but he did eat it and enjoy it.

"Every visitor was welcomed. If people were hesitant about coming in, he would go out and invite them in. No one left without some leaflet or booklet to take along.

"Humming birds outside his window were a sight he thoroughly enjoyed. Always he praised God who gave us such happiness.

"Every little animal and bird was a thing of wonder. One morning he was ecstatic when he discovered two rabbits, several squirrels and five various birds all enjoying the feed around the bird feeder.

"Mary's Rosary was a constant companion. We prayed the rosary in the morning, in the afternoon, in the evening—any time of the day! Sometimes we said all fifteen mysteries in the same hour. We knelt for all fifteen decades.

"Father Murphy thoroughly enjoyed VCR's, which showed God's love for people and nature. TV dramas interspersed with commercials annoyed him; he'd lose the story. He always enjoyed the VCR of the first Folkmoot in Maggie. He liked the music, the dancing, and the many people present. We attended that first performance together."

Bill Higgins

In 1946, Father Murphy (not a priest at the time) took his mother, Margaret, to Lourdes in France to the Eucharistic Congress. I was just four years old and had polio. Margaret Murphy brought back some Lourdes water and gave it to my mother to rub on my legs. She also prayed over me. I was cured of my polio.

In 1978 my wife, Sue, and I came from Michigan to settle in Maggie Valley. When we heard that Father Murphy, the pastor at St. Margaret's, was from Detroit, we wondered if he was by some chance related to Margaret Murphy, the lady to whom we attributed my cure. I found a holy card, which Margaret Murphy had given to me tucked away in an old prayer book. She had written on it. In order to find out if the two Murphy's were related I showed the holy card to Father Murphy. Immediately he said, "My mother! My dear, sweet mother!" He acknowledged that the handwriting was indeed his mother's. We then spoke to my parents about it and they confirmed the story of my cure. We wanted my parents to know that Mrs. Murphy's son was now our pastor.

Shirley Hillyer

Father Murphy believed in physical fitness. In a letter I received from Father Murphy and Sister Agnes conjointly they said, "Father Murphy is now 96 1/2 years old and is still going strong. We take our walks down the hill to the road when the weather permits. We walk slowly and notice many things along the way. We stop to listen to birds in the trees; we notice the newest green plants coming from the ground. We even walk the steep hill to the Sisters' Convent. We rest a while and then walk back home."

Some of Father Murphy's strength came from his love of good food. He loved to eat. The Sisters and I took him to the Cracker Barrel and he ordered a waffle with strawberries. It came to the table loaded with fruit and whipped cream. He just sat there for a while, looking at it, and saying. "Oh my! Oh my! Oh my!" After he got through with the exclamations he dug in, and ate the whole thing with gusto!

On Wednesdays a group of us from St. Margaret's would go to Duvall's for breakfast. Ernie, the owner, would fix Father Murphy a plate without even asking what he wanted. Ernie had come up with his own idea of what Father liked. He would bring him a platter of eggs, bacon, pancakes, etc.

Each time it was a little different but Father always ate whatever was put before him. He made sure he gave a blessing before he–or anyone else–began to eat. But he never gave that blessing until the filled plate was in front of him."

One year "Christmas in the Valley" got the British Brass Band to play. When Father Murphy heard about it all he could say was, "Oh, my goodness! Oh, my goodness!" He thought a brass band was inappropriate entertainment for Christmas, particularly if it was a BRITISH Brass Band.

Jim and Irene O'Neill

In 1984, we were on our first visit to Maggie Valley and went to daily Mass. We spoke with Father Murphy and he asked why we were here (as he did most everyone—we later found out). We told him that we thought we would look for a piece of property to build a home on for relief from the Florida summers.

He surprised us by telling us that he had several pieces of property and asked what size we were looking for. We decided to take a look at the one-acre piece on which he had once intended to build St. Margaret Church.

We loved it and we told him we were interested in buying. We went to the rectory to discuss purchasing it. We settled on the purchase of one-half acre and arrived at a selling price. Since we did not have the entire amount, Father Murphy said that he would finance the balance. At that time the current interest rate was between 14% and 16%. We told him we would be willing to pay the current rate. When we told him that, he responded, "ANYTHING ABOVE 7% IS USERY," and he refused to hear anymore about the current rate.

We were astonished at what he said. Because of his kindness to us in not accepting the higher rate of interest, we were able to pay the note off much quicker. We built our home and moved in after Jim retired, in 1987. It became a place we chose to stay in year round.

Father Murphy visited us at this home many times. Each time Jim would ask him to play a little tune on the violin and Father Murphy always said, "I don't know how to play the violin" and then when Jim would hand him the violin, Father Murphy would break into an Irish jig. We loved him and miss him very much.

Brenda and Joey O'Keefe

We arrived in Maggie Valley in May 1966. At that time we purchased "The Pancake Pavilion" business from Thelma and Spec Pettison of St. Louis. When we bought the business, the lease on the building and land were owned by Wm. Michael Murphy, an elderly gentleman from Detroit, Michigan. Mr. Murphy was thrilled upon meeting us because it was obvious that Joey was also a northerner with Irish blood.

After finalizing the deal to purchase the pancake house business we, Brenda Strickland and Joe O'Keefe, made plans to marry. Mr. Murphy attended our wedding, a wedding between a Catholic and an Episcopalian, held at Dellwood Methodist Church, and conducted by a Baptist minister, Rev. John Finger. A reception followed at the Pancake House with Mr. Murphy joining in the drinking of Champagne and hailing the glories of God.

Joey's mother had divorced her husband, an alcoholic, in the 40's and had been denied communion in her church. Her son, Joe, "resented the church" even though he had been educated at all Catholic schools and attended St. Margaret's occasionally. Mr. Murphy thought Joe did not attend church because his wife was Episcopalian.

During those years, which included the building of St. Margaret's Church, Mr. Murphy dined only occasionally at the Pancake House. We often lost our water supply due to the fact that we shared a water line with the Falling Waters Motel. The last two years we were on a year-to-year lease because Mr. Murphy had plans to do something to the building.

Father Murphy was a very tough man to do business with, driving a very hard bargain, and this caused us to seek another location, which turned out to be a blessing. The Lord works in mysterious ways. We stayed in the original location, now called "Murphy-Garland Hall," for six years until buying a permanent location one half mile away from the original pancake house.

We attended Father Murphy's ordination. It was a moving sight to see this little man prostrate on that hard flooring. He often spoke of his mother. We knew his niece very well. After his ordination, he often came with family and friends to our new restaurant, now called "Joey's Pancake House." He always liked to say, "What a glorious day this is!" Over the years we came to know many priests and sisters from the church and the retreat center."

Edd Mills

I really never got to know Father Murphy personally but I sure have heard a lot about him and I feel like I know him. I've seen the heritage he left when he died. The Church and the Reflection Center for retreats gave several of us a good place to work and good people to be with, and I appreciate it very much. The Reflection Center and the Church would not have been here if it had not been for Father Murphy. I am sure he was a great person and loved by all who knew him. Opal, my wife and I, have lived in Maggie Valley for a long time and we can see how everyone loved Father Murphy.

Jim Ellerbrock

I remember watching Father Murphy play Pedro with my wife and Shep and Velma Altman. When he was asked if he wanted to change any of his cards he hesitated, stalled, and finally said he guessed he had better play with what he had. What he had was a perfect hand. He got every trick and then turned around to me and said, "I played that pretty shrewd, didn't I?" He had a good sense of humor.

Alvina Ellerbrock

My greatest memory of Father Murphy is in the way he celebrated Mass. He was so devout at the consecration of the Mass and even cried. In the winter, when he celebrated Mass in the rectory, his dog followed him to the altar, squatted down by the altar with his paws crossed in front of him, and remarkably never made a sound. The moment Father gave the final blessing the dog would rise and then walk out behind Father Murphy back to the sacristy. He acted almost as if he thought he was an altar boy, a server.

"I also remember the first time I saw the church. I said to Father Murphy, "Father, how can you pray in a church like this with all the beauty you see around you as you look through these windows?"

He replied, "You are admiring God's work and that is a prayer."

Pat Kreinbrink

My most memorable time had to have been when I attended Mass in St. Margaret's for the first time. I remember how remarkable it was to pray "The Lamb of God" and look to the left side out the window and see sheep grazing in the grass on the hillside. I also remember how emotional Father Murphy became at the consecration and how someone needed to wipe the tears away. That was very touching to me and that's a memory I'll never forget. It's as clear in my mind today as it was at that moment. I think St. Margaret's is one of the neatest churches I have ever attended Mass in. Every time I'm there, it seems like I can't get much closer to God. Up in the mountains, seeing all the beauty God created is breathtaking, and if you are lucky and sitting in the right place you can see the image of Margaret reflected in the trees. She seems to be watching over all of us and she is looking at us as if she couldn't be prouder.

Jim and Joan Rubenacker

We are very thankful to Father Murphy for building such a beautiful church here in Maggie Valley. We retired to the Valley in 1987 from a Chicago suburb in Illinois, and love these beautiful mountains! It is nice to be near our church, too. This is a "great place" to live, as Father Murphy would say. Father Murphy was a SAINT. He was such a nice person and did so much for our community. We enjoyed playing checkers with him, even though he won most of the games. God bless you, Father Murphy!

Ralph Boyes

Many times we had Father Murphy in our home for meals. And on other occasions my wife, Fern, cooked meals and took them to the rectory. That was a perfect match, as Fern loved to cook and Father Murphy loved to eat and talk, mostly about things in the past.

On one occasion, Fern cooked rice with a meal and Father Murphy shifted it all over his plate. He did everything but eat it. Fern said, "Father, I don't think you like rice, and I won't cook it for you anymore." She added, "What else don't you like?" He said, "Cucumbers and oysters I don't eat, and fatty meat." Then he said, "Rice is no good unless you put something on it. And cucumbers are worthless. You can dump a truckload of them in a hog pen and they would climb atop of them and go to sleep. I won't eat anything that a hog turns down."

Fern then questioned his dislike for oysters. He quickly answered, "I didn't say I disliked oysters, I just don't eat them as I am afraid of what they will do to me." That ended our conversation that day.

On another occasion I was taking care of Father Murphy while the Sisters attended a meeting in Asheville. I took him for a ride on the Parkway as it was in the fall and the leaves were beautiful. I drove several times between Soco and the Waynesville exit at his request. He asked me to pull over on an overlook and said, "You know, if this is this beautiful, can you imagine how beautiful heaven must be?" I have never forgotten that day and the look on Father Murphy's face when he said that. He was quite a man!

Ron and Terri Van Dyck

In 1980, we came to Maggie Valley with our two youngest sons. We were told to see the beautiful Catholic Church there. That's when we met Father Murphy. After many visits to the area we decided to move here permanently. It didn't take us long to know and love the verbally quick-witted little priest.

We can remember the time we had him up at our house high in the mountains. Father Murphy could only say, "If this is so beautiful what must heaven be like?"

We also found out how much he loved wood-burning fireplaces and how amazed he was that we had a fireplace that was open on both sides–a double-sided fireplace. He would go into one room and look at the fireplace. Then he would go into the next room and look at the same fireplace from that room. He marveled at the ingenuity of a fireplace that was a see-through, a sort of "double-duty" fireplace, heating two rooms at the same time.

We asked him to bless our house. He went from room to room with his blessings. He finally came to the bathroom. He said, "God bless this room and everyone who uses it." Then he left.

"One morning I was in the rectory and said, "Good morning, Father Murphy." I felt his face and said, "It feels like you haven't shaved in a while." With his quick wit he looked at my bearded face and said, "You look like you haven't shaved in twice-a while."

One evening, we went with Sister Francine and Sister Agnes and Father Murphy to dinner at a restaurant. We asked Father Murphy to give the dinner blessing. He said, "I can't do that."

We asked why not?' He said, "Because the food hasn't been served yet." He couldn't bless what wasn't there.

We always had to watch that not too much food was put on his plate because he was taught not to waste what was put before him. Sometimes he struggled to eat it all rather than to waste it.

Rev. Joseph Kelleher

I took the youth from Annunciation Parish in Albemarle to Maggie Valley on a ski-retreat. I said to Father Bill that I was amazed at how quiet they all were and then he told me of his ingenious way of placing the "uprights" in the walls of the building in such a way that the rooms were sound proof. My response was "Glory be to God, they could have been as boisterous as a riot and I couldn't have heard them!"

Every time we met I used to call him "Uncle Bill" because his mother was "Margaret Mary Murphy" and my mother was "Mary Margaret Murphy" before she married. Every time I would say, "How's my Uncle Bill?" he'd shoot back with "That's worth another dollar in my will."

I remember during the Priests' Retreat, towards the end of his life when he was not remembering too well, I sat beside him on the sofa. I was not in "clericals. "He said to me, "Are you a priest?"

I said, "I must be. I've been saying Mass for 38 years."

He fired back, "I can say Mass in fifteen minutes."

I preached at his 95th birthday Mass. Bishop Donoghue was the celebrant. I knew Father Murphy couldn't hear me so at the end of the sermon I turned to him and said: "And, Bill, you didn't hear a word I said, did you?" He just laughed.

I also recall that during one of the diocesan clergy retreats Father Murphy and Bishop Begley were climbing up to the church from the Center. Bishop Begley complained about being out of breath and Father Murphy enlightened him, 'The secret is to keep walking and stop talking."

Trudy Cinque

In 1979, my husband Jim and I spent the Christmas Holidays in our cabin in North Carolina. Jim had to be back to work on January 2, so we planned to go back to Florida on New Year's Day. I had asked Father Murphy if he planned to have a vigil Mass on New Year's Eve. He said, "Of course." So on December 31, in the evening, I went to St. Margaret's but no one else was there. The church was dark but the door was not locked so I went into the rectory where Father Murphy was sitting in his comfortable chair. Again he said he would offer the Mass.

After he had his vestments on he tried to find the Mass prayers. The nuns were gone and Father was used to their setting up the altar for Mass and getting everything ready for him. When he couldn't find the right place in the missal he phoned the nuns. He knew where they were. In the meantime, I found the correct place in the missal. He was so excited that I had found the Mass prayers that he phoned the nuns back and said excitedly "The lady found it! The lady found it!" So he offered Mass—just for me. No one else was there.

Jim was showing Father Murphy some card tricks one day. After Jim palmed a card for him, Father said, "Where did that sucker go?" He wasn't accustomed to being out-smarted. But he was accustomed to looking up to people. After looking up and down at Jim who is quite tall, he would say, "How high are you?" Because Father Murphy was short everyone else looked tall to him.

The story goes that a man came here wanting to buy some property from Father. The man said, "Money's no object." Father Murphy said, "The land is not for sale." Then the man said, "I've got a million dollars, so how about it?" Father Murphy answered, "Well, the last time I checked I've got seven million, so the land is still not for sale." With that the prospective buyer backed off.

On certain occasions Father would play the fiddle. "The Irish Washer Woman" was a favorite. His fingers were stiff but he played his tune very well. On his 95th birthday an Irish River Dance group danced for him at the Stompin' Ground. He liked that. On his birthday and on St. Patrick's Day he wore the leprechaun hat someone gave him and his "It's great to be Irish" green apron. Of course, Sister Agnes saw to that!

When Fred Woodall and Jim were interviewing Father they always ended up in the church. Jim asked Father about the stations, thinking there was a special story about them—like who designed them? Where did they come from? Instead of answering the questions Jim had in mind, Father started explaining each station. After the third station Jim explained that wasn't really what he meant by his question."

Mary Witte

Harry and I felt privileged to have had the opportunity to pray with Father Murphy and to assist at his celebration of the Eucharist. He was such a marvelous priest it was hard to believe that he had not always been a priest, that he was a construction man at one time. We also felt privileged to have had him as a guest at our supper table. We loved his appetite! We also loved the stories about his early years, especially about the farm and the berry picking. He, in turn, loved to look at Harry's artwork and to hear what we had to say. He was such an enjoyable guest. He always seemed so happy, so radiant in the Lord. We feel that his holiness and manners were influential in our decision to purchase our home here in the mountains.

Mary Jo Holmes

Father Murphy's life was a witness to the Gospel ideal for everyone who knew and loved him. I met Father Murphy when I was attending summer school at Saint Meinrad School of Theology while pursuing a degree in religious education. He was then Will Murphy, a "young" man in his late seventies, and he was studying for the priesthood! He was already well on the way to becoming a legend.

Will and I did not attend the same classes, however. What I vividly remember about him is his faithfulness in participating in the daily Mass and the liturgy of the hours with the monastic community and the summer school students.

One of Father Murphy's mentors at Saint Meinrad was a dedicated scripture scholar and professor who became one of Father Murphy's good friends, Father Conrad Louis, OSB. For years Father Conrad traveled to Maggie Valley during Holy Week to assist Father Murphy. For many of those years my family and I accompanied Father Conrad to Maggie Valley for the Holy Week and Easter services.

I could see a deepening of Father Murphy's faith life. Now he was a priest and the pastor of his own parish. He was now the celebrant of the

Eucharist. Father Murphy's encounter with his God in the Eucharistic celebration seemed to overwhelm him emotionally, especially during the consecration of the Mass. He was brought to tears at this time. That phenomena gave those attending Mass cause to reflect on the question, "What does the Eucharist mean in my life?" One could readily see that the Mass was of great value to Father Murphy.

The first time I visited Father Murphy in the valley, I had two of my teenage children along. He gave us a gift of money for tickets to visit Ghost Town in the Sky. He wanted us to go up to the mountain top just to see the beautiful valley down below. On one of our visits after the House of Prayer burned he told us that immediately he celebrated a Mass of Thanksgiving that no one was injured in the fire. That was the real Father Murphy. In the midst of tragedy he counted his blessings and thanked God for them.

Many are the times I heard Father Murphy speak of the good people of the valley. Often while he was praying silently, he would suddenly pray aloud for the people of the valley. It was edifying to see how the people gathered around him before and after Mass.

Margie Duncan

One day back in 1989, I was talking with Sister Agnes, Father Murphy's housekeeper. I told her how I always cry when I have to leave St. Margaret's to go back home. We shared stories for an hour or so, and finally I told her about my dearest friend, Brother Dick Walsh, a Glenmary Brother, and how he told me he was going to North Carolina for an ordination. He said he would see me when he got back. Well, he came back in a casket, and it broke my heart. Sister Agnes said, "Margie, you are standing here in the very room where Brother Dick died." We both cried, and I then knew a piece of my heart would always be in Maggie Valley at St. Margaret's and that is why I cried when it was time to leave and go home. I was privileged to be in the very room where my very best friend had died at Father Murphy's ordination.

Ray Walker and Rev. Dan Shashy

Ray Walker, a former newspaper correspondent, tells of the impact that Father Murphy had on a friend of his.

A cold, misty, gray blanket covered the still green lawns of Sacred Heart Seminary in Hales Corners, Milwaukee, Wisconsin, as 64 year-old Daniel Shashy from Jacksonville, Florida, stared out his bedroom window. This was the first morning of his four-year academic journey to the priesthood but, instead of feeling elated as he had imagined, his mood was somber—even morose. A thought flashed into his mind that startled him, "What in the hell am I doing here?"

Dan's wife, Bernice, had died some fourteen-months earlier. Dan reflected that for several years before her death, he had found himself drawn into more and more church activities. He had planted a beautiful rose garden beside the Chapel entrance; he often cut the grass at the church; he taught RCIA; he became an Eucharistic Minister. It came as no surprise that after Bernice's death the priesthood became increasingly more attractive to him. Finally, he approached Monsignor Mortimer Danaher, his pastor at Christ the King Church, and stated, "I want to become a priest!"

Danaher was shocked. No 64-year-old man had ever said anything like that to him before. Immediately, though, he was pleased. "There is an old priest in Maggie Valley, North Carolina, who became a priest when he was 80. Go and talk to him." It was Father Michael William Murphy, of course, the pastor at St. Margaret's Church. Dan called Father Murphy the next day and made an appointment to visit with him.

Maggie Valley in the Great Smoky Mountains had been the vacation focal point for Dan, Bernice, and their four children for many years. Driving down US 19 South, which runs through the Valley, was like coming home to Dan. Father Murphy was a joy to meet. There was instant rapport between the two men. For two hours questions were asked and patiently answered while the younger man was strongly encouraged to follow his "call." As departure time approached Father Murphy invited Dan to come to St. Margaret's and help him after ordination.

Upon returning to Florida, Shashy submitted his request to go to the seminary to his Bishop, John Snyder, in St. Augustine, Florida. Hesitant at first because of Dan's advanced age, Snyder agreed to accept him. Thus it was that on this dismal fall morning in 1987, Dan found himself on his first morning in Sacred Heart Seminary, staring out the window, full of trepidation and doubt.

After breakfast, Dan and 160 other similar, older candidates gathered together, seated in a giant circle, with their instructors. It was a "get to know you" meeting and Dan volunteered to talk first. At the end of his introduction, he told the group about his earlier, disturbing thought, 'What the hell am I doing here?' By the time the other men had participated, Dan was astounded how many other men echoed the same sentiments. Dan was at ease now. He was with kindred souls who felt as he did. He said later that the four years in the seminary were the happiest in his life.

Dan Shashy became Father Shashy in the Cathedral in St. Augustine on May 18, 1991, nineteen years after Father Murphy was ordained in Maggie Valley, and one year after Father Murphy's death.

Because Dan had raised four children and had lived through the traumatic experience of losing a beloved wife, he became an instant hit with the people, not only as a compassionate reconciliation counselor but also as the founder of a far reaching Bereavement Ministry. As Father Dan says, "I was there; I had done that." Everyone who came to him knew and appreciated his background, his down-to-earth family experience.

Dan also says that without the love and background of his mentor, Father Murphy, there is a good possibility that none of this would have happened. Now, in his own way, Dan tries to encourage other older and wiser men who think they have a "call" to trust God and 'GO FOR IT!'"

Reverend C. Morris Boyd, D. Min

In April 1978, my classmate, Michael Seger, and I traveled to Maggie Valley to spend our pre-ordination retreat with Father Murphy. We were both deacons and were preparing for ordination as priests. Michael and I studied at St. Meinrad School of Theology, as did Father Murphy.

Father Murphy allowed us to stay in the rectory with him. Each day, Michael and I would go out in the mountains with a picnic lunch. We would climb a mountain, say our prayers, eat our lunch, and then come down in the evening. We assisted Father Murphy at the late afternoon Mass, and then joined him for dinner and conversation.

I will never forget one evening over dinner, when in the middle of our conversation about St. Meinrad, Father Murphy asked us if he was celebrating Mass correctly. He thought perhaps things had changed a bit since he had finished his studies six or seven years before. Of course, NO priest would ever ask a lowly deacon if he were celebrating Mass correctly. But Father Murphy did. What we discovered that evening was that Father Murphy wanted to learn. Michael, who was a student of the liturgy, gave him a few pointers.

But the greatest surprise I had during my time with Father Murphy was the last evening Michael and I were there. Over our last meal with Father Murphy, the Sister who prepared the meal for us said to Father Murphy, "Father Murphy, you might want to get these two young deacons to help you before they leave. You know you have that wedding this weekend and you don't want to marry them three times like you did the last couple!" Michael and I looked up at each other at the same time and then it hit us. "Three times," Father Murphy didn't realize that in the marriage ritual book the rite included options. He thought they were all required. He apparently had led the previous couple through the vows THREE times, and he prayed the nuptial blessing THREE times. That couple was REAL-LY married!

After dinner Michael took the ritual book and went through it with Father Murphy. Whenever there was an option in the book, Michael asked

Father Murphy which formula he liked, and then he crossed through the other options.

Needless to say, my classmate and I had one of the best ordination retreats ever. I have never forgotten Father Murphy and the humility he displayed when asking two young hot-shot deacons if he were celebrating Mass correctly.

Bishop Begley's Encouragement

If it had not been for Bishop Michael J. Begley's encouragement after the fire destroyed the House of Prayer, there probably would not be a "Living Waters Catholic Reflection Center" in Maggie Valley today. After the fire the House of Prayer staff offered to return to Ohio. The Bishop would not accept the offer. Instead, he encouraged the staff to continue in the retreat ministry. He appreciated the work of the staff, which he knew was made possible only because of Father Murphy's generosity.

On December 4, 1984, Bishop Begley wrote the following to Father Murphy, "As you know, the Revised Code of Canon Law provides for a bishop to retire at seventy-five. Having attained that age, I am now able to let another Bishop assume the responsibilities of the Diocese of Charlotte.

As I relinquish responsibility to my successor, I want to thank you, once more, for the wonderful facilities at Maggie Valley. You have helped our non-Catholic friends to become aware of the Church by encouraging their visits and also, by letting the beautiful chimes from St. Margaret's resound throughout the Valley. You have certainly evangelized in your part of the mountains! God love and bless you, Father Murphy, for all you have done to make the Church known in western North Carolina.

The following have generously shared their photos for inclusion in this book:

Mary Jo. Holmes
Sister Francine Sartor, OSF
Sister Laura Will, CPPS
Rev. Ralph Lynch, OSB
Shirley Pinto
Trudy Cinque
Sue Higgins
Olan Mills
Our Sunday Visitor

Epilogue

Father Murphy, the storm that was brewing when I began this book of memories never materialized. In its stead there came a gentle breeze, the breeze of your spirit, the spirit that you left with us when you died. I can think of no better ending to what I have written than to give back to you your own words:

"The High Priest has spoken."
With Love!
With Gratitude!

Father Michael William Murphy

Entered this life
August 08, 1891

Entered Eternal Life
April 25, 1990

Services
Tuesday

May 01, 1990
2:00 P.M
St. Margaret's
Catholic Church

Officiating
Most Reverend John F. Donoghue

Interment
Holy Sepulchre Cemetery
Southfield, Michigan